Increased Profits
Through Better Control
of Work in Process

Increased Profits Through Better Control of Work in Process

Frank S. Gue

Reston Publishing Company, Inc.
A Prentice-Hall Company
Reston, Virginia

Library of Congress Cataloging in Publication Data

Gue, Frank S
Increased profits through better control of work
in process.

Includes index.
1. Inventory control. 2. Production control.
I. Title.
TS160.G83   658.7'87   79-23233
ISBN 0-8359-3062-9

© 1980 by
Reston Publishing Company, Inc.
A Prentice-Hall Company
Reston, Virginia

10 9 8 7 6 5 4 3 2 1

Printed in the United States of America

This book is dedicated to the many mentors and associations who, through the years, have taught me what I know, and have challenged me to think through what I did not know, to prove it on the shop floor, and to write it down here.

Contents

Preface

This book is devoted to understanding the principles controlling one segment of inventory, work in process (WIP).

Many industries make assembled products. The longer the cycles, the more levels of assembly, the fewer the stock parts, the more expensive the product, and the more the customer has to say about the product's design and manufacture, the more difficult WIP control becomes. Builders of machine tools, power generation and transmission equipment, cranes, ships, and so forth spend months in the construction of one item. Builders of automobiles have collapsed these times to days. The industrial equipment builder cannot excuse himself by protesting that he is not in the automobile business. If he identifies the *principles* that make it possible to build so complex a product so quickly, he can reduce *his* cycle times too—and hence his demand for capital and human resources. As Henry Kaiser once remarked, "There's no money in a slow job."

My background is in medium to heavy industry. In the early days of manufacturing resource planning (MRP), either it wasn't for us, or we'd been using it always—we weren't sure which. Every heavy equipment builder for generations has used crude requirements planning, if only identifying his forging and casting needs in the first week after the order was landed and getting these to Purchasing at once. Sadly, the dates often read "ASAP" (as soon as possible), and castings often went to machining, red with months of rust.

Computers came and we could plan better. We fought the Battle of the Bills—getting an amazed organization to realize that the bills of material had to hang together somehow: that if Engineering didn't do it, Manufacturing had to; that we had to identify parts uniquely; and so on. We began to think that we really were *planning requirements* because we could date everything back from the ship date. Some of us were pioneers in putting tools, maintenance, labor, drawings, and so forth in with the rest of the "requirements." It all looked so good—on paper. But the exectution improved slowly—ever so slowly. If only the shop would just follow the dates. . . .

Back we went to management texts, our experience, and the MRP books with their talk of power tools, toys, and hair dryers—things built by the thousands, from stock parts, with only a few levels of assembly. Somewhere there must be *principles* which apply to *our* business. What are they? How do we apply them?

The principles are, indeed, there. They flow from old and new management writing and from patient analysis of experience, good and bad. Some sound so trite they don't get the attention they deserve, such as, "Plan the work; work the plan." Some are like Einstein's $E = mC^2$: so simple an engineering freshman can prove it in 30 seconds of dimensional analysis, yet so profound that 40 years, two world wars, and the labors of thousands were needed to turn it into an atomic reactor. "Plan and control capacity and priority" is one of these.

So we did what so many do: we tried this and tried that. We tried shop floor control, cycle-time reduction, manufacturing cycle efficiency improvement, input-output control. Sometimes we succeeded but weren't quite sure why. We reduced planned cycle times 10% and saw inventory drop 50% while on-time deliveries rose 60%. Elated, we used the same techniques elsewhere with so-so results.

But there were glimmers of light. We learned about handling primary and secondary work centers, the big difference between working on *orders* and working on *flow,* and the importance of balance and sequence, especially in a job shop where the activities seem aimless and disconnected. We learned that one of the similarities between a job shop and an automobile plant is that the job shop *does* have a production line; only it's invisible, and its location, speed, load, and capacity keep changing daily. The glimmers of light spread until there emerged a body of knowledge worth passing on to others: an orderly set of rules that can be used to assure efficient, economical, on-time manufacturing in most kinds of shops. This text identifies the *principles* underlying these rules and demonstrates how they can be successfully applied.

These principles are applicable to large and small factories. However, the problems in a small plant are typically the responsibility of only one man or, perhaps, a small group of people. Like the pilot of a small aircraft, he can steer his way through small problems at low speed without needing to understand much about the complexities of instrument flight. But when a job begins to include a few dozen work centers, many foremen and subforemen, staff aides, and financial people, fifty jobs in the plant instead of two or three, the plant manager is faced with a coordination problem that can no longer be "flown by the seat of his pants." He has to use every possible navigational aid and fly by the book.

This text owes much to people with keen minds. I acknowledge particular indebtedness to W. G. Ratz, a boss who encouraged innovation; Dr. A. Szendrovits, a teacher who knew whereof he spoke; and N. C. Sirianni, a kindred spirit in the search for sound principles. Westinghouse Canada, through many stimulating managers including my present superior, Ray McCormick, has provided opportunity for the development of the material. My wife Fern has read much of it and filtered out a lot of mud. I also recognize that there are others who should be mentioned, and these are the Browns, Everdells, Garwoods, Orlicklys, Plossls, Welchs, and Wights within the profession. To all of these I am grateful.

WHAT THIS BOOK IS:

This book is a blend of good theory, old and new, with proven, practical procedures for direct application in the real world of manufacturing assembled, multilevel products. It identifies *principles* to apply to ensure reliable deliveries with good labor efficiency on a small inventory base. It encourages the practitioner to fall back on these principles when in difficulty, rather than upon some recent fad in systems or computer programs.

WHAT THIS BOOK IS NOT:

This book is not a complete text on production and inventory control. Many such books exist and will be referred to throughout. It is not a book for, against, or about MRP (Manufacturing Resource Planning), ORP (Order Review Point), or the other tools in the practitioner's kit.

WHOM THIS BOOK IS FOR:

This book is for managers of plants with large WIP investments, their staffs, and their line people. It is for students who want to know something of the world of manufacturing before they are hurled into it. And it is for those people in higher levels of management who often admit that they know little of the shop but are puzzled and disappointed at the inability of apparently good people to hit delivery, cost, and asset turnover objectives consistently. Management, it is said, is the search not for the right answers, but for the right questions. This book identifies the right questions to ask about WIP.

Frank S. Gue

Chapter 1

Introduction

WHAT MANAGEMENT WANTS FROM INVENTORY: A DISCUSSION OF INVENTORY POLICY*

A fanatic, it is said, is one who, having lost sight of his objectives, redoubles his efforts. There is plenty of room for fanaticism in the field of production and inventory control. That firm whose objective has become the installation of a manufacturing resource planning (MRP) system or a sales replacement system or the introduction of shop floor control is in trouble.

These are all very good means to certain ends. But those ends need to be stated clearly by the management of the firm and reviewed frequently by all who manage inventory. They need, in particular, to be stated specifically as applying to work in process in firms whose WIP investment is high. If one asks any ten management or supervisory people in such firms to name their segments of inventory, only two or three of them will include WIP in the list; one or two more may add it hastily as an afterthought; but *most will not name WIP at all*. Inventory, in the thinking of many of our key people, means *ledgered materials only*. This unfortunate and very fundamental management error can result in our completely overlooking WIP as an asset to be controlled. I once heard from an executive, "Why worry about WIP? We've got it because we have customer orders and shipping stocks to build and sell. That's good, isn't it? That's good, sold material." Few of the people who will open this book are victims of such mistaken thinking, but all of us would be wise to assume that it is more prevalent than we might hope or expect.

Most managements are aware of the need for policies in sensitive areas such as safety, manpower development, customer and supplier relations, and so forth. Well written, framed copies of these policies hang on many an office wall. But we may be hard-pressed to find an inventory policy. In part this is understandable, for a separate inventory policy risks straying from, or even going contrary to, other key policies such as incentive sales programs. Nevertheless, if management does not form a policy, the ledger clerks will, in order to do their job. Although it will not be written down, the policy will be formed as subconscious reaction to the stimuli

---

*Much of this material first appeared in *Production and Inventory Management* 17, No. 4 (1977), p. 83. Used with permission of the publisher.

received, such as the boss's dislike for too much stock, mismatched stock, and too little stock.

The most common unwritten inventory policy (which you can easily confirm by asking tactful questions of the right people) is, "Don't run out!" Now every reader will understand what that policy can cost. But let us not criticize the user of such a policy until we find out what he or she has been told to do.

If society generally gets the government it deserves, industry generally gets the inventory it deserves, often by failing to give clear policy guidance to the people with their hands on the inventory valves. Words similar to these can be found in many books; yet seldom does one read a specific inventory policy. Specifics are dangerous in an area like this, because a specific example can be taken as a recommendation or a model to be followed, with regrettable results. Nevertheless, if the reader will recognize that what follows could be very good policy in one setting but incomplete in another, I offer as a point of departure a policy statement synthesized from several I have seen in actual use.

Purpose of an Inventory Policy

In many companies inventory is the largest single material asset. The purpose of the following inventory policy is to provide a framework within which this asset will be best managed.

Inventory Policy

1. Every decision to invest in inventory, including decisions to reorder, must support either service or economy. The scope and level of the necessary review must be appropriate to the financial impact of the proposed investment.

2. Control of inventory shall be assigned to a specific person (or persons, if complexity of the firm warrants). The use of the production authorization and manufacturing commitment procedure (for manufacturing firms) is recommended.

3. Inventories shall be held at the lowest average level needed to support the service levels stated elsewhere or as directed by management.

4. Inventory levels shall be planned for each forthcoming period by use of sound inventory objective-setting methods.

5. Inventory funds may not be used to speculate. Hedging against foreseen supply problems is permissible if the hedge is identified and approved in advance at the appropriate management level.

Note that this policy is comprehensive but flexible. No specific numbers are stated. Any number of strategies could be fitted to it without strain. Provision is made for its revision and an annual review is mandatory. It forms a clear framework for action, in which many requirements and a few specific prohibitions are spelled out. It is directly linked to the two functions of inventory—service and economy.

Finally, it gives the thoughtful materials manager a good feel for the company's posture with respect to inventory so that he can adjust his local policies and procedures accordingly.

THE KEY WORDS

Scope

We must concentrate on where the payoff is. Some inventory decisions are made in 10 seconds by the ledger clerk. He knows the cost is low, the part has been in use for thirty years and is likely to continue indefinitely. Others require high-quality, high cost input from marketing or engineering before being reordered. To a considerable extent, production and inventory control (P&IC) systems are designed to sort out which is which.

Level

Inventory investments having high impact upon the business require approval by a high level of management. This approval may be for an entire year's production plan or for an individual high-cost purchase.

Financial Impact

This is not the same as the dollar value of the purchase. Financial impact has two elements: dollar value and time. Every decision to invest in inventory displays these two elements, but the dollar value is usually much more apparent than time. Impact is measured in dollar-months or dollar-days, and a sound restocking decision cannot be made without recognizing this (Gue 1976, p. 88).

Production Authorization

This is Marketing's undertaking to Manufacturing to sell forecast amounts of certain products at certain times, and an order upon Manufacturing to produce in support of this plan.

Manufacturing Commitment

This is Manufacturing's undertaking to Marketing to produce an agreed amount and mix of product over an agreed period.

Specific Persons

Something which is everyone's business is no one's business. Inventory falls into this category. Most factories splinter their expense accounts to assign responsibilities accordingly. Tool maintenance is assigned to the foremen; materials handling is assigned to material control; quality costs to the quality assurance (QA) manager, and so on. It is time we directed a part of our inventory control efforts similarly. Who in your plant accepts responsibility for the WIP investment which results from the myriad of work dispatching decisions made every day? If you aren't sure, you probably have a WIP problem.

Lowest Average

Here again, time should be emphasized. If I borrow money, the banker charges me for the dollars I have and the days I have them. If we consume company resources to invest in inventory, we are demanding dollar-days from the treasury. It is not sufficient to have low inventories at specific times (for example, at the end of the fiscal year). Performance must be measured on the average level of inventories throughout the year.

Service Levels

This requires that we have service level goals, which should be written down, tracked, and compared with actual performance. Elementary? Probably. Obvious? Certainly. However, again using the WIP example, in how many plants is on-time delivery from feeders to assembly targeted, tracked, reported, and acted upon by a responsible person? Again, if it isn't in yours, you have a WIP problem.

Sound Inventory Objective-Setting Methods

Rules of thumb such as, "we need 23¢ of inventory to support $1.00 of sales," are still prevalent. P&IC can claim to be a science when it is capable of developing reliable predictions of minimum inventory investment needed to support specific manufacturing and marketing activities. These minimum investment levels are always far lower than we are accustomed to carrying, and the difference between what we have and what we might have is always a worthwhile turnover improvement objective (Plossl 1973, p. 59; Sirianni 1975, p. 73).

Speculation—Hedging

What's the difference? While recognizing the wide gray area between, it is easy to pick out the extremes. If a buyer in a copper-using industry acts on a hot stockmarket tip that copper is going up again next week and buys far above his needs, he is probably speculating. If, however, he notes that labor negotiations in the trucking industry are going badly and that there's a 90%

chance they won't be rolling next week, and brings in one more truckload, he's probably hedging. But in any case, if the impact (dollar-days again) of his decision is above a trigger level, he needs his boss's approval.

ORP, MRP, ABC analysis, forecasting, tracking, and so forth are tools in our kits, nothing else. They are not ends in themselves, but means to ends. If we do not have these ends clearly in view when we open the tool kit, we will not make best use of our tools. An inventory policy is needed which focuses on objectives without dwelling upon the means of reaching them.

You have a policy, whether written or unwritten, wise or unwise. If your company does not have a written inventory policy, you owe it to yourself and your company to get one if you can. If you cannot, write down your own policy for guiding yourself and your staff and for the information of your superiors.

WHERE WORK IN PROCESS FITS IN THE PRODUCT FLOW

Inventories are often classified by their state or condition at the time. This leads to the following conventional classification, or some variation of it. (See Fig. 1–1.)

Raw material. These include chemicals, steel plate, wood, cloth, and so on, which will be subjected to primary "make from" operations. Some firms subdivide this class into "raw" materials such as bulk minerals and preprocessed materials such as electrical insulating tubing and steel plate.

Parts. These are bought-out or self-made articles ranging from products of a single process (like castings) to intricate and costly subassemblies (like keyboards or radio systems) which will be used at some assembly level.

Work in process (WIP). This includes everything that has been issued from stores to manufacturing for inclusion in the product and has not yet been shipped to a customer or a warehouse (or back into a storeroom as a stocked part). This can be a deceptive classification, for some firms use a "four-walls inventory system" in which all receipts are immediately included in WIP. When identifying your inventory opportunity watch for this peculiarity.

Finished Goods. These are ready for sale as the name implies; or "almost-ready-for-sale" needing only some final item (e.g., a label, paint finish, or a carton) to make them saleable. They may be warehoused at the factory or in the field, and this classification is often subdivided in that way.

Before undertaking any inventory turn improvement project, we must have confidence that the work will be effective; that is, concentrated on a significant inventory element whose performance improvement will be worthwhile. Zimmerman's "The ABC's of Vilfredo Pareto" (1976, p. 1) will help us rank inventories

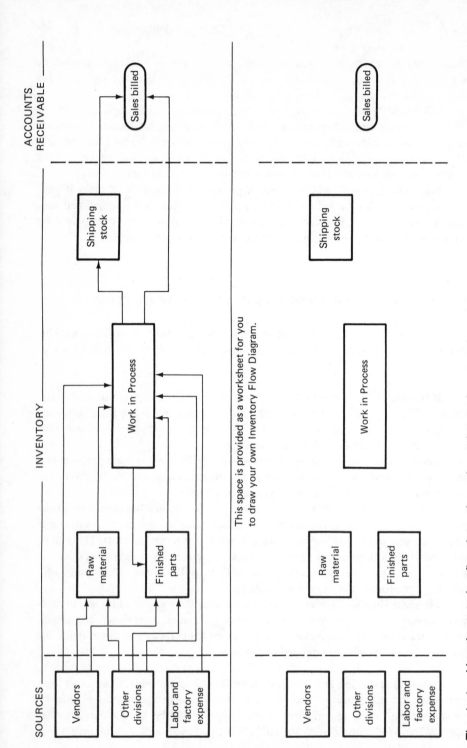

Fig. 1-1. How inventories flow into, through, and out of a manufacturing business. (Courtesy of Westinghouse Electric Corporation)

according to their importance. Let's look at a simulated accounting statement which tells us where our dollars are:

Dollars in Thousands		Turnover Times Per Yr.
Raw Materials	$ 4,000	6.5
Parts	400	1.8
Work in Process	7,500	1.2
Finished Goods		
Factory	250	4.0
Districts	-	
Total Inventories	$12,150	3.0

At first glance, we would rank these segments for attention thus: No. 1, WIP; No. 2, Raw Materials; No. 3, Parts; No. 4, Factory Finished Goods. Turnover gives us a second glance, but, probably, we would still not depart much from our first ranking. If, however, the turnover figures for Raw Materials and WIP had been inter-changed, we might well have pondered a good deal and could easily have settled on Raw Material instead of WIP as our improvement candidate. This illustrates the importance of looking at inventory (or any other) problems in several ways before deciding upon an approach.

It is, unfortunately, characteristic of industry that firms with large WIP investments tend to turn them rather slowly. Makers of heavy hard goods have turnovers of WIP ranging from as low as 1.0 to as high as 4.0 or more. It is not possible in a book like this to suggest what *your* turnover ought to be. Keeping in mind the 1 to 4 range in turnover, the following suggestions will help you: 1. Split up inventories as in the example and calculate a turn rate for each piece before deciding upon WIP, or any other segment, as your target; 2. Be creatively discontented. Find out what other divisions in your company get and, if you can, what the competition, or similar industries, get. You will be either better or worse than they. If you are worse, there is an important competitive opportunity going to waste. If you are better, you can be sure someone is gaining on you unless you are actively working upon the problem and can see your progress. In either case, creative discontent is in order.

SELF-CALIBRATION: DETERMINING THE NEED
FOR WORK IN PROCESS CONTROL

Still another way to set priorities is by checking a list of criteria for firms needing WIP control. Such a checklist follows, along with two example scores to illustrate the process (see Fig. 1–2).

There are 11 factors each with a possible score from zero to three. Give a factor a high score if it is extremely important. For instance, an automobile maker would have to assign a maximum score of three to the "many options" criterion. There are 33 possible points: the higher a score, the more important WIP control is to the profitable operation of the firm.

Factor To Be Considered	Example Scoring for Maker of	
	Appliances	Large Motors
1. Market:		
Make-to-order business	1	3
Many options for user	1	3
Late delivery penalties	0	1
2. Product:		
Long manufacturing cycle	0	2
Many assembly levels	1	3
Many processes	3	3
Many parts and materials	2	3
High labor content	0	3
Many make-to-order parts	0	3
3. Financial:		
WIP is a large part of the firm's assets	0	3
Machines & equipment are a large part of the firm's assets	2	2
Total Score	10	29
Need for WIP control	Low to moderate	High

Fig. 1–2. Self-check: the need for WIP control.

In the example, which was chosen to illustrate firms close to the two extremes, the appliance maker has much less need for WIP control than the motor maker (but note well that even the appliance maker has *some* need). If a firm's score is high, it should have a continuous program of WIP turnover improvement in place.

Remember, though, that while deciding what programs are needed, addressed to what segments of inventory, we must not lose track of the system of which MRP, shop floor control, master scheduling, and so forth are *parts*. To emphasize this, Appendix IV shows a system model, not much different from those seen in many good articles and books. The subject matter of this text fits into Blocks 11, 12, 15, 16, and 17, which are no more nor less important than the others. Look at the model now. Look at it frequently. Build your system wisely and in a way which ensures that the gears mesh.

THE OBJECTIVES OF BETTER WIP CONTROL

Referring back to the sample inventory policy, recall that inventory is an investment in service and/or economy.

In the WIP context service can be rendered in several directions:

1. Balance among different production rates can be provided by buffers of WIP which carry a work center through a second or third shift, when its feeders need to work only one shift.

2. Scheduling inaccuracies, either built into the plan or creeping into its execution, can be tolerated if some level of idle, unsynchronized WIP is permitted.

3. The simple physical fact that not everything can be done at once, particularly where there are many levels of assembly, is cared for by spreading the operations, and therefore the WIP investment, over time.

4. In some industries, WIP performs an indirect but important service to customers: it permits their inspectors to satisfy themselves that construction is proceeding in an approved manner and that the tests contracted for have been carried out and passed.

Economy is provided by WIP.

1. Parts the firm makes for its own manufacturing stocks are less expensive when made in quantity, which may call for appreciable WIP.

2. Because of limitations of skills, departmental capacity, and so forth expensive parts which are needed in sets and which require long manufacturing cycles, are made in sequence rather than in parallel; the first ones made must wait for others to catch up. For example, coils for large power transformers, each weighing many tons, are required in sets of three, six, and sometimes nine or more. This avoids the high cost of duplicated facilities and parallel learning curves.

3. Heavy manufacturing typically employs general-purpose work centers capable of doing many jobs reasonably well. For example, a fabricating shop might house a big welding platen. Positioners and handling devices, teamed up with minicomputers and automatic welding machines might be many times more efficient but might require an unattainable degree of product standardization. The firm cannot afford high-cost equipment standing by for only infrequent use. The price it pays is in long setups, prolonged processes, much waiting and handling, all of which takes time—WIP again.

The objectives of better WIP control, then, are to identify which of these benefits are necessary to the profitable functioning of the firm and to provide them at least cost in terms of direct labor costs, managed costs, and opportunity cost. We will thus raise return (R) and reduce investment (I) in the ROI equation.

Here, we should touch on something that will be dealt with more fully later. It is that tight WIP control, as well as having present benefits, can defer, sometimes for years, the necessity to expand the physical plant. This is a big contribution to the strategic goals of the firm, and one which is usually overlooked.

One final consideration is job satisfaction in the workforce and preservation of the sane peace of mind of supervision, one of the most neglected groups in industry. Typically, an inventory drive is dreaded by these people; it means still more frantic expediting, increasing demands for ever quicker decisions based upon an ever reducing information base. There is no need for this approach to WIP control. The work force and its supervision are composed of reasonable, intelligent, responsive men and women. They will react positively to a WIP program based upon their own needs for meaningful work, their own view of their prime job, and upon principles of simple survival.

The following sign, seen on a shop superintendent's office wall, summarizes the main job and priority of most supervision as they see it.

> If I miss my cost reduction target, my boss will chew me out: but
> if I miss my shipments, *I'll get fired.*

A vital objective of any WIP control program, therefore, *must* be to help the factory to ship its products on time. No set of objectives which does not include this at or near the top will be credible in the eyes of supervision; and without the steady, knowledgeable dedication of supervision, a WIP turn improvement program will not happen. No foreman needs much coaching in the simple truth that a satisfied customer will return, enabling the firm to earn another ROI another time.

THE RESULTS OF BETTER WIP CONTROL

Better WIP control, quite simply, results in better return on investment (ROI). Over the years, many have challenged the place of ROI as the undisputed queen of objectives (Blake and Mouton 1968, p.7). But the simple economic facts of life always win out. For example, any endeavor which fails to earn more than is invested in it (in money, time, care, prayer, or any other resource) ultimately vanishes from the scene; and natural competitive forces, sometimes augmented by society's controls, will limit the size of the return, even to a monopoly. Between these extremes of zero return and excessive return most firms must operate, and do (Cool and Reese 1978, p.28).

The mechanics of how inventories impact ROI is well illustrated in the Du Pont model of the firm (Hessler and Cline 1960, p.797). This model is built backward from the fundamental relationship of

$$ROI = (\text{Profit Percent}) \times (\text{Investment Turnover})$$

The accounting statements of any firm will yield most of the required numbers. One, the carrying cost of inventory, is discussed in Chapter 4. Refer now to Fig. 1–3 which shows this financial model. Points worth noting include:

1. Inventories appear in both the Investment and Income branches of the model, therefore they have some leverage in their effects upon ROI.

2. Changes in investment turnover have small effect on taxation (in most jurisdictions) but have full, 100% impact upon ROI. Therefore turnover improvement is a means of improving profitability while attracting minimal extra tax.

3. The nature of product life cycles is such that, for most of their lives, most products earn steadily shrinking margins (Boston Consulting Group 1968). Therefore, with mature products, one strategy for maintenance of profitability is to increase turn rates.

Fig. 1–4 illustrates some typical figures for a firm with high WIP investment, earning a modest ROI of 10% after taxes. The accounting department in any firm can supply the figures and adjustments necessary to develop these relationships for the particular firm.

Fig.1–5 shows how the ROI would be increased 16% by a modest 10% decrease in inventories. In this example, all else has been held constant. In real life, all else would *not* hold constant: an aggressive management would see to it that such an asset reduction would be accompanied by corresponding reductions in managed and other costs. However, the assumption understates the impact of inventory turn improvement and is therefore conservative. For this firm, we could say the inventory sensitivity is 1.6:1. That is, a 1% change in inventories will have a 1.6% influence on ROI.

Let's now inquire what change in sales volume, with other costs and investments in proportion, could yield the same improvement in ROI. Fig. 1–6 shows that volume would have to *increase 53%* to get the same effect as a 10% reduction in inventory would yield. There are endless reasons why a 53% increase in sales volume would be exceedingly difficult to get in any short period of time. For example, physical capacity would likely be insufficient without heavy new investment: price levels could well be reduced; and 53% more business might just not be available through the existing distribution channels. Yet a 10% inventory

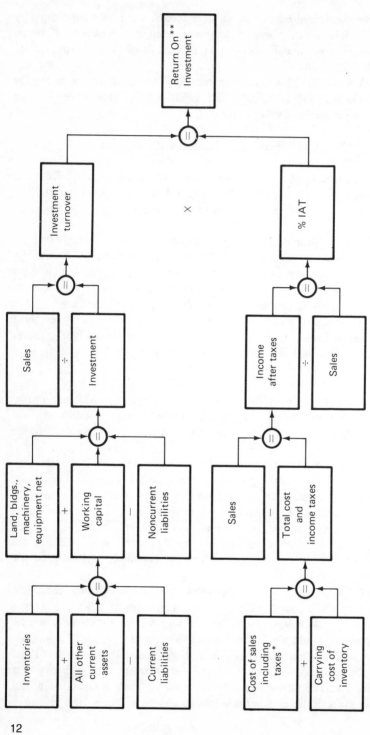

*Excluding carrying cost of inventory
**P & L statement ROI is adjusted for interest and other tax adjustments

Fig. 1–3. The Du Pont model: how inventory and its carrying cost affect ROI.

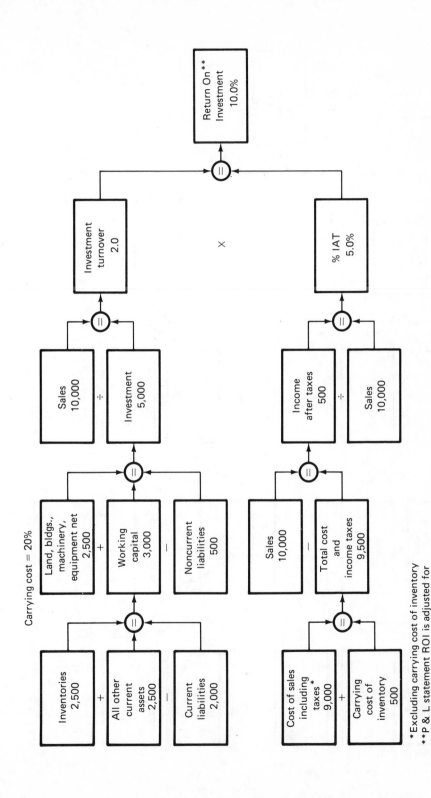

Carrying cost = 20%

*Excluding carrying cost of inventory
**P & L statement ROI is adjusted for
  interest and taxes

Fig. 1–4. Example of a firm with low investment turnover and medium ROI.

13

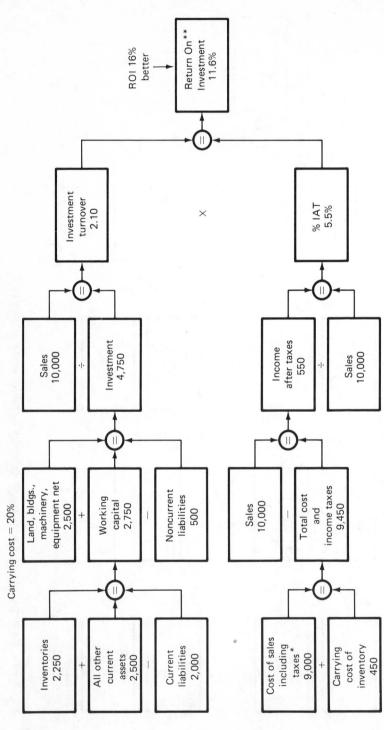

Carrying cost = 20%

ROI 16% better →

Return On** Investment 11.6%

Investment turnover 2.10

×

% IAT 5.5%

Sales 10,000

Investment 4,750

Income after taxes 550

Sales 10,000

Land, bldgs., machinery, equipment net 2,500

+

Working capital 2,750

−

Noncurrent liabilities 500

Sales 10,000

Total cost and income taxes 9,450

Inventories 2,250

+

All other current assets 2,500

−

Current liabilities 2,000

Cost of sales including taxes* 9,000

+

Carrying cost of inventory 450

*Excluding carrying cost of inventory

**P & L statement ROI is adjusted for interest, tax, etc.

Fig. 1–5.   How a 10% inventory reduction affects ROI.

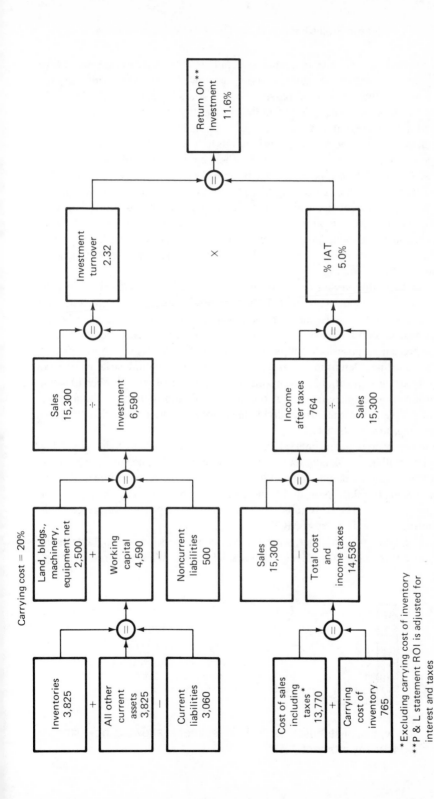

Fig. 1-6. Volume increase required to yield the same ROI improvement as a 10% turnover improvement can yield.

15

turnover improvement is quite attainable, generally in a much shorter period of time than any major increase in sales volume, at lower cost, and with ongoing cost-decreasing influence as time passes. Furthermore, it attracts negligible additional tax and little or no attention from the competition. If we consider ourselves business men, we can not ignore the messages from the Du Pont model.

With the Du Pont model examples in mind, let's look at Fig. 1–7 to see how a firm typically uses its investment in WIP. The important part of the picture, of course, is the large *slack time* bar. This is time during which, for any one of a myriad of reasons, the job is standing idly somewhere in the factory; waiting to be moved, waiting to be set up, waiting for matching parts, and so forth. The very name, *Work in Process,* implies that here is material upon which we are happily busy, secure in the knowledge that it will soon be a neat entry under Accounts Receivable. Alas, it would be quite in order to retain the acronym WIP but change the meaning to *Waiting in Patience*.

If you doubt this, try a Manufacturing Cycle Efficiency (MCE) study in your own plant. It can be done with great simplicity and directness, giving an accurate but not unnecessarily precise answer; or it can be done with a very elaborate procedure that accounts for every move and labor operation. Each method has its place. For present purposes, the simple approach is better. Select any representative product in your line. Determine from the cost department, the industrial engineers, the manufacturing requisitions, or any other reliable source, the number of labor hours consumed in its manufacture. Along its critical path, determine the average number of people at work at a time; divide the labor hours by this number to get an equivalent elapsed work time (t_w).

Now ask Planning the interval they use when they talk to Sales about the product. This will be in calendar days or weeks or months. Reduce this to operating hours by eliminating weekends and holidays and multiplying by the number of shifts per day and hours per shift. Now divide these operating hours into t_w, the equivalent elapsed work time. The resulting decimal (multiply by 100 for percent) is manufacturing cycle efficiency or MCE.

Now we know why it is that, when the president shows his personal interest in an order, a 12-week interval suddenly becomes 4½ weeks. We simply followed that

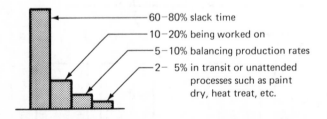

60–80% slack time

10–20% being worked on

5–10% balancing production rates

2– 5% in transit or unattended
processes such as paint
dry, heat treat, etc.

Fig. 1–7. A typical distribution of WIP investment, showing how little is actually in work at any moment.

particular order closely enough to ensure that its MCE, for once, was 55%. (Do not ask what became of other orders in the production stream at the same time!)

We should now touch on a matter that we will deal with more fully later in our discussion of the objectives for WIP, viz. the influence of time upon inventory levels. We have to recognize that when the job is on the shop floor we have little or no control over the *amount* of WIP it will ultimately represent. Its cost has been built into its design and depends on the quantity and kind of materials in it and the work content. Over none of this do we, as material control people, have much influence so far as current production is concerned. What we can and should influence is the *time* over which this investment must be held. There is a direct and simple relationship between WIP inventory and cycle time:

$$\text{WIP} = (\text{Production Rate}) \times (\text{Cycle Time})*$$

This simple formula seems to suggest that, if we cut our cycle time in half, we will have half as many units in production to maintain the same shipping rates. And that is exactly true. Enjoying such stunning benefits is not quite as simple as the preceding equation suggests; therefore, cycle-time reduction will be discussed more fully in Chapter 5. The important message for present purposes is that *time,* specifically product cycle time, is *inventory.*

Getting back, then, to Fig. 1–7 with its 75% slack time bar, we can see that there is a very large wasted potential in most of our shops. If we can cut out some of this 75% (and we must, or others will leave us behind in the accelerating technology of the next few years), we can maintain shipping rates with fewer jobs on the floor, higher turnover, and higher ROI. Fewer jobs on the floor means fewer headaches because, what we do not have, we cannot lose, damage, manage, move, find, repair, repaint, and move some more. We do not find ourselves tripping over tomorrow's problems while trying to solve today's. And perhaps we won't have to extend the assembly bay out into the employee parking lot next year, after all.

Old habits of thought die hard, none harder than the mistaken belief that we need much physical evidence of plenty of parts awaiting assembly before we can confidently begin assembly. As a means of persuading yourself and your line people that this is a fallacy, do this simple thing: check a random sampling (or perhaps all) of the parts awaiting assembly. How many of them are needed today? If most of them are not—and you will find they are not—then what are they doing there? Their presence doesn't help, it hinders us in doing today's jobs. It's a security blanket. In this book we will find out how to keep the unneeded parts from being made and to increase the proportion of our manufacturing effort dedicated to making things we need next.

Then what should we expect from better WIP control? For most of us, improved ROI is a laudable result, and once a month or once a year it's nice to see we "made it." But we want and need more frequent reinforcement for our efforts;

---

*Rate in units per week or month: time in weeks or months.

more concrete signals that we are really doing better; things we can point to in our own sphere of operation which convince us that we are doing our share and doing it well. Watch for signals like these:

Late shipments to customers and to assembly: DOWN 60%–75%
Visible WIP inventory on the shop floor: DOWN 20%–60%
Labor efficiency (ratio of productive hours to attendance, or in-plant, man-hours): UP 10%–20%*
Emergency overtime: DOWN 50%–75%

Any plant setting out to improve its WIP control should set its sights on benefits like these and not rest until it gets them. There is no need to settle for less.

GENERAL PREREQUISITES TO BETTER WIP CONTROL

The prerequisites to a successful program of WIP control are: people and an organization recognizing a need for better profits, better customer service, and less nerve-wracking lost motion, hence fewer disagreeable surprises; a good, simple system to help the people; good information to support the system; careful use of words in communication; and probably a computer to do the clerical work, the arithmetic, the remembering, sorting, and other things the computer does well.

The *recognition of need* has happened at least one place in the organization, or you would not be reading this book. Part of your job is to propagate that felt need.

Simplicity will be stressed here and at every other opportunity. Bluntly, we have no place for systems artists in the factory. This means, among many other things, never use exponential smoothing if a moving average will do; learn to fear and mistrust the word *automatically* when applied to computer programs—it often means a result which is unexpected, unwanted, or just plain wrong; learn and apply the distinctions among system features, that is, (1) must have, (2) nice to have, and (3) gingerbread. Stick with Category 1.

Good information, as so often noted, is the basis of any good system. But we learn so slowly. An American Production and Inventory Control Society (APICS) survey some years ago showed that the vast majority of practitioners felt a need for better systems; only a small minority wanted better information. A decade later, under the heading of older, sadder, and wiser, the same survey showed almost exactly reversed results: the majority wanted better information.

---

*There is typically a snowballing effect. A WIP turnover improvement drive in a feeder section will improve labor efficiency in the following department, even though a program may not have been started there; parts are now coming in a steady flow of matched sets and there is less need to search, switch from job to job, move unwanted items, and so on.

It is commonplace to note that good systems fail because of bad information—the GIGO syndrome (Garbage In, Garbage Out). Studying this subject of information and asking ourselves exactly what *good information* really is, we can suggest a broad-brush definition: it is

- accurate,
- current,
- accessible.

"Accurate" means just that: correct enough for the purpose. (Note a distinction: Accuracy is freedom from blunders, and all our work must be accurate. Precision is closeness of measurement, and we can afford only a limited amount of that. Taking inventory of a small machine screw by weighing a bucket of them is an illustration of obtaining the necessary accuracy without unnecessary precision.)

"Accessible" means that the user can get what he needs to know directly without searching. Line 24 on Page 386 of Book II of the Master Ledger File printout is definitely not accessible—particularly if the user then finds that he needs Book III, not Book II, because that's where Superseded Material is.

"Current" means milliseconds or days, depending on the environment. In most manufacturing plants, currency within a few minutes or at the most hours is usually acceptable. But if we are looking at an order status printout produced last Friday night from cards sent in Thursday which were keypunched in stages over the prior week and represent a report made sometime in the week prior to that (not too far-fetched in some of our plants), we just don't have current information. And if it isn't current it isn't safe, because it just can't be accurate.

Concerning Words:

The following quotation was seen on the wall of a programmer's office.

> I know you believe you understand what you think I said, but I'm
> not sure you realize that what you heard is not what I meant.

Words are both the building blocks and the stumbling blocks of communication. A costly advertising campaign by GM is said to have failed because the proud motto, "Body by Fisher" translated literally into "Corpse by Fisher" in another language. A production manager and his new boss wasted a few minutes and irritated each other until they realized that "dispatching" meant authorizing labor to one, sending out taxis to the other. "Order" may mean an authorization to do one labor operation, or to make one part, or to make an entire apparatus worth a million dollars, depending upon the factory one is in. Some linguists go so far as to say that no word means precisely the same twice in succession (Hayakawa 1964).

The P&IC practitioner cannot take on the role of company linguist. He must, however, insist on that precision of word usage in his work which marks a professional and ensures that communication is open and is two-way. The APICS dictionary is helpful, as are IBM and similar manuals. But P&IC is not yet mature enough that all definitions will agree. As a minimum, we must

- recognize there will be a language problem.
- watch for symptoms of it; the puzzled look, the silence.
- assume we will be misunderstood at times and seek feedback.
- avoid gobbledegook, computerese, and ''in'' talk.
- study and use the rules of clear writing and speaking.
- study the simplicity and power of some of the most effective writings of the ages, from the Bible to Shakespeare to Churchill. Note the scarcity of words above two or three syllables.

We can succeed only by working with others, and this means using words. In P&IC, as in any other science, it is essential that the words be well defined, carefully chosen, and used with precision and simplicity. Concerning the computer, we have probably said enough for now. It is a powerful tool, used correctly. Throughout our discussion we will identify where to use it and where to avoid it.

Additional Considerations

Sadly, *too much experience* can be a handicap. An expediter who has spent thirty years in the order-launch and expedite mode will need a great deal of upgrading before he can be brought even to believe in a printed schedule or load summary. We must recognize psychological and social factors too: firefighting is often fun, and brings its moments of high accomplishment and camaraderie when a shop ships a job everyone said couldn't be shipped this month. The people who burned the midnight oil to get that job out the door are a loyal, tightly knit crew who will resent being told there is a better way. Their temperaments may simply not be well suited to a calmer, steadier mode which tries to get as much out in the first week of the month as in the last.

But upgrade we must. And education is the way. But the education must be followed very shortly by reinforcing events such as real success in improving on-time performance. How to get this improvement is the subject of this book.

SYSTEMS PREREQUISITES

Our discussion assumes that many systems components are in-place and working properly. (We must distinguish carefully between a system that gives a ''not wrong'' result—a system we can probably afford, and a system that gives the ''right'' result—the search for which we cannot afford. A system that is working properly gives ''not wrong'' results.) We will discuss briefly some of the more important of these system components to ensure that the assumptions upon which the techniques in this book are based can be understood.

A Stable Master Schedule

A good quality master schedule is quite recognizable. First, it is the only door by which parts requirements can be entered on the factory. It displays them all. Second, it has been built up in a way which does not grossly over- or under-load the factory. Front-end overload, a common sin of organizations having inadequate MRP systems, has been avoided. While there may be overdues, they are not the automatic result of forecasting, say 50% or 100% more than the plant ever turned out. Overdues have resulted from the usual emergencies of manufacturing and are under constant review for rescheduling if necessary. And finally, a good quality master schedule is stable. Priorities, while having the necessary flexibility, do not jerk back and forth unnecessarily. This stability can result only from proper respect for time fences and for the accumulated lead times with respect to them. Instability results when the computer is allowed to change dates automatically or when schedule changes within the time fences are permitted.

There is a vicious cycle worth noting which creates master schedule instability in make-to-order plants. As a given month approaches, the various shortage lists are consolidated and someone—usually a very senior shop superintendent or manager with a phenomenal memory and intimate product knowledge—forms a judgment concerning which orders have the best chance of getting shipped and consequently issues a "ship for sure" list. All expediting effort is then directed toward the shortages for these orders. This, in turn, so disrupts the rest of the schedule that some of the next month's scheduled load slips. And so on. If the firm adopts MRP, there is a strong tendency to use the immense power of the computer to accelerate this vicious cycle by rescheduling jobs which, it is felt, will slip anyway. This creates chaos in the feeder departments, where items appear on schedules, disappear next week (perhaps after they have been started into work), reappear three weeks later far down the sequence list, then are suddenly brought to the top of the list by an expediter who authorizes overtime to ensure immediate delivery. For a better way to mangage overdues, see "Managing Overdues for Profit" in Chapter 6.

A Properly Structured Product

The bills must be structured the way the product is manufactured. There is simply no alternative. Having said that, however, we must immediately acknowledge that there are many schools of thought on structuring. The user must choose one which suits his purposes and is "not wrong." We must also acknowledge that other arms of the organization have need of the bill structured in a variety of ways (Bourke 1975; Carruthers 1976, p. 401; Garwood, et al (b); Hoffman 1977, p. 48; IBM 1975, p. 16). It is worthwhile for a firm to retain a good consultant for this work. It tends to be expensive, hard on the organization's nerves and good humor, and easier to do twice wrong than once right.

Bill structuring is outside the scope of this book, but one point should be emphasized: that is, the structuring method chosen should be useful to *people* as well as to computers. Scattered throughout this text you will find a method of structuring product, problems, causes, and effects that has many appealing attributes. It was developed before computers and, therefore, can be readily used on-sight. Products can be "symbolized" to show their relationships internally. This technique lends itself to computerization and the creation of such useful tools as indented parts lists and schedule summaries (see Fig. 1–8).

Symbol	Name of Component	Comments
-M	Main assembly	"-" forces the computer to sort this to the top.
A	A component of -M	Strictly should be "-MA"
AA	A component of A	but would waste space.
AB	Another component of A	
AB1	A component of AB	Note that level is built into
B	Another component of main assembly -M	symbol: B is level 1 (1 character) while AB1 is level 3 (3 characters).

Fig. 1–8. Fragment of an indented parts list illustrating "symbolization" as a structuring aid.

One organization* has used this technique for many years and finds it an invaluable common language among manufacturing, design, purchasing, and related functions. It has never been found necessary to take it beyond six characters. While many products have more than six levels, they tend to be detail items made within departments. Identification down to six levels, supplemented as it must always be by level number and of course the actual part or drawing number, is more than sufficient.

The Computer

"Computer programs never run the first time. Complex computer programs never run" (Gall 1975, p. 130). Don't confuse the fact that the program is running OK with any suggestion that the *system* is working. Many expensive programs have run for years quite independently of the system of which they were supposed to be a part. Their outputs are useless, and the users know they are useless; the users have found out how to operate in spite of the computer. This does not seem to deter the people who designed and installed these systems from taking visitors on tours to explain to them the joys, say, of an on-line, real-time dispatching system.

You must find or develop a system that fiils your needs simply and understandably. This book describes the elements of a simple system which will

---

*As far as I know, this was developed at Westinghouse Canada Ltd.

care for parts of the System Model of Appendix IV dealing with WIP: chiefly Blocks 11, 12, 16, 17, and 19. This is not to be misunderstood as a suggestion that you go and design such a system. Good software packages now exist which have most of the attributes described and can be customized to provide the rest. With the cost of one hour of programming now exceeding by far the cost of the CPU of some of the smaller computers, it is folly to launch into a major in-house manufacturing system development. It can cost millions. Nevertheless, in a shop of any size, a good computerized production, planning, and control system is a necessary but not sufficient condition for good control. The factory is run by people, not computers.

This field is moving so fast that any advice on specific kinds of software or hardware would be out of date before it was printed. But some very general observations can be made.

Expect the computer to do these things:

1. Generate listings, such as schedules and load summaries, which are simple in concept but impossible to do by hand because of sheer data volume and speed required.

2. File-and-find. Always question whether a piece of paper is required at all, and if it is, make sure it isn't produced until the last moment. Learn how to use the computer to do special file searches and to sort and list things in cunning ways.

3. Track and report critical indicators such as days overdue by work center, out of sequence operation.

4. Remember unfailingly and prompt on an exception basis when the time is right. It can be the perfect b/f (bring forward) clerk.

5. Help in doing, quickly and economically, things which couldn't even be attempted before, such as tracking down the entire effect of a change notice and calling for appropriate action from those people, and only those people, who are affected. If all you ask your computer to do is a mechanized version of what you've always done, you've entirely missed the boat.

6. Provide information on request—quickly, accurately, preferably without paper.

A warning about computer programs: they almost automatically become complex. There is a very real risk of buying $100,000 solutions to problems that seldom exist. The more complex the programs are, the more they cost—exponentially; and the less likely they are to work—exponentially; and the less likely the user is to have confidence in them, because he cannot understand what they are doing.

It is increasingly apparent as the years go by that we are headed for an era in which we can no longer afford to write our own programs, except in specialized cases. We will increasingly be buying more and more inexpensive hardware fitted with more and more expensive software, the cost of which can be amortized over hundreds of installations, not just one. It is highly unlikely that a program available to a user contains all the features recommended in this or any other book. The options open in such cases are the usual ones: settle for the most you can get, buy a package which can be adapted, or plug in modular programs.

Or, you can watch for the forward-thinking software houses who, aware of the principles outlined in books like this, begin to offer equipment that will do all of these jobs. The specific suggestions made in this book are, in the main, from experience: they can be done, they have been done, and they are being done as you read this.

One sage, many years ago, remarked that the firms which would cash in on the third generation of computers would be those who would keep their second generation computers and learn how to use them. Many firms are in exactly this situation with their manufacturing systems: they have had, for years, textbook systems which they have not learned how to use or have prostituted to support their old, order-launch and expedite mode of manufacturing. Before assuming that this or any other text requires that the old system be thrown out and a new start be made, examine the old system thoroughly. It may well be found that, with a few of the unsound modifications it has accumulated stripped out, a few malfunctions repaired, the data base cleaned out, and a few revisions to the logic to provide such things as priority index, it will do most or all of what is needed.

Another phenomenon that is receiving increasing notice is the tendency of the user to become "hooked" on the computerized system as if on a hard drug. It has become so embedded in everything the firm does that it cannot be removed without major surgery with a very real risk that the patient might die. (How many of you know full well that you still have running on your latest generation machines programs originally devised for a tabulating card machine or a hard-wired program board, which have gone through several generations of conversion to more modern equipment?) Under these conditions, it becomes not only desirable, but perhaps unavoidable, that the existing system be studied to determine how it could be upgraded where necessary to do what we now recognize has to be done.

If this becomes the only feasible route to take, it is essential to document what is done, even though the system to which the changes are being made is poorly documented.

The subject of user involvement will come up again and again in preparation for, development, and installation of any shop (or other) system. Some consultants go so far as to suggest that a top-flight member of supervision be put in charge of the systems effort. We disagree. These people's invaluable qualities and talents are far more useful and effective managing the factory than they would likely be in systems work.

There must be deep and continuous user involvement when a new system is being installed, specified, chosen, or enhanced. But it must be done on their terms, not on the terms of a systems department. Systems must learn to talk to the shop in shop language, not vice versa. Once in a long while there emerges a shop supervisor who is also a natural systems man. If in management's judgment he would be better used on temporary assignment in charge of a system installation or enhancement, so be it; but such persons are very rare.

A Good Material Supply System

The scope of this book is WIP, and we cannot digress too far into the realm of MRP with its various and changing definitions. Nevertheless, it is quite obvious that WIP cannot be successfully controlled if there are chronic stock part and material shortages. Nor does it do much good to control WIP tightly by backing up production with such excessive parts and materials stocks that we are never "out." It is essential, therefore, to plan material requirements at least as well as labor requirements. We will examine labor requirements planning in Chapters 2, 5, and 7.

Integration

It is no longer practical to have separate purchasing systems, payroll systems, shop floor control systems, and so forth. Truthfully, it never was; but with so much manpower around, it was always possible to stagger through somehow. We can no longer afford the manpower we once could, and what we can afford is increasingly (and rightly) unwilling to do drudge work which can be done orders of magnitude faster and more accurately by machine. We must strive for integrated systems that talk to each other in machine language where human decision and judgment are not required but where purely clerical messages must be transmitted. We are entitled to expect that, when a receipt is registered, the ledger balances will be adjusted, open purchase orders decremented, accounting entries set up for later summarization and posting, receiving reports stored for the matching function, and an appropriate message sent to the right person if this is a high priority item which production is awaiting—all by machine.

Response to Change

Increasingly, net-change systems are essential. They make it possible to work smoothly over a long production cycle without huge paper regenerations and intercycle delays. The good ones will take a change notice of any kind (such as quantity or date) and with excellent selectivity trace down all affected functions, change records silently where that is safe, and ring alarm bells when that is needed. Appendix IV is based upon net-change thinking. Principles and teachings discussed here are much easier to implement if the factory system is net-change.

THE SYSTEM AND THE WORK IN PROCESS

WIP is hard to control because it moves so quickly from one state to another without passing through a control point such as a storeroom. Each time a labor operation is performed or even a move is made, a piece of WIP should, technically, change its identity, be counted, or be checked into and out of some "stores" or a storeroom. But this is quite impractical in most environments, simply because of data volume and the other costs of controlling such minute detail. (It is worth noting, however, that more and more practitioners are insisting that activities like part movements be reported quite separately from operation completion.)

So we must develop other methods to control the thousands, perhaps millions, of part numbers which exist in our plants at any given moment. We must prevent the escape of these transient, phantom parts (such as a part which has gone through three of its seven needed operations) into the vast WIP swamp where the only method of finding them again is to send someone (an expediter) after them.

In one way or another, all WIP control systems attempt to build a model of the factory and its contents, then keep that model up to date as manufacturing activity proceeds. Every production meeting, whether the environment is manual or computer-aided, is an updating of the model—usually only a partial updating of the sections of most pressing concern.

Our ability to manage WIP, in the end, depends critically on the validity and visibility of the model we are using and upon the system's ability to select from that model, which contains so very many parts, critical items of immediate concern. As the time horizon recedes to weeks, months, and quarters, the WIP manager must, of necessity, be interested in more and more summarized, and less and less detailed, information. The system must support him in this, neither flooding him with too much information which he cannot use nor concealing from him information he must have immediately.

Another dimension of the systems problem is perspective. The supporting system must, at the same moment, make it possible for a machine operator to determine his next operation and for the plant manager to identify which of his ten departments is most in need of additional manpower input. Concurrently, the system must summarize the status of perhaps hundreds of orders open, making it possible at a glance to determine, for a given order, how current it is or, if there is a holdup, where the holdup is and how bad it is. These are very different kinds of information, but they must be extracted from the WIP data base in an efficient and orderly way. The system user must be able to look at the WIP control job from close up, from far away, and from many perspectives.

Most of our systems do not provide this quality of support. They are too slow, inaccurate, incomplete, full of bad records, or based upon misconceptions of what constitutes effective manufacturing.

In what follows, we will identify the principles of effective manufacturing and build upon them a WIP control system that will strike this essential balance between information which is too much and too little; too soon and too late; too detailed and too general. And we will spend a great deal of time exploring how people, system, product, and plant must interact to assure effective manufacturing. (To paraphrase Drucker, efficiency is doing the thing right, while effectiveness is doing the right thing. Both are essential, but it is more important to be effective than to be efficient.)

Chapter 2

The fundamentals of Manufacturing an Assembled Product

AN OVERVIEW

Let us inquire what we have to do in order to manufacture a product economically, on time, out of a small asset base, and without crises or unpleasant surprises.

Without apology, we must begin with a schoolboy maxim: Manufacturing is a constant repetition of two processes, which are going on concurrently at all times.

- plan the work
- work the plan

These are equally important and interdependent. They must link with measurement, comparison, and feedback in a closed loop control system.

To get behind the maxim and to identify the sources of its power, we can employ several pairs of principles. For instance, "plan the work" can be split into two basic parts: (1) enough time to make each part; (2) synchronization between part and parent throughout the order. As a framework for our thinking, refer to Fig. 2–1, where the pairs of principles are diagrammed in their correct relationship to each other.

THE PLANNING PHASE

As previously stated, a good manufacturing plan has two basic parts: (1) enough time to make each part, including many elements typically not spelled out, such as stock picking and drying paint; and (2) sychronization among items and their assemblies.

These ideas are carried to their ultimate in automobile and other high-volume assembly operations. Most of us, however, live in a world between "continuous" and "intermittent" production (Greene 1970, p. 13.5). Our work centers are organized functionally (e.g., lathes and mills in one place, steel fabrication in another). The product moves from place to place in a fashion which is only generally predictable, and individual orders will have wide variations in routing. Parts must be entered into the production process over a period of days or weeks in order to link properly with their parent subassemblies and with final assembly which may be many weeks away.

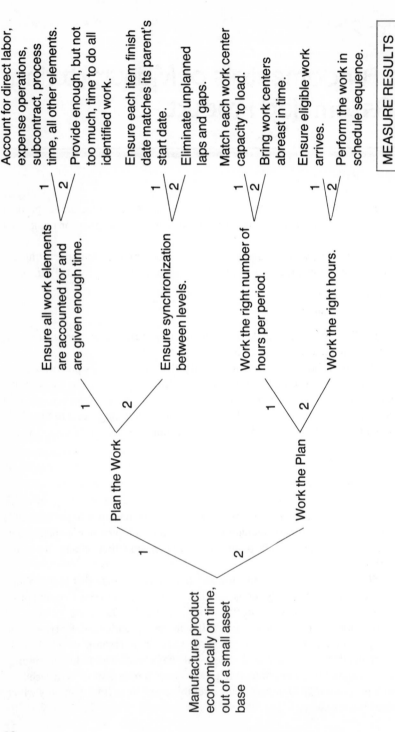

Fig. 2–1. Broad-brush picture of manufacturing activities.

It becomes hard to determine what is "enough time" because variety hinders effective work study. Synchronized production is even more intricate to plan, let alone execute, because so many pieces, needing such a variety of cycles, entering into so many subassemblies, for so many orders, are involved. Inevitably, slack develops in the plan because of the planners' uncertainty or lack of knowledge; unsynchronization may be present in the plan itself and is sure to develop in its execution. This is what brings us to the situation presented previously in Fig. 1–7; that is, the low utilization of our work in process capital.

It is not safe to assume that because we have MRP these problems are taken care of. We should always nurture the seeds of wholesome skepticism. Later we will see how to do a system check-out to ensure these things are provided for.

It now becomes important to specify the method of transmitting the good plan to the people who must translate it into shipments—the foremen, production controllers, and their staffs. Referring to Fig. 2–1, we find that we will ask these people to work the right number of hours and work the right hours, work center by work center. (This pair of principles owes its existence to the advice that we "control priorities and capacities" and was developed both before and after Plossl and Wight's landmark book in 1967. Some of us had groped for some years toward a rationale for effective manufacturing, doing many of the right things without having specifically identified *why*. Finally, with "control priorities and capacities," we found a fundamental idea upon which to grow and expand.)

This suggests that the planning system must output two documents: (1) one which will enable operating people to see easily what the right number of hours is likely to be, and (2) one which shows the sequence, or priority, of the operations to be done, viz., the right hours.

The first document is often called a *Load Summary* or *Load Report,* while the second is customarily termed the *Schedule* or *Short-Term Schedule* (STS). We must consider these outputs in detail, because they are the heart of a good manufacturing system. We want to see how they allow us to (1) clear up once and for all the confusion between load and sequence control, (2) accurately define, and take advantage of, the important differences between load and capacity, (3) provide the user (foreman, production control man, and operator) with direct, helpful measurements of how he is doing and in which directions his plans should change for the oncoming day or week, and (4) link load, capacity, and priority control.

Henceforth, for consistency, we will refer to these two key outputs of the planning system, as the load summary and the STS, the schedule, or sequence control list.

Developing Factory Loads

This will not be a discussion of computer programs, computer techniques, or software packages. We must explore here concepts and principles which have governed the manufacture of assembled products ever since one of our ancestors tied a sharp rock to a stick and assembled the first axe. The computer's priceless contribution has been an ability to handle data faster and more accurately than the human can. This makes it easy to do things which are readily understood (like MRP) but very hard to do manually. Our explanations, therefore, will be of procedures which could, at least in principle, be done with pencil and paper, although the typical factory now uses a computer to do them. (Refer to Appendix IV, Blocks 2 [Bill of Material Processor] and 11 [Schedule and Load].)

The bill processor (electronic or human) reads a bill of material for a product whose manufacture has been authorized and for which a completion date has been established. Fig. 2–2 shows, in its simplest form, such a product. Whether this is a complete product, a planning bill, or a part to be made for stock is of no importance to the present discussion.

The processor will combine the variable, or order, information he has received with the above product characteristics and with scheduling reference information which is also available. With this brief reference, we must pass over a complex process involving item master files, product structure files, and explosions—computer-oriented terms which have their functional equals in manual systems. (Sources of additional information concerning this process appear in the Reference List—see especially IBM Publication # G-320-1978-0; Wight 1974, p. 81; Plossl 1973, p. 105; and Belt 1978, p. 13.) Fig. 2–3 summarizes the results of Bill of Material Processing, Block 2 on Appendix IV, and Schedule and Load, Block 11 on Appendix IV.

If we had no other orders, we could now proceed to write a load summary for the three work centers in our model factor. (See Fig. 2–4.) Noteworthy points about these load summaries are as follows:

1. There is no mention of order number or part number, but only of the number of hours to be worked per period.*

2. Less time is required to do the jobs than is provided during the loading process. The shop, therefore, has some planned slack to work with, in recognition of the fact that job shop loads never, in real life, pass over work centers precisely as scheduled, and couldn't be handled in that way if they did.

3. Even without any of the additional informational tools which will be introduced later as belonging on a load summary, these summaries provide

---

*A good quality system will retain a record of where this labor requirement is to be used (i.e., in a form exactly similar to a where-used listing in MRP). Labor must be pegged to its parent just as parts must. This is in the interests of keeping the system clean at all times. Loading of a week's bucket of time, unloading of this same bucket, and the effects of the many inevitable changes of date, quantity, and so forth cannot be done safely and correctly without pegging. The system model shown in Appendix IV has a Block No. 2 called "BOMP and Change." In a capable, integrated manufacturing system it will be found that this function is a big and important program: it is the throat of the venturi through which all system activities must sooner or later pass. It can function effectively only if all labor, as well as material, is pegged.

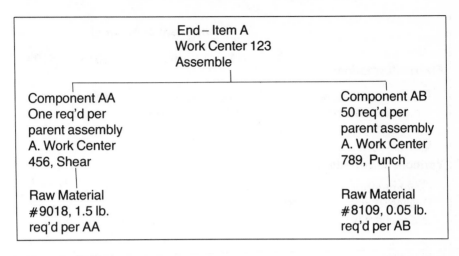

Fig. 2-2.   Model of a simple assembled product.

sufficient planning information to enable a foremen to identify loads, overloads, and underloads by period, and to match these loads with his skills as identified by the work center number. It is extremely clear that, if either feeder load (Work Center 456 or 789) were to slip, the ship date of end-item A would probably slip also. It is also quite clear that, if the shear operator can also run the punch press, we had best have him doing it in the week of Day 80, where the press is loaded and the shear is not. Similarly, if the assembly operator can run the shear, it would be useful to have him do it in the week of Day 85, when he has no assembly work but both feeders are busy. If we fail to take these opportunities, we will have idle time during several periods yet run a risk of going overdue because of transient overload on a feeder work center (unless, of course, we lay on emergency overtime in assembly after we missed this chance). This situation (idle time, overtime, late shipments, and mismatched inventory) is already, perhaps, beginning to sound familiar.

4. Loads in most practical systems are spread throughout the interval provided for them. For instance, assembly hours in Work Center 123 are arbitrarily divided equally between two weeks. In a practical case, many operations would be present, few of them arriving precisely as scheduled. Spreading the load in this fashion provides more flexibility, is simpler, and is more readily understood than more sophisticated systems.

Experienced P&IC practitioners will wonder why the example stops short of so many things, such as load levelling, queuing, adjustment of intervals for number of shifts, and so forth. In part this is to keep the example deliberately simple so that the basic principles it illustrates come through without confusion.

More experienced P&IC practitioners, however, will recognize that this scheduling and loading function can become a systems man's and computer

| | **Component or Material** | | | | |
	A	AA	AB	9018	8109
Fixed Information:					
Qty per next assembly	1	1 pc	50 pc	1.5lb.	0.05lb.
Time value, hrs/pc	0.1	0.01	.00048		
Interval, days*	10	1	5		
Offset, days†	0	10	10		
Variable Information:					
Order number	1	1	1	1	1
Delivery date	100				
Order quantity	500 pcs				
Calculations from the above fixed and variable information:					
Order quantities	500 pcs	500 pcs	25000 pcs	750lb.	1250lb.
Labor content, hrs	50	5	12		
Start dates, day no.	90	89	85	89	85

*Interval is the number of shop calendar days allowed by the planner for manufacture of this part or assembly. Different systems applied to various products, of course, make various kinds of adjustments for order quantities, batching, etc.
†Offset is the number of shop days before final delivery by which this part or assembly must be finished.

Fig. 2–3. Results of explosion and dating.

programmer's playground. The resulting system can be so opaque* to users (and indeed also to the designers) that normal operation cannot be distinguished from malfunction, and user confidence in it is then quickly lost.

Consider, for example, that load levelling shifts labor loads so that peaks can be clipped to fill in the valleys. But this action should shift the clipped peaks only earlier, not later, because shifting later destroys synchronization and causes late

_____

*An opaque system is one whose operation cannot easily be understood by the user, who then will usually be found working *for* it or *against* it, when he should be working *with* it.

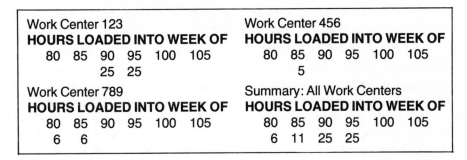

Fig. 2–4. Three load summaries resulting from the scheduling and loading of end-item A due Day 100.

shipment. Further, as the effect ripples down into the lower levels, it repeats. The system schedules the same product over a 6-week interval one time, 11 weeks the next.

And as more load arrives for future periods, complex rules of logic must govern what happens when a fresh overload arises; is it first-come, first-served, longest (or shortest) interval which gets the capacity, or what? Very soon we have long computer runs, unstable loads, unacceptable intervals, unintentional under-loading, blizzards of change notices, and so on. Certainly, elaborate routines can be developed to control all this. And the result is more programming, less predictability and transparency, less user confidence, more computer time.

There are simple, transparent systems with shortcomings they unashamedly display to their human masters. There are sophisticated, elegant systems that delight the incurable system designer but conceal what they have done, delivering mysterious results that the user is supposed to take on faith. *Pick the simple one* and thankfully make provision for its shortcomings. People can judge; the computer cannot. People are flexible; the computer is not. Use the computer for what it's good at: arithmetic, memory, sorting, fast data handling. But leave the running of the factory to the people.

Coming at the problem the way we have, it seems trivial, obvious, and hardly worth the explanation. But this is only because we have waded (probably impatiently) through the front end of the process and we understand all too well the implications of the various kinds of failure to perform. It is also because the example is oversimplified. Think now about obscuring it by

- having hundreds of jobs present, not one or two,
- suffering parts shortages, illness, and so forth,
- having a mix of skills which seldom fit exactly the loading we have this week,
- putting pressure on our supervision for high labor efficiency, which we believe we can measure, to the exclusion of load balancing, on which the

information system gives us no guidance and which we therefore cannot measure, though it is equally important,

● and all the other exigencies of daily factory life,

and we may recognize the value of having a system that does nothing more for us than compile and present information in summarized, action-oriented form. In fact, however, there are many more things the system can and should do for us, and it is essential to proceed from the simplest possible example to the explanation of the much more complex situations which will follow. We are searching for *principles*, which are usually surprisingly simple but have generally been obscured by complex thinking, requiring us to excavate to the bedrock and build back up again.

Ensuring Accurate Intervals for Production

Bear in mind our definition of accuracy: it is freedom from blunders, not pseudoscientific precision.

Developing factory loads is more complex than our example of the prior section. Some of this complexity must be dealt with properly now. The discussion which follows is intended for the *user,* not the designer, of the system, since it is assumed that most users will buy software rather than develop it. But buying the best software package available will not guarantee good results if the user does not do his part.

For example: Consider one of the common ways of scheduling a product or part. The computer record for this part contains a standard interval for its production. This interval has little to do with the standard labor hours required. The interval typically is a flat number of days. (This kind of production model is common in shops that build only one or two expensive, long-cycle end-items per customer order; e.g., large generators, ships, heavy ac motors.) If the bill of labor for this product accidentally or carelessly omits important elements such as time to dry paint or to impregnate, the program will do what it has been told to do; that is, distribute the operations listed across the time interval in the model. Fig. 2–5 shows what might be the result of such an omission.

The result of the omission of operations that bear no standard times (which is a commonly found error in some computerized manufacturing systems) is that, if the shop adheres faithfully to the schedule, the assembly will be delivered 18 days late. In our example, this is how it happened: The program complied with its logic, distributing the standard labor hours across the 45-day standard interval for the product. Since the careless routing omitted most of the elapsed times, however, the program spread the first two operations over 39, not 9, days as it did for the routing that correctly included subcontract and paint-drying intervals, which had no labor hours. Therefore the paint operation, though scheduled to start Day 139, could not even begin until Day 161, even though the factory may have adhered exactly to the schedule given to it. Allowing for paint to dry, the fabrication would not be ready until Day 163, 18 days after the wanted date of 145.

Part A	Correct Method Subcontracting Included in Ops		Wrong Method Subcontracting Omitted		
Operation Number and Name	Std. Labor Hrs.	Sched. Start Date	Sched. Finish Date	Sched. Start Date	Sched. Finish Date	Result: Finished by
1 Assem., tack and weld	48	100	109	100	138	109
2 Prep. to ship out	1	109	109	138	139	139
3 Stress relieve (sub-contract)	240	109	138			158
4 Sandblast (subcontract)	24	138	141			161
5 Paint	8	141	142	139	145	162
6 Paint dry	24	142	145			163

Fig. 2–5.   Example: scheduling incorrectly—process times omitted.

There are many ways of providing schedule intervals used by various scheduling systems, and the above example is not likely to match many of them exactly. However, that aspect of the situation is not important. What *is* important is that any rational scheduling system can be thrown so far off by bad input that its outputs are useless. It takes only a few experiences like this to teach the shop people that they cannot depend on the schedule, and since they have no way to know what part of it is likely to be wrong, *they must check and replan it all.* Without realizing it, many firms have evolved two planning systems: the formal one which cannot be trusted, and the informal one which fixes up the formal one—often, alas, too late to salvage the ship date of the order. The production and inventory control practitioner may or may not be responsible for the routing function, but in either case he must, for self-preservation if for no other reason, assure himself that it is being done right (i.e., accurately, not necessarily precisely). I was once told in all seriousness that the standard time for installing the stator coils in a certain electrical generator was 407.325 hours. It would have been much more helpful for scheduling purposes to know what the winding foreman already knew; namely, that with a four-man, one-shift crew the job would take about three and a half weeks if there weren't too many tight coils.

To be sure the routing is being done accurately, it is well to check for the presence of commonly omitted production events which usually have no standard labor hours attached, such as:

● inspect,
● process time (vacuum, dryout, heat treat, paint dry),
● pick and kit-up stock materials for assembly,

- cut stock raw materials to length in stores,
- long unattended tests such as heat runs,
- time taken in a subcontractor's plant and in transportation to and from.

Any good scheduling system must be able to handle batching (where some definite number of pieces can go through heat treat together, for instance); crew sizing (where the program divides the labor hours by the crew size specified using a crew of one if not specified); and overlapping (where the first items of a long run can be sent onward to assembly before the last are done). The system must discriminate between shift time (which governs the scheduling of labor operations) and clock time (which governs the scheduling of processes like paint dry); and must be able, if instructed, to bring some items in the bill of material of a long-cycle assembly job up to assembly partway through. Although this is not a treatise on system design, these warnings must be sounded so that a user can be sure of getting what he needs.

A good program must be matched by an understanding in the user's rate-and-route department of how to use and manipulate these program rules of logic. System documentation is vital, and training of people in the services peripheral to production planning, such as route-rate, cannot be bypassed. Good planning of production depends on many properly coordinated inputs, and this is one of the most important.

Before passing on to other topics, we must touch on a subject of importance to factories that run large assembly bays where heavy apparatus is assembled and tested. The load on such a facility is difficult to estimate in meaningful ways, because shop supervision can assign any reasonable number of people to a job; therefore, standard hours may be only one of several useful measures of load.

The capacity of such an assembly bay will depend, at any moment, on one of three things:

1. Machine capacity. Typical examples of machinery limitations are a finite number of test booths, positioners, and so forth.

2. Manpower capacity. Naturally, there is a limit to the number of people who can be effectively employed in a given space, and frequently there is a limited pool of assembly talent, which tends to be slow in growing if the product is at all complex.

3. Area-time, the simple ability of the available floor space to accommodate the jobs that must be laid down in it.

Unfortunately for the P&IC practitioner, these capacities do not remain constant, and depending upon load mix one or the other may be the limitation during some week.

For instance, if the mix leans toward a few large jobs, relatively few assembly crews can be employed and manpower is therefore not a limitation. Similarly the few jobs make relatively few demands upon equipment, which is not the bottleneck.

Yet it may be essential to go to a second or third shift simply to move the big jobs through the facility faster; their area-time consumption is very high, and area-time has become the limiting capacity this week. A capable routing-rating function can take this in stride, again providing an accurate, if not too precise, estimate of the area occupied by the assembly in question. This area must include access space—a share of aisles and walk-around room. A computer program can be enhanced to recognize this situation and print the area-time capacity requirement beside the manpower requirement on the load summary. This is a warning or exception column only; the area of the assembly floor is known, the hours it is available for production are known (80 hours per 2-shift, 5-day week, for instance), and therefore the area-time capacity of the bay is known. If the area-time loading approaches this figure, supervision must take necessary and appropriate steps to avoid a holdup in shipping product.

Similar specialized program subroutines can be fitted to many shop floor control systems to detect overloads on equipment such as test outfits, which do much of their work unattended and thus may not otherwise show up on a load summary couched in man-hours only. Square foot–hour computations develop very large numbers; it is necessary to publish them in thousands.

A word of caution: It is very easy to so overwhelm operating people with the sheer elegance of the scheduling and loading outputs that they cannot or will not attempt to absorb them in their busy day. Loading area-time is best left as an enhancement after the major project has been installed successfully and has gained credibility.

The influence of schedule adherence upon interval must now be examined. Figs. 2–6 and 2–7 show two possible kinds of performance of a work center in delivering its output on time.

Fig. 2–6 shows an idealized point of reference. The work center suffers no delays, is in complete control of its input sequence, hence its output sequence, and is capable of making a perfect match between labor required and labor available. (While called *idealized*, this condition is actually approached quite closely on paced

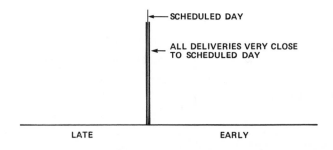

Fig. 2–6.   Ideal case of a work center delivering all items on time.

production lines.) The interval required for work to pass across such a work center is simply its labor content plus a move allowance.

Fig. 2–7 shows a practical case. The work center, on average, is delivering its output on time. However, it has its share of delays, feeder falldowns, and sequence mixups, and, therefore, is not perfectly on time with each and every output; some output is late, some early. Its performance can be visualized as a distribution of deliveries clustered around the due date as an average. The interval required for work to pass across such a work center is its labor content plus move times, queue times, and so on, plus an allowance for these random events. The frequency and severity of these random events govern the slack component of production interval needed to make the part.

Since the slack component is the very focus of our attention in WIP turn improvement, it will pay us to study this factor and its implications with great care. One important implication is that *the production interval is governed much more by factory characteristics than by product characteristics*. So let us turn our attention away from the product for a while and look at the factory through which it must pass.

Fig. 2–8 is a model of a factory manufacturing an industrial product. For simplicity, it shows only the major flows. It is, in effect, a picture of the invisible production line in the plant.

This model shows the three distinct kinds of work centers in most factories: (1) gateway or primary feeders whose inputs are raw materials such as plate steel, semiprocessed materials, such as castings (i.e., work centers that are devoted to doing Operation No. 1 on piece-parts); (2) secondary feeders, such as winding machines, drills, brakes, benches, or bake ovens, whose inputs are the outputs of other primary or secondary work centers; (3) final assembly work centers whose inputs are either collations of parts from the feeders or else partly completed final assemblies from earlier final assembly work centers, requiring no parts but only added labor.

Hybrid work centers also exist, such as shipping, where product, packing materials, trucks, and so forth must be coordinated; but we will discuss only the three major types just mentioned. These three kinds of work centers have

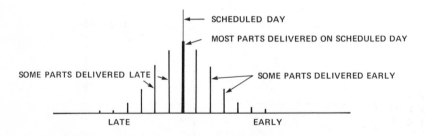

Fig. 2–7.   Practical case—job shop work center delivers mostly on time.

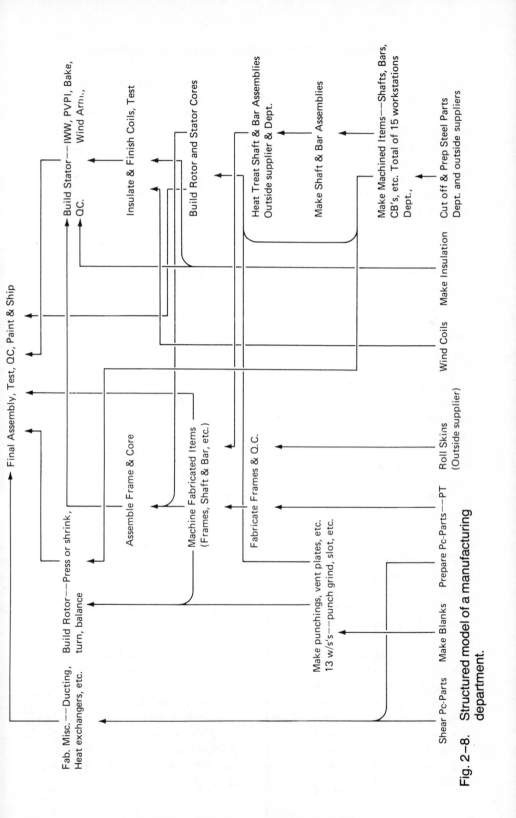

Fig. 2–8. Structured model of a manufacturing department.

significantly differing characteristics, hence differing demands upon the system. For instance, primary work centers can control their sequence much better than secondary because input to the secondaries tends to be randomized much more by the facts that (1) several work centers may be feeding them, and (2) their work tends to come in pallet loads that have been accumulated for transportation efficiency rather than for schedule adherence.

Subassembly and assembly work centers are at the mercy of everyone feeding them; primaries, secondaries, outside suppliers, the stockkeeping system. They are profoundly affected by both this variety of sources, which brings a variety of potential problems, and by the cumulative effects of the randomization of sequence that occurs constantly upstream from them. *And the longer the stream, the worse the randomization.*

From these considerations, therefore, we can predict what Fig. 2–7 can be expected to look like for the three kinds of work centers we have identified:

Primaries: narrow, tall.   Primaries, particularly if working from general-purpose raw material stocks such as wood or plate steel (as distinct from historically troublesome materials such as castings), should be able to adhere closely to schedule sequence.

Secondaries: wider, flatter.   The higher the level the secondary work center occupies in Fig. 2–8, the worse this poor sequencing can be expected to be.

Assembly and subassembly work centers: Widest and flattest of all.

Later, we will quantify these effects, but for now let us take note of a useful rule of thumb for developing estimates of the nonworking portions of the intervals. (Recall that we do not claim or wish to be able to eliminate slack production time—simply to reduce it from perhaps 80% to something more economic.) The rule of thumb is this:

1.   Different kinds of work centers require different slack allowances, hence different intervals.

2.   Single-item work done on stock materials at primary work centers will require the least slack time.

3.   Multi-item assembly work done upon stock, purchased, and self-made items will require the most slack time (particularly if scarce and/or expensive labor is involved).

4.   Any work which seems to require a very high proportion of slack time (such as 80% or more) is probably not in control, and allowing so much slack is making the control problem worse, not better.

5.   The farther downstream from primary feeders is the work center under consideration, the wider its distribution of parts delivery dates around the average (i.e., the poorer its sequencing is likely to be), and thus the greater its requirement for slack time. Refer to Fig. 2–8 and note that some work stations are very far from the gateway work centers, others quite close; the farther away, the more slack needed.

The importance of a careful examination of this principle is hard to overemphasize, because (as will be reiterated often throughout this text) plan execution depends, obviously enough, on the plan; only if the plan is good will execution be good.

What we are trying to do is improve the probability that matching parts will arrive at an assembly work center. Since assembly is fed from a variety of work centers, it must wait until they have all performed their jobs before it can begin any given customer's assembly.* Each of the feeder work centers will be delivering parts ahead of, on, and behind schedule. Since almost everything that happens to the flow of work through the factory tends to randomize the exact parts which are ahead, on, and behind schedule, it is safe to assume that a complete set of matching parts will be available to assembly only after the most-late work center has delivered its most-late parts.**

Accordingly, an interval must be allowed which is as wide as is necessary to span a suitable part of the distribution of the work center in question, so that there is an acceptably high probability that all matching parts are available to assembly. As will be dealt with more fully in our discussion of plan execution, this requires operations to be completed, on average, near the middle of the work center's interval. That is, every work center should be completing is operations, on average, about one-half of its allowed interval ahead of schedule. This permits those items which are out on the tail of the delivered late part of the distribution to be ready when assembly (or secondary work center) needs them. (One way to guarantee late shipments and high WIP is to sequence the STS by finish date and print those dates on the STS!)

Students of statistical inventory control of independent demand items will be struck by the close similarity between the principles just explained and the principles which have been used for years in setting safety stocks. Just as with safety stocks, there is a percentage of safety we can and cannot afford. It is uneconomic to be 100% secure against failure to deliver a key, needed-first part to assembly. An attempt to do so would result in the development of extremely long intervals.

Students of the old, familiar lead-time game will also recognize elements of that game in the previous discussion. For if a work center is given excessive intervals in recognition of its history of erratic delivery, it will have scope for even more departure from schedule discipline, hence even more erratic delivery, which will demand even longer intervals.

Notice that we have made an important departure from most ordinary methods of establishing intervals for parts and for products. We have blended the characteristics of the part (its labor content, number of operations, process times, crew sizes,

---

*Exceptions are made daily, of course. Every experienced assembly foreman grudgingly accepts the fact that he must often start jobs with parts missing which he can do without for a short while.

**One job of expediting, of course, is to make the distributions nonrandom by finding and resequencing the items occupying the very tail of the distribution. This is one of the kinds of expediting which is likely *always to be necessary*.

and so forth) with the characteristics of the work centers through which it must pass (whether primary or secondary, whether many or few manufacturing levels away from assembly).

Dating algorithms that do this are not common, but they do exist. Somewhere in every scheduling system there is a file that records the work center data (identification number, description, customary number of shifts worked, alternate work centers, move time to be allowed, and geographic location). The system user must classify each work center according to its position in the factory model (Fig. 2–8) and find a data item that can be manipulated to give the desired interval. *Move time* is often used for this purpose.

The dating algorithm, then, must build in this interval allowance while dating the order.

Our discussion may suggest to some readers that a vast and comprehensive operations research project is necessary to find some ideal combination of numbers which will result in "correct" scheduling under all conceivable conditions. Such is not being suggested at all. What we want is a solution to the problem of setting a production interval which is "not wrong."* This is one of those innumerable production problems which has no right answer but has many not wrong answers.

In summary, then, the process of ensuring suitable production intervals involves the following steps by the system user. Include in the production interval the following:

1. Setup and run times, divided by crew size if more than one man.

2. Move times that are sensitive to geography and facilities (e.g., the move time needed between work centers connected by a moving chain is quite different from that needed if they are in different plants connected by a once-a-day truck).

3. Nonlabor intervals such as heat treat, paint dry, inspect.

4. A provision for doing some work, such as annealing, tumbling, and so forth, in batches appropriate to the facilities.

5. A provision for sending ahead parts of a batch when assembly can begin that way.

6. A provision for out-of-sequence working, based on the work center's status as a primary, secondary, or assembly, arrived at most usually by a judgment call based on experience and what the planner feels should be tolerated.** (This will strike many as dreadfully unscientific. We wish them all good luck in arriving at a scientifically correct result. As will be dealt with later in our discussion of objectives, we may well content ourselves with adjusting our scheduling system to

---

*Our thanks to R. G. Brown for drawing this incisive and helpful distinction between the unattainable "right" answer and the readily attainable "not wrong" answer.

**There are ways of measuring, tracking, and controlling this out-of-sequence allowance that will be dealt with shortly. Here, we are describing what typically happens (subconsciously) in most factories whose systems have, like Topsy, "just growed."

do no better than we have ever done; and then, using operating tools which are not generally used but which are readily obtainable, simply tighten shop management in an orderly, controlled way over a period of time. The process is far more easily handled empirically than theoretically.)

7. If the type of product warrants it (products which warrant it are ponderous things like hydraulic turbines, ships, heavy utility transformers, which are custom designed and built one at a time), back up this scheduling system. Use a computer-housed model against which the final schedule is compared and either stretched or compressed to fit the model. This is strictly a precaution against blunders, which are far more likely in one-off, long-cycle, multilevel plans that will be used only once. Here, one interval blunder high up in the structure can destroy the entire plan. Train the system to notify the user if expansion or compression has exceeded some limit.

An Example of a Factory Load Plan

Fig. 2–9 shows a factory load summary for a work center which embodies the principles we have discussed so far.

LOAD SUMMARY WORK CENTER 123								RELEASED STANDARD HRS. 140				
DEMONSTRATED CAPACITY 69 HRS								IDEAL WORKING RATE 77 HRS				
WORK REPORTED LAST WK 64 HRS								WEEKS OVERDUE	1.3			
AVERAGE DAYS LATE	4							PRIORITY INDEX	2.4			
OVER	HOURS OF KNOWN LOAD FOR WEEK STARTING										FUT	TOTAL
DUE	855	860	865	870	875	880	885	890	894	899		EXCL FUT
90	50	61	49	58	42	70	52	39	41	28	191	580

Fig. 2–9. Load summary for a factory work center for a 10-week horizon.

Load Summary

Data names are in plain language, with no computerese. Don't force the user to look up in a manual what "IGL 6.2" might possibly mean. Don't code or abbreviate if it can be avoided, unless the abbreviation is readily understood and in everyday use.

The load summary is for 5-day periods except for the week of 890, which apparently contains a holiday. Some summaries go out 7 weeks plus 3 quarters. Ten weeks is convenient because the "Total" column can readily be divided by 10 to track load changes as they occur.

Some summaries contain additional information, such as the split between planned and released hours.

The heading block contains both backward-looking and forward-looking information. *Backward-looking,* or "how are we doing?" information includes:

- *Demonstrated Capacity,* which is the moving average (preferably exponentially smoothed)* of the past three or four weeks of labor unloads.
- *Work Reported Last Week* is a quick check on whether we are raising or lowering our demonstrated capacity, and is also useful to supervision for miscellaneous minor purposes.
- *Weeks Overdue* is a computer calculation of the overdue hours divided by the demonstrated capacity.
- *Average Days Late* is the computer calculated average of day reported minus day scheduled for each operation reported last week. If the number goes negative, the work center is working ahead, which is a useful signal for shop management. Note that there can be a minus *Average Days Late* and a positive *Overdues.*
- *Priority Index* is the computer's calculation of the standard deviation of the distribution of labor reports around the average (the average being Average Days Late). The practical uses of this information will be explained in our discussion of executing the plan.

Forward-looking, or "what should we be doing?" type of information includes:

- *Ideal Working Rate,* which is a computer calculation of the hours per week that the work center would have to generate in order just to clear off its overdues and its first four weeks of load in four weeks. It's strictly a rough cut at the problem. It gives the foreman a point of departure in planning his capacity. For good reasons which will be discussed later he would seldom be found working that exact rate.
- *Fut* is the total future load which the computer "sees."
- *Total Excl Fut* is just that—the horizontal total of overdues plus 10-weeks load. This is an important number to monitor for load buildups and fall-offs.

---

*Exponential smoothing is a much overused technique, but this is one of the places where it is better than a simple moving average. It gives most weight to the most recent performance of the work center, progressively less weight to any earlier week. A moving average gives equal weight to all elements in the average, which is more suitable if, for example, we were tracking the average inventory through several periods. Computer capability is so much greater now than it was when exponential smoothing became popular that it is no longer necessary to coddle the computer by making do with exponential smoothing in cases where a moving average would be more suitable. However, where exponential smoothing is indicated, the standard formula for picking an alpha factor when n, the desired number of periods to be covered, has been decided, is

$$\alpha = \frac{2}{(n + 1)}$$

A typical application of exponential smoothing is given in Plossl and Wight 1967, p. 37.

- *Released Standard Hours* is an agreed multiple of demonstrated capacity and tells shop management how many hours are accounted for on the STS or sequence control list. In the example the multiplier is evidently 2. If the system is capable of doing it, the release of printed manufacturing requisitions should be triggered by this same number of hours. A useful rule is: When Operation No. 1 of a manufacturing requisition falls within the released standard hours time horizon, print the requisition and work packet for all work centers to which the piece is routed. This keeps the paper work inside the computer until the last minute, eliminates voluminous filing, and reduces change-notice confusion. The multiplier must be user controlled and, of course, the load postings themselves are the source of the shop management's short-term planning activities.

We would not suggest that this load summary would be completely suitable for every circumstance. However, the principles which have been used in its creation are universal, and any load document should use these principles in its preparation. Disagreements will tend to center on peripheral matters such as whether moving averages or exponential smoothing should be used, or whether planned orders should be shown separately. Every operating environment needs its own picture of its own business.

But we do need, in every firm which has persuaded itself that it needs a load summary, all the header information shown in Fig. 2–9 in some form or other. Information such as *average days late* and *priority index* provide to shop management the surgeon's scalpel in place of the caveman's club.

This same shop management also requires that these loads be summarized at the level above the work center level; that is, we need a *summary of summaries* giving one load summary for an entire department. It has probably become obvious by now that principles which apply among work centers (such as the need to have all work centers running as close as possible to the planned average days early) apply equally among departments. Such a summary of summaries is a superintendent's tool. It will be discussed more fully under ''Reaching the Goals.''

Some large shops have still another level of summarization above these two, giving yet more condensed information for a higher level of management. While the process could be carried on indefinitely, it is unlikely that three levels would be exceeded; but two levels is a minimum.

Load Leveling

Much has been written about this subject. Only some of it is useful and helpful. Let us start from the beginning by defining what we wish to discuss.

Load is the demand made upon a factory, department, or work center for the output which it is equipped to produce. This output may be measured in hours of work, tons, pieces, numbers of purchase orders, or drawings.

Leveling is the process of adjusting these demands so that they are spread uniformly through time. That is, a level load at a work center might be a steady 32 standard hours per week, week in, week out.

Load leveling can be defined, therefore, by simply stringing the two definitions together. We want to have little or no load variation over time.

Let us set the tone of this discussion by stating flatly that in a job shop, load leveling is impossible. What is possible, however, is to reduce and adjust for the impact of nonlevel load so that effective manufacturing can proceed. "Effective" means assuring on-time delivery at least total cost. Consider the points at which load leveling could be a problem:

1. Every firm makes conscientious efforts to level out its shipping load, to adjust it when necessary in an orderly and gradual way with sufficient advance notice to all concerned (factory and suppliers). The people who can do this, however, do not and cannot possibly have much idea of the detailed changes to departmental loads that their leveling activities create. Consider, for instance, the common situation of a firm that makes several products in the same plant, some with long intervals, others with short. As the financial year goes on, perhaps the sales of long-cycle work taper off. As it becomes apparent that the planned billings may not materialize, strenuous efforts are made to fill in with short-cycle work. Assuming this is successful, the billing load in prospect is restored to its former healthy condition. However during the process, some early feeder department began running out of work as fewer of the long-cycle jobs were started. Its load may have fallen to a very low level before the sales department was able to fill in the billing load with short-cycle work. Now, suddenly, the load on the early feeder is restored—but to a much higher level than before the fall, because although the amount of product to be shipped is the same, the feeder production must be over a much shorter period (i.e., the output per week must rise dramatically). Fig. 2–10 illustrates this. In this model, the billing load is absolutely level at $1,000 per week. However, the mix has shifted from all large, six-week delivery work to all small, three-week delivery work, then back to all large work. This model shows the work that must pass through the earliest feeder. It demonstrates that, through this period of mix change, its load has varied from six jobs in-work, down to three, up to nine, and then will of course subside back to six.

2. The department manager will see this coming on his load summaries and will consult with his boss, with Sales, with anyone who can improve his visibility. Decisions may be made such as building components for inventory; moving men to departments where the load is temporarily high; layoffs for short periods; or enforced vacations. Planners may be able to move some of the peak which begins in Week 10 back into Weeks 7, 8, and 9.

Note, however, that an important change has taken place. The plant's ability to level the load has diminished drastically. Many of the actions that have to be taken at the department level will affect *capacity* rather than *load*. The firm must pay the cost of unused machine capacity, but has a lot of control over unused man capacity and at the departmental level it must use this control.

3. The work center supervisor's plight is even worse. If his gateway work center is, say, a steel shear, he has no work for it in Weeks 7, 8, and 9. But then in

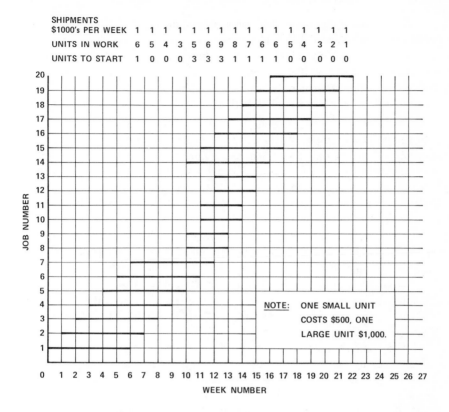

SHIPMENTS $1000's PER WEEK	1	1	1	1	1	1	1	1	1	1	1	1	1	1	1	1	1
UNITS IN WORK	6	5	4	3	5	6	9	8	7	6	6	5	4	3	2	1	
UNITS TO START	1	0	0	0	3	3	3	1	1	1	1	0	0	0	0	0	

NOTE: ONE SMALL UNIT COSTS $500, ONE LARGE UNIT $1,000.

Fig. 2–10. Wide changes in factory activity caused by mix change even though the shipping load has been leveled.

Weeks 10, 11, and 12 he must shear material for one large and two small jobs—200% of his normal load. In a four-week period his load has gone from 100% to zero to 200% of normal. Small wonder factory subforemen tend to be a bit grumpy at times and suspicious of "systems" designed to help them.

It is tempting to use the power of the computer to level out these loads. But there are constraints so numerous that the rules of logic begin to fill books of COBOL coding. Among the constraints:

- Don't move load later, only earlier, because later will threaten the ship date,
  - unless it's an order for stock replenishment, in which case *if* the stock level is _____, then _____.
- If you move load earlier, check the material source.
  - if it is from stock, then tag the record for MRP.
  - if it is from a vendor, then

- if the change is less than 5 days, then _____ .
- if more than 5 days, then
  - if vendor is _____ , then _____ ,
  - but if else, then _____ .
- if it is from another work center, then
  - if it's in Plant No. 1, then _____ ,
  - but if it's in Plant No. 3, then _____ .

And so on. This example is only a little bit facetious. In real life, these condition statements would be only a fragment of a fragment of the start of the decision tree. And the number of times the machine would have to go through the tree when there is a date change or when a new order drops into the stream, will result in long computer run times, many schedule changes, unwanted system results, and nontransparent outputs.

This is probably the place to demonstrate that people are superior to computers and can do a job simply and straightforwardly if the computer will give them the information without trying to make the decisions for them.

What this leveling problem tells us is that, while it is difficult at best, and often impossible, to level the load on the *facilities,* it is possible, it is necessary, and it is not hopelessly difficult to level the load on the *people*. The computer can be a big help but must not be allowed to run things.

The computer help is in the form of presentation of such information as current booking rate; ideal booking rate (an average—about the only form of leveling the computer should be permitted to do); total 10-week load; weeks overdue: average days late; and so forth.

Given this information, local supervision can do, basically, two things:

1. Their own leveling. If load variations are not too drastic, and if the planning models used provide sufficient flexibility, simply working at the ideal booking rate and augmenting capacity occasionally with planned overtime, may be all that is necessary. (One of the earliest production games that every factory should play when the new reports become available is to compare how they did last month on a troublesome work center with how they would have done if they had worked the ideal working rate. The results are often strikingly in favor of working the ideal.)

2. Adjust capacity to agree with the load. This is a high-quality supervisory job calling for careful development of multiskilled people and adroit internal movement of them from week to week as load peaks and valleys come and go. Skills can be grouped; for instance, most machinists take pride in being able to run a variety of machines; and machines like shears, nibblers, Weidemann presses, brakes, and ironworkers require very similar skill levels and product knowledge and should be run by a pool of people whose number is deliberately kept less than the total number of machines to be staffed.

So once again we have a pair of principles. Load can be leveled by either adjusting load to capacity or adjusting capacity to load (or a combination).

At times, transferring people has its problems, such as when skill or knowledge levels are very different. A shear operator can hardly stand in for an electrical tester. But he can often stand in for an assembler or crane driver. This will cause problems with job classifications and rates of pay, and will cause resentment because "She's doing *my work,*" unless handled with care and skill by supervision. This is high-quality supervisory work. Chasing shortages is not.

Creating a Sound Schedule

Refer again to Fig. 2–1 and note that, in creating a schedule, we are providing one of the means for the shop to work the right hours; that is, remain in sequence.

We can continue to use our loading example to develop a schedule for our three work centers. But we must, for the schedule illustration, add another order; Order No. 2, for 500 of a similar product having a part BC instead of AB. BC has an interval of 10 days, not 5, and its labor content is double that of AB. Fig. 2–11 summarizes this end-item:

Fixed Information:	Component or Material				
	B	BA	BC	9081	8109
Qty per next assembly	1	1 pc	50 pcs	1.5 lb.	0.05 lb.
Time value, hrs/pc	0.1	0.01	0.00096		
Interval, days	10	1	10		
Offset, days	0	10	10		
Variable Information:					
Order number	1	1	1	1	1
Delivery date	103	93	93		
Order quantity	500 pcs				
Calculations from the above fixed and variable information:					
Order quantities	500 pcs.	500 pcs.	25000 pcs.	750 lb.	1250 lb.
Labor content, hrs	50	5	24		
Start dates, day no.	93	92	83		

Fig. 2–11. Example of bill explosion and schedule-and-load for a simple product.

Now blend the two orders and create a schedule for the three work centers, as shown on Fig. 2–12.

Schedule for Work Center 123			Schedule for Work Center 456		
Order No.	Part No.	Opern No.	Order No.	Part No.	Opern No.
1	A	1	1	AA	1
2	B	1	2	BA	1

Schedule for Work Center 789		
Order No.	Part No.	Opern No.
2	BC	1
1	AB	1

Fig. 2–12.   Schedules for the three work centers in the example.

Noteworthy points about these schedules are as follows:

1. They have no dates. The shop should work to sequence, not date. How overdue we may be is load intelligence, not sequencing intelligence. And, as explained earlier, to assure on-time delivery of a finished product, a work center must be delivering, on average, ahead of scheduled day. Strange as it may seem, in a properly functioning shop floor control system, *a date on an STS is a confusing, ambiguous, and dangerous piece of information*. It leads to local replanning for local convenience, storing up untold trouble for work centers down stream in the production flow. The best way to discourage this bad habit is simply to suppress dates from the schedule printout.

2. The start sequence of parts does not necessarily follow the ship date sequence of the orders. Note that parts AA and BA for the two orders should start in the same sequence as the ship dates of the orders, while parts AB and BC start in reverse order. This is a simple and obvious outcome of the scheduling process which is often overlooked, especially by shops in the expedite mode. Such shops expedite by order number, not operation sequence, usually calling for "all the parts for Order No. 1." In the example, this would have displaced parts BC for Order No. 2, which then would have become an expediting crisis a few days later.

3. Operations are scheduled (sequenced) by *start*, not *finish*, dates. The common practice of manufacturing to due date would have guaranteed that a large percentage of operations would have been completed late. If we start on time, we have a good chance of finishing on time; we should not obscure valuable information.

4. No time values are displayed. Labor content is loading, not scheduling, information. Time values may well appear on the shop manufacturing instructions, labor reporting ticket, or other document, but should not appear on the schedule because, among other things, they are one more encouragement to pick and choose jobs. Easy jobs with long run times have a strong tendency to be done first. This practice can be de-emphasized by suppressing information which leads to it. Another disadvantage of displaying the time values is that wasteful arguments often arise over the accuracy or inaccuracy of the allowed time. The heat of battle is no time to be arguing over the size of one's boots; we use what we have and press on. "Accuracy of time values is important for reasons *other* than the control of production."*

Again, the examples are stripped to their bare essentials to emphasize basic principles without which a schedule is not valid. Examples will be given later of schedules with more information on them: things every shop person needs to know at one time or another, such as where the item came from, the operation name, and so on.

How long should a schedule be?

Here is another of the strong links between load and capacity control and sequence control, because the length of the schedule should be related directly to the rate at which the work center has been working; that is, proportional to its recently demonstrated capacity.

Refer to Fig. 2–9, the example of a load summary, and note that its demonstrated capacity is 69 hours of work actually unloaded per week. This is typically the moving average of the past three or four weeks. The basic principle of input-output control at the work center level is: In a steady state condition, reload only what has been unloaded. If shop management, using whatever analytical and judgmental tools are available to them, have decided that the schedule should display, say, two weeks of work, then the computer should list jobs whose content sums to about 138 hours. (We must say "about" 138 hours because, of course, there is no way to assure that a random sequence of jobs will hit the desired figure exactly.)

If the state is not "steady," the computer, under the rule of logic just stated, will immediately begin to compensate by closing or opening the throttle in response

---

*Our thanks to Romeyn Everdell for this deft way of stating an important point without starting an unimportant argument.

to reduced or increased working rates. That is, the schedule will become shorter if demonstrated capacity falls, longer if it rises—the exact effect we desire. The STS becomes not only the schedule but a dynamic log of released work. This is the key to input-output control and queue-size control.

This idea is worth exploring thoroughly to ensure we understand its implications.

Principle. The schedule should contain an amount of work equal to some agreed multiple of the demonstrated capacity of the work center. "Agreement" may be between, for example, a foreman and his boss or a foreman and production control.

Corollary No. 1. Unreported work will diminish the amount of freshly released work. Suddenly the shop has a very big stake in keeping its labor reporting up to date. System discipline will be tighter by an order of magnitude.

Corollary No. 2. Undone work left behind will prevent the release of more work (will prevent the system's reaching into the future for more hours). Every shop has work that takes a back seat all the time, every time. In a job shop, it is often the orders for stock parts that are pushed aside while we work on customer orders, until, of course, customer orders are held up because of stock part shortages. When we break into a setup to make one stock item, we destroy not only the economies of stocking, but our hope of delivering on time the job which was stopped by the shortage, and also very likely our chances of delivering on time the job whose setup was broken into. With the above principle in force, the only way the work center can get more work issued to it is to finish what has already been issued to it.

Corollary No. 3. The planning dates had better be good. One common result of installing input-output control is that the stock supervisors are suddenly flooded with parts they don't need and don't know what to do with; parts inventory rises sharply, and management wants to know why, with this fine new system in-place, they have to invest more, instead of less, money for inventories. What has happened, of course, is that the priorities in the shop are now actually being observed and honored; something perhaps unheard of in the past. Ledger supervisors, their hides thickened by years of experience with parts intervals that vary from 1 to 14 weeks, are shocked to find that most of their parts now are available in, say, 1½ weeks after the order hits the floor. They will need to be educated to expect this pleasant outcome and to clean up their stale orders before the effect hits them.

Corollary No. 4. The rate at which work is released to the work center is adjusted effortlessly and automatically by the computer, yet is under the control of the owners of the system, shop supervision and their staff aides. For instance, if the work center breaks down over several computer cycles, and no work whatever is reported, the demonstrated capacity will begin to drop at once, the length of the STS will remain what it was when the breakdown took place, and the reload rate will fall to zero. (*Caution:* The system must provide for a manual override, because the day the machine is repaired it may well go three-shift and consume its backlog entirely before the demonstrated capacity can recover.)

Corollary No. 5.   Work routed to another work center to offload in time of overload must be properly accounted for. That is, it must be removed from the schedule of the original work center and rerouted to the relieving work center. This is one of the less well-done paper work chores in most shops; it is poorly done because so many systems are so full of stale work or wrong priority work, that the continued presence of the rerouted work doesn't make much of an impact. It's another case of the informal system not requiring accurate records because it ignores the records anyway, being constantly in the expedite mode. When we move to a formal system that depends upon good records, self-policing features are invaluable.

On-line systems:

Job shop industry is moving toward dispatching on-line. Whether or not such systems are necessary is discussed elsewhere. For present purposes it is necessary to point out a potential serious pitfall with tight input-output control in combination with on-line dispatching.

The commonest reason for on-line dispatching is that it eliminates system lags and identifies genuine expediting needs by establishing the point in time when an operation is "eligible" to begin. An operation is eligible when material, manpower, drawings, and so on have been supplied. On-line systems typically are designed to collect information about each of these requirements as time passes and perform the same kind of check off that a clerk must do in a manual system. Then, when the computer is satisfied by its rules of logic that the operation is eligible or "go" and also that its turn has come (priority control), it releases or dispatches it to the work center. (The rules built into such systems must also include what to do if the scheduled time approaches and the go status has not been established, but that is another subject.)

Many on-line systems are not real-time, however. That is, to conserve line cost, or to reduce load or cost on the big computer, there is a minicomputer or smart terminal which is "up" at all times but is reloaded periodically by the host computer. Or else the host computer performs a full analysis of eligibility only periodically (e.g., once per day) and between these cycles merely acts as a mini or smart terminal, serving the demands of the work center's display and dispatch device simply by displaying the next record.

This means the host or the smart terminal must accumulate the equivalent of an STS to see it through to the next cycle. If one of the requirements of the system is that an operation be eligible before it may join this queue, then obviously enough, sufficient time must pass between the operation's becoming go and its being displayed for all operations ahead of it in the queue to be completed. Therefore the factory has suffered a pure delay in manufacturing introduced by the time needed for the newest go operation to rise from the bottom of the list to the top. If the list is one day long, the system has introduced one day of delay into every operation manufacturing must perform.

From this it follows that, if a plant intends to go on-line with its dispatching function and combine it with an elegibility test (which is a perfectly logical thing to do), it must go all the way and be truly on-line, real-time, with no compromises. The delays introduced should, in most plants, be no more than an hour or two; and if the machine must cycle this often to keep up, it should be running the system real-time. There should be *no* accumulation of go or eligible labor operations and in truth there should be no STS, unless perhaps one considers the single record displayed on the screen as the entire STS (Gue 1976, p. 117). The previous discussion, which addresses the problem of schedule length with on-line eligibility and dispatching systems, applies also, with full force, to operations based upon printed schedules, which we will continue to have for many years. The following principle must be observed:

Principle.   A printed schedule without an eligibility test to permit an operation to join the queue can say only what should be done, not what can be done. If an eligibility test is added to such a system, permitting an operation to join the queue only after all requirements for its commencement have been checked off, then the time for the latest added operation to work its way to the top of the schedule and to be started will be, at worst, as long as the time between computer cycles plus the time represented by the length of the queue. At best this delay will be equal to the time represented by the length of the queue.

Corollary No. 1.   Computerized dispatch and eligibility systems using printed schedules more than one operation long have the potential of adding considerably to the slack time during which the product cannot be worked on. Such systems can force the factory to wait for the system to cycle.

Corollary No. 2.   Factories not ready or able to go the whole way to on-line, real-time systems for dispatch, eligibility test, and queue control, should not become too rigorous in their use of eligibility-testing systems. It is very helpful to the factory to have information printed alongside the dispatched operation which indicates whether or not it is go, and if it is not, what is holding it up (e.g., purchased item, earlier routed operation, or stock shortage). This gives Production Control its last chance to put the schedule into a go state before the operation actually rises to the top of the should-do list (the STS). This is one of many places where genuine, firefighting expediting is necessary and will continue to be necessary as long as there is industry on the planet.*

An Example of a Short-Term Schedule

Fig. 2–13 is an example of a schedule for a work center which embodies the principles we have been discussing. As you will notice it is not called a *schedule!* The title *sequence list* was deliberately chosen to emphasize the major purpose of

---

*The word *expedite* has received such a bad name that it is fashionable to claim to believe that all expediting is bad. This is not true. It's when expediting is the only way we know to get out production that it deserves such scorn.

Sequence List For Work Center 12345   Printed Day 854
Burgmaster Drills

Seq No.	Order No.	Identifi- cation No.	Name	Op No.	From	Reason For Holdup
1	98765	K5095-03	Basepla	03	54321	
2	39495	R1509-82	Brg Cap	01	Store	
3	44586	L9596-05	Rail, L	11	45678	OPN 8 W/C 45987
4	84068	J95876	Bracket	02	6C123	Purch Item Not Rec
5	59687	J44786	Pan	01	Store	

Report stops when an agreed multiple of demonstrated capacity has been accounted for.

Fig. 2–13.   Example of short-term schedule for a secondary work center.

the list, which is to present work to the shop in the sequence in which it should, ideally, be done. Although no dates are shown, the list is sequenced by start date, and the user is told from where to expect the item to come.

There are only three possible sources: an earlier work center, a storeroom, or purchased directly against the order. Examples of all are shown. If the item is held up (is ineligible to go), the user is told where. For example, sequence No. 3 is "nogo" because operations 8, 9, and 10 have not been reported complete. Operation sequence No. 4 is nogo because of a purchased item shortage.

Items in sequence positions 3 and 4 are not prevented from being on the list because they are ineligible. There are many reasons for this which were dealt with in our previous discussion. One other reason should be mentioned; that is, if one looks far enough ahead, everything will be ineligible. In a tightly scheduled, fast paced shop, it might not be in the least unusual for an item a few positions down in sequence to be nogo when the computer analysis was made, and then to be go in sufficient time to be done in its proper sequence a few hours later.

The main difference between this schedule and that for an assembly work center is that provision would be made to print any necessary number of lines in the Reasons For Holdup column, since more than one item on an assembly bill of material might be missing.

There is no superfluous information on the sheet. And in fact, it would have additional information. For instance, the word *Store* would be replaced by a storeroom designation; or proper account would be taken of the fact that the raw material identification is not the same as the piece-part's identification. Typically this STS would be printed in the long direction of the paper to accommodate these extra data-items. But there is seldom a good reason for going to paper larger than letter size. This is an irritating and unnecessary imposition on the people who must handle, carry, file, keep on their desks, and page through their working information.

Planning the Work for Critical Work Centers

Many WIP (and other) control systems fail or are unnecessarily expensive because the ABC principle has not been applied to *the system*. This text emphasizes the need to control flow of WIP at the work center level. Many principles are explored and their application recommended. It will always be found, however, that some work centers need more control than others. That is, they are "critical." Just like the AA parts in a ledger inventory, whose controller checks his on-hand balance every morning before eight o'clock and places the day's order before nine, a few work centers need intensive application of every principle and technique that will help. Most of the rest will require diminishing amounts of application of control; a few will require little or none except the occasional check to ensure that nothing is falling behind. It pays to know which are which and to set up the control systems accordingly because control costs money.

Recognizing critical work centers

The attributes of criticality can be identified readily. A work center is potentially critical if it has some of these characteristics:

1. It is heavily loaded.
2. It uses scarce labor skills.
3. Its load is highly variable.
4. It is not a primary work center, but is far downstream in the product flow.

A *heavily loaded* work center is sensitive to small load variations because of queuing and other problems. It can be shown that, for a work center (e.g., machine, toolcrib wicket, supermarket checkout) subject to random arrival of work having random service times, as the load approaches 100% of capacity, *the queue length approaches infinity*. A graph can be drawn of wait time vs percentage of load, and the most notable feature of this graph is that it rises steeply after about the 70% point. If you think back to any experience you may have had in machine shops, computer rooms, supermarket checkouts, and so forth, you may recall that, as load passed about 70% of capacity, the problem of getting the load through the facilities, for no obvious reason, became acute. (See Fig. 2–14.)

Automakers and other assembly line industries overcome this and reach loads in excess of 90% of capacity by detailed planning, relentless scheduling, millisecond precision in their time values, paced feeder chains, mechanized handling, and pitiless expediting when parts go late. In other words, they can and they do accept a very high cost of control. They eliminate the randomness.

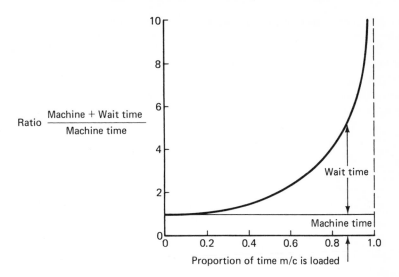

Fig. 2–14. Wait time vs machine load. (From K. Shone. The queueing theory. *Time and motion study.* (U.K.). 1960 and 1961.)

Job shops cannot entirely eliminate the randomness, but not all of it is inevitable: this will be dealt with later. In general, however, set an alarm bell to go off when load approaches 70% of capacity, because the organization is going to have to shift into another gear when that point is passed. Critical work centers are usually already well known to the people who have to plan and execute factory loads. The coil-winding machines in a large transformer plant; commutator building or thrust bearing building in a large rotating apparatus plant; high priced, specialized test equipment in an electronics plant; or, in general, facilities that require a lot of capital to augment or a highly skilled, highly paid work force to operate, are likely to be the critical ones. Consciously or unconsciously, the management has accepted the cost of an occasional production delay or upset, or even chronic trouble, in order to avoid the high cost of standby machine and manpower capacity. Whether this decision has been a good or bad one is outside the scope of this book; we want to know how to live with the problem.

In what follows, we will assume that such safety valves as subcontracting are unavailable. This is often true, because the nature of the work done in a critical work center is usually at the technological heart of the firm's business, and it is unlikely that subcontracting capacity is readily available. For example, it is fairly easy to subcontract a welded tank for a large power transformer, but most unlikely that the winding of its coils could be done outside. Further, most shop managements prefer to keep work inside the plant if at all possible, in order to retain their skills and spread their overheads.

Scheduling the critical work center

Earlier, the basic technique of back scheduling from the finish date was explained. Obviously, this will result in the imposition of loads at random times upon any given facility, even though the end-product billing load has been reasonably well leveled. And the more custom-made the product, the more random the service times (allowed standard hours) will also be. As a result, the conditions necessary for the wait time to climb toward infinity as the load passes 70% of capacity have been set up. For the same reasons that this is a critical work center (high investment, high skills, or both), the management's tolerance for slack time is rightly very low, because the work center is actually controlling the volume of business which can be done by the plant. So we have to use this spare 30%, or as much of it as we can.

Since this critical work center is controlling factory output, it becomes a direct concern of the marketing department, because the promises it can give depend upon the load on the critical work center at the time their current negotiation would impose additional load.

Earlier, we commented that the work center load can be forced toward 100% without excessive queuing only by removing the randomness from either or both the arrival time and the service time. This means that, in the planning stage, the load on the critical work center must be leveled and plan dates established so that, if the plan matures as expected, jobs will arrive in a nonrandom fashion. This simple sounding sentence has profound implications for the work centers, suppliers, and stores which feed this work center: they must be managed so that they very seldom fail to feed on time as required.

Instead of pure backward scheduling, a compromise of forward then backward scheduling is needed. The procedure is as follows:

1. Establish the first date by which work on the new job to be scheduled could begin. In the simplest case, add the new job to the end of the waiting line of jobs already in queue.

2. From available information (standard intervals, estimated time values, crew sizes, and number of shifts worked), schedule forward to a finish date on the critical work center.

3. From this point, using whatever model the firm has adopted for the product in question, continue the forward scheduling process until an end-item finish date is arrived at. This (in absence of management intervention) is the earliest shipping date that can be attained for the new order.

4. Back schedule from this date in the normal way, retracing the path from the critical work center and creating new paths for the rest of the order.

Important corollaries arise from each of these steps.

Step 1. *Corollary (a):* We don't always enjoy the simplest case. The more custom-building the factory does, the more likely it is that isolated pockets of load already exist scattered through future weeks and months. The likelihood that the fresh load will fit neatly into some space between these pockets becomes very slim. Again, we must depend upon averaging to help somewhat; as commented elsewhere, the interval for a component is always much longer than the pure allowed times would indicate. This provides the shop with its needed flexibility (if, as deserves repeating, we do not provide too much slack). And so, if job intervals overlap, which they are sure to do, we must count on shop supervision to keep machine utilization high at all times and work religiously in sequence. So long as total load over a reasonable period (say a few weeks) does not exceed total capacity which can be made available over that period, we are still safe.

Step 2. *Corollary (a):* This is one of the relatively few times that the standard time values allowed for the job and the labor efficiency to be expected become of critical importance to the planning people. We have commented elsewhere that the precision of the standard times is important for reasons other than control of production; but in the case of the critical work center, this comforting generalization has to be abandoned. By definition of a critical work center, we are usually running it flat-out; obviously, therefore, we must have a good idea at the planning stage of what the actual applied labor time is likely to be, or our delicate balancing act will collapse at the start. The alternative is to provide a cushion in the estimate; in other words, to plan in some slack. It isn't a good alternative, if only because Murphy's law will guarantee that the general manager will walk past the critical machine on two consecutive occasions while it is idle.

Corollary (b): Planning must be in close and continuous contact with supervision, who have things to worry about like vacations, training, retirements, overtime, and overhauls, so that unavailable capacity is well identified in advance.

Step 3. *Corollary (a):* Management intervention could take several forms: for example, negotiating a later shipping date; deciding upon an earlier shipping date and accepting the inventory holding cost; building components in the critical work center in advance of need and holding inventory at that level. In any case, a "what if?" capability in the planning system is a necessity.

Corollary (b): The result of the work to this point will often be unsatisfactory in some way (unacceptable shipping date, too much overtime). There is a temptation to get rid of the problem by entering the order on a compressed schedule. While this has often been done successfully (if we are not too careful about our definition of *success),* it is not recommended. A compressed schedule does not make additional capacity available; it just forces the problem underground where it doesn't show—for a while. Furthermore, it uses up some of the flexibility we need when a genuine, emergency requirement to compress a schedule arises because of the usual manufacturing difficulties—supplier falldowns or illness, for example. Compressing schedules is something to do when forced to and as a last resort, not to be deliberately done in the planning stage.

Step 4. *Corollary (a):* As the back scheduling is done, work centers feeding the critical work center will, of course, be loaded. These work centers must now be regarded as at least potentially critical; in other words, they become really extensions of the critical work center and must be actively managed even though, viewed in isolation, they do not display the appearance of criticality. *Actively managed* means given at least some of the attention due a critical work center during the planning stage, for example, a little extra care is taken to assure adequate intervals; a little extra safety stock or safety time is provided in the raw materials stocks backing them up; or care is taken to ensure they have physical facilities to maintain an orderly output queue. It does not mean giving them additional production interval over that normally required, for reasons which are explained elsewhere. The aim of this extra attention, of course, is to ensure that the critical work station can, in fact, start close to its scheduled time, job by job. It is part of the program to take the randomness out of the job arrivals at the critical work center, randomness which will cause its practical capacity to gravitate back toward 70%.

Overall corollary: It is worth repeating that these discussions refer to industries with high custom-building elements in their work. Industries whose products are highly standard will use classical MRP, where the randomness of job arrivals can be almost eliminated, and in which detailed time studies and repetitive manufacture eliminate most of the randomness of service time.

The *principles* will remain identical but their application becomes quite different as one moves toward the continuous production end of the product spectrum. As one moves toward the custom-engineered end of the spectrum, requirements planning itself undergoes profound changes in appearance and application. As one important example of this, many heavy equipment builders have in stock only raw materials and a very small amount of piece-part stocks: things like plate steel and hardware. Where piece-parts are engineered for each order (as they are near the extreme custom-building end of the spectrum), the existence of very critical work centers becomes more and more likely and their management typically more and more difficult. Requirements planning, then, is likely to be found loading work centers with lot-for-lot orders: typically all are different and few or none are stocked. Concepts of a best (economical) order quantity, safety stock, and so forth do not apply; the firm makes exactly what the order requires, no more and no less. The practitioner must decide where he is in this spectrum and treat his critical work stations accordingly.

Another overall corollary: If there are two or more work centers of similar criticality, the necessary juggling can, quite literally, go on forever if allowed to do so. The compromise that is ultimately made will invariably express itself as added WIP inventory held, hopefully, at as low a value and for as short a time as possible. This balancing inventory or buffer stock detracts from the firm's capital turnover objectives. Only the particular firm, in its own circumstances, using its own cost of capital and other business analysis tools, can ultimately decide whether the time has come to eliminate buffer stocks by augmenting capacity and/or improving the flexibility of the work force. Both courses of action have their prices, which must be offset against the cost of carrying the buffer WIP.

We should now review just how far we have progressed on the paths outlined in Fig. 2–1. We have planned the work and have load summaries and schedules to show for it. The plan recognizes the difference between the allowed labor time and the anticipated elapsed shop time. Although the example was too simple to bring it out, presumably we have identified everything that has to happen to every part and have allowed enough (but not too much) time for it to happen. Also, we have taken care to make the finish date of each component the same as the start date of its parent, so we have synchronization between levels. There is no point where we have unplanned gaps between component end date and parent start date; nor have we places where component end date is after parent start date. So we have no laps or gaps. So far so good; we have a plan.

We must now trace down the elements of working the plan, which is our next subject.

THE WORKING PHASE

The elements of good plan execution, as shown in Fig. 2–1, are "working the right number of hours" and "working the right hours."

Working the Right Number of Hours

The load summaries we developed earlier are an estimate of the way in which load will arrive, period by period, at a work center. Simplistically, if we work these numbers of hours each period, we will have worked the right number of hours. But it is not practical to do this in most cases, because the load is so variable. At the work center level, it is quite common to see the capacity requirement swing plus or minus 100% and more about its average. It is not usually practical to operate three shifts one week, one or none the next. Some compromise is necessary. The compromise always ends up being some kind of average. Then what kind of average? Over what period of time? It is helpful to back into the answers to these questions by identifying how serious (or trivial) the consequences of *not* working the right number of hours may be. Therefore let us ask, "So what if we don't?" We will, as usual, use a model to explore this. (See Fig. 2–15.)

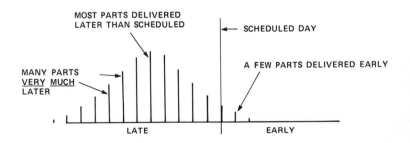

Fig. 2–15.   Poor practical case—job shop work center delivering late and out of schedule sequence.

This distribution will have an average which measures the average days late that the work center is reporting in its operations. It will also have a deviation, which is the measure of its width or, in real terms, a measure of how far from sequence (schedule sequence or priority) it departed during the period being investigated. Thus, in one simple plot, we have revealed the work center's quality of plan execution. Its average days late is a measure of its recent successs in balancing load and capacity, and its width (or deviation) is a measure of its recent ability to stick to the schedule, or sequence, or priority.

If this work center were the only one in the factory, the consequences of its performance would be extremely simple to explain from the figure; that is, (1) the customer orders, on average, are being delivered a certain number of days late, and (2) a few will be delivered early, and a lot will be delivered very late.

But it is *not* the only work center in the factory. Refer again to Fig. 2–8 and note that every work center is related to every other work center; each one feeds others, and/or is fed by others, and/or must work with others to supply parts to assembly.

Let us consider a model of a simple factory having only two feeder work centers that provide parts to a single assembly work center. Work Center No. 1 is running later, on average, than Work Center No. 2. They have similar schedule adherence, that is, their distributions of work-done around the average days late are similarly shaped. We would like to examine this model to identify its effects upon such things as on-time shipment and WIP.

Therefore, let us draw these distributions which have different average days late and see what the resulting picture is trying to tell us. (See Fig. 2–16.) We can immediately, without mathematics, say several things about this typical condition:

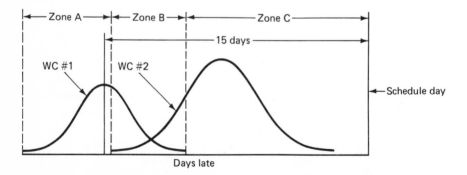

Fig. 2–16. Distribution of finish dates of labor operations done in two feeder work centers which are not the same degree late to schedule.

1. The assembly work center will, on average, run more than 15 days late, since it must await feeder items from Work Center No. 1, which is averaging 15 days late.* (In real life, as this effect penetrates further into the factory, away from the gateway work centers, it becomes worse as the downstream people struggle to unsnarl the unsychronized inputs from upstream.)

2. Work produced very late (Zone A) can be used at once, because the matching parts from Work Center No. 2 were made long ago and are waiting to be assembled. Additional time is, of course, lost in collating these items for assembly, because of the FILO effect. (FILO is an acronym for first in, last out.)

3. Work produced in Zone B (earlier than Work Center No. 1's average, later than No. 2's average) may or may not be usable at once, depending on whether they are matching parts, which is mostly a matter of chance.** A statistical optimist might hope for a 10% parts match up.

4. Work produced in Zone C (by Work Center No. 2, much earlier than matching parts being made in Work Center No. 1) cannot be used at all for some time; not until matching parts from Work Center No. 1 catch up.

Now let us turn our attention to a real-life situation. Refer to Fig. 2–17. Here we see a partial family tree of an industrial product. However, instead of being drawn in the usual way, showing the production intervals required for the various parts, it is drawn to show the average days late of work being reported by the various work centers in the plant. (This is the average days late shown on the example load summary of Fig. 2–9.)

From this figure, without much arithmetic, some interesting observations can be made:

1. Both rotors and fabrications, on average, wait two days for stators to catch up.

2. No downstream work center is more current than the most-late work center feeding it.

3. Starting a long series of operations (such as those leading to the building of the stator) early does not guarantee that they will finish early (the stator is the latest component of the three, and its coils started earlier than anything else). It is quite apparent that something else has to be done to assure finishing on time.

---

*Unless, of course, the assembly work center can catch up, i.e., compress its own interval. Typically the final assembly work center can and does do this when subjected to heavy month-end shipping pressures; but the cost is high and the effort is always only partially successful.

**There are many ways to bias this result favorably so that less chance is involved and more matching parts are made. Expediting is one, which is not necessary or desirable for routine production and is not recommended. Another is a form of critical ratio which develops a priority ranking which is allowed to override simple start date sequence. (See Appendix V.)

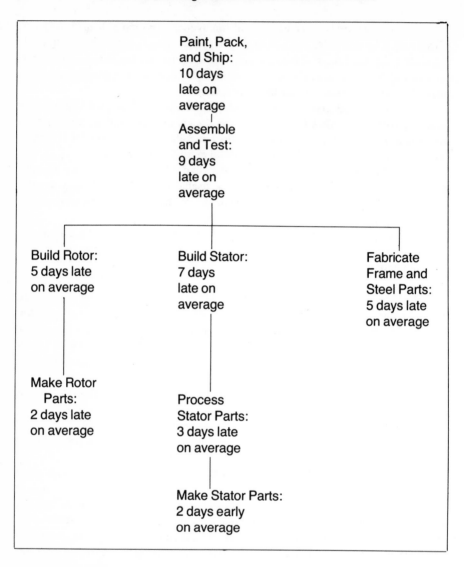

Fig. 2–17.   Partial family tree for an industrial product showing synchronization worsening from level to level.

"Something else" is working more of the right number of hours (load-capacity balancing) and more of the right hours (sequence control). Without these, starting early does not help and may, in fact, hinder on-time shipment if, by starting early, we provide more opportunity to mix the sequence.

Of course, this is a dynamic condition; if one looked at it another week, he would see a different picture. However, the messages would remain the same because the appearance of the picture is necessitated by basic principles of the interaction of sequencing errors, loading errors, number of levels, and product characteristics that are discussed in this chapter.

Their consequences can be held to tolerable levels by good WIP control. Or, if they are not recognized, they will be intolerable, yet will survive through generations of shop management and will continue to plague the factory indefinitely.

The picture shown in Fig. 2–17, by the way, might be quite tolerable for a given product, market, and style of management. Some other management, in some other environment, might find such figures intolerable and set much closer limits upon how late the product shall be permitted to be, on average. It boils down to economics again; control has its price. Every factory has some form of control and pays some price for it. Application of the principles of good WIP control can improve the control and reduce its cost.

We have answered one of our two questions; namely, what the effect upon on-time shipment will be if we work out of sequence and varying degrees late among work centers. The brief answer is that final assembly and shipment to customers will not be, on average, any better, and might be even worse, than the most-late work center feeding it.

Now what about WIP? Let us continue to use the model of two feeder work centers supplying parts to a single assembly work center. Let us make some additional financial and other assumptions that will highlight this WIP aspect. These are as follows:

1. The annual cost of WIP flowing through each of the two work centers is the same.

2. The curves for the two work centers are sufficiently separated to ensure that the match up of parts in the overlap zone, Zone B, is negligibly small; that is, none of Work Center No. 1's early parts match any of Work Center No. 2's late parts.

The assumptions combine with Observation No. 2 on Fig. 2–16 to show that half of the feeder WIP can be used immediately: there is zero idle WIP out of work center No. 1.

The assumptions combine with Observations No. 3 and No. 4 (Fig. 2–16) to show that half of the feeder WIP (viz., that out of Work Center No. 2) cannot be used immediately but is completely idle for the length of time it takes for parts from Work Center No. 1 to catch up.

The model as a whole demonstrates that, given quite typical factory conditions, half of the feeder WIP is performing no useful function whatever, and indeed is a drawback in every way, being nothing but expensive clutter preventing

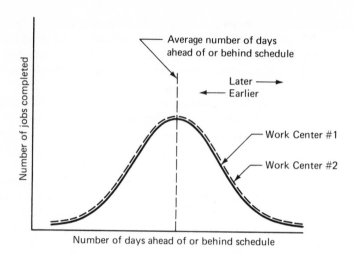

Fig. 2–18. Two work centers working precisely the same number of days early or late to schedule, with the same distribution of reports about their average.

efficient work, while at the same time being damaged, lost, and so on. It should not be necessary to press the case further by explaining that abandoning the assumptions or considering a more typical (i.e., more complex) factory, would have only marginal effects on the result, being as likely to raise the 50% figure as to lower it.

Working the Right Hours

The second component of working the plan is working the right hours, i.e., sequence or priority control. Let us suppose that, using methods explained later, we succeed in getting all work centers exactly abreast; that is, all working the right number of hours, all equally late, early, or on time. Refer again to Observation No. 3 (Fig. 2–16) and extend the reasoning. If the work centers are now abreast and performing identically, what is the probability that, at any point in time, two matching parts are ready for assembly? Fig. 2–18 illustrates this condition.

Looking at the extreme left end of each bell curve it is obvious that there is effectively zero chance of matchup. Extremely few parts have been made. The likelihood that any two of them would be mates is certainly small.

Looking at the extreme right end of each bell curve it is obvious that there is effectively a 100% chance of matchup. Nearly all parts have been made; the likelihood that any given part would have a mate is extremely high. At points between these extremes, the probability of matchup rises from left to right: at first very slowly, then extremely rapidly as one follows the curves toward the right through the average; then slowly as the 100% probability level is approached at the right ends of the curves. And even though, in an actual case, the curves would not be normal distributions, the probability of matchup would begin to rise steeply at about the average of the two curves and would reach effectively 100% at perhaps two standard deviations to the right of the average. Figure 2–19 illustrates qualitatively this phenomenon.

The fact that these distributions are not normal does not change the force or direction of the our arguments; just the numbers that would result from any analysis.

The significance of these observations is that, to assure delivery of matched parts to the assembly work center in our model factory, we dare not assume delivery on schedule; and that the amount by which we routinely depart from schedule will govern the manufacturing interval required through that part of the factory. Therefore, if we can measure and control the amount of this departure, we can control the amount of interval, product lead time, and WIP we need to do our job.

This development is one of the central principles around which WIP turn improvement must be built. It is worthwhile to review it before reading on.

Departures from the Model

Let us consider the main influences that will make reality different from the model and estimate their impact upon the principles that we have been discussing.

1. There are not two, but many work centers feeding assembly. This will sharply reduce the probability of matching parts arriving at assembly until nearly 100% of the total time interval shown in Fig. 2–16 has elapsed. The S curve of Fig. 2–19 will move to the right. There will be more and more instances of assembly being ready to start except for two or three parts. Ship dates are less dependable.

2. Not all work centers have the same distribution curve. This will mean that assembly will have to wait until most of the right-hand tail of the distribution of the

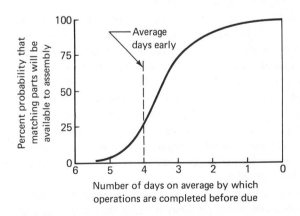

Fig. 2–19. The probability that matching parts will be available from a two-feeder factory as time goes on. Figures are illustrative only.

worst work center has passed. That is, WIP will become proportional to the schedule performance of the worst performing work center.

3. The distributions are not normal. As commented frequently, we can, indeed, be sure that they are not normal. The main job of expediting and priority rules like critical ratio is to ensure that they are not normal. The result will be to skew the distributions so that the average lies somewhat closer to scheduled day and so that the right-hand tail of the distribution is cut off, at least for the parts we really want. If the factory is in the order–launch and expedite mode, the load figures are more or less unreliable anyway and it may seem as if there is a lot of overdue load; but some of it (probably most of it) is not really wanted. This problem will be discussed in some detail later. But the practical effect is that parts will be made, on average, less early (probably late, in most of our shops).

The qualitative, rather than rigorously quantitative, treatment of these principles may trouble some students. But for the purposes of practical shop management the scatter of work-done dates around their scheduled dates does exist; it does have the effects on deliveries and on WIP that we have predicted. The analyses of the shapes, corrections for skew, and other mathematical exercises are probably not warranted because the answers will be different tomorrow.

In what has gone before, you have probably noticed that the commentary has swung back and forth between load-and-capacity control and priority control and has not at times focused exclusively on one subject. This is because the two are tightly intertwined. Some of us may still recall the mild surprise with which we discovered that algebra and trigonometry were not really two different subjects but, if we expected to get much farther in school, had to be used together. Priority control and load-capacity control are just such a pair. One can readily imagine a situation in which well-meaning people have set out to fix one or the other without paying enough attention to its companion set of principles, with the result that the factory has almost as much WIP as before.

This, in fact, is one of the reasons that shop floor control systems or input-output control, for example, sometimes have disappointing results. If load balancing among work centers is given equal emphasis with sequence (priority) control, the groundwork for success in reducing WIP, labor costs, and late shipments has been laid. If sequence control is overlooked or considered a secondary matter, as it often is, the seeds of failure have been sown.

Hopefully this discussion has reinforced the importance of measuring both load balancing and schedule adherence and the importance of displaying them prominently upon the computer outputs. If we do not measure the factors that control effective working of a good plan, then we deserve—and will get—all the WIP our buildings will hold.

One of our pressing concerns, therefore, is to learn how to measure our performance in these two vital areas in ways that will enable us to take quick, effective action to make the steady improvements in productivity of capital and people which industry increasingly requires.

Being Current to Schedule: Definition

We have dwelt at length upon the fact that a work center is very unlikely to be on schedule in the rigorous sense that it is delivering today all the things and only the things it is scheduled to deliver today. For many practical reasons, it will be delivering some things early, some things late. Or we can view its performance as delivering some things earlier than its average days early (or late) and some things later than its average days early (or late).

However, the customer's ship date is a very specific date, with none of the vagueness that seems to be embedded in our emerging concept of a work center as being current. To meet this ship date (i.e., for the final assembly operations to finish on a specific date), all work centers must feed final assembly on schedule; their dates cannot afford to be vague when the desired ship date is quite specific.

We have seen how the randomness of deliveries from feeder work centers is the major factor requiring that our allowed production intervals be much longer than the standard time values. We have seen that one of the requirements of a sound plan is that each feeder interval be synchronized with the next level of assembly. We have seen that, to be 100% sure of having everything we need to begin assembly, we must allow the tails of all the distributions of deliveries from all feeders to pass (or else to be truncated by expediting or, better, by management by exception). And we have seen that a short-term schedule should be sequenced in start date sequence (i.e., the start date of the interval in the production model we are using).

From these observations and principles, it is apparent that routine production of any one leg of the structure of the product we are building will see a few of the parts delivered very early in the allowed interval; a few delivered very late in the allowed interval; but most delivered near or after the middle of the allowed interval. This, in turn, means that the feeder work center should expect to be working, on average, ahead of schedule if assembly is to have a chance to deliver on time. This is very uncharacteristic of most factories, especially job shops. And it is one of the reasons for suppressing the date from the STS: because there is no right date to print. If we print a date, we can be sure that most of the work will neither start nor finish on that date, and the shop operating people know this too. If a piece of information is demonstrably wrong, or if not wrong at the very least unhelpful, it should not be displayed. Date on a short-term schedule is such a piece of information.

These observations refer to routine production. Of course, some of the time we do not have routine production. One of the main functions of shop management and staff is to care for the nonroutine. Because this is so, it sometimes seems to us as we are caring for the running of the shop that nothing which happens is routine. But that is not so. The usual ABC distribution exists; we spend 80% of our time solving problems affecting 5% or 10% of the production flow. The existence of the nonroutine does not destroy principles that apply to the routine events—simply makes them more difficult to care for and less apparent to the eye.

Further, one of the main objectives of any WIP turn improvement project is to move more of the nonroutine events into the routine category. The best example of this is seen when we move from the expedite mode into the requirements-planned mode of production. In the expedite mode, almost everything that happens is nonroutine; most things don't progress until the expediter makes his lists and his calls. In the requirements-planned mode, by contrast, a good plan ensures that we know what to do and when to do it; while good execution ensures that most of it gets done as a matter of course. This leaves us free to deal with the genuine expediting emergencies—the porous castings, the machine breakdown, the 'flu epidemic.

So now we know, qualitatively at least, what *current* means to a feeder work center. It means working far enough ahead of finish date, on average, that the vast majority of parts, whose deliveries are scattered around this average, are delivered before the scheduled finish date. Now it remains to clothe this general statement with some practical, numerical criteria. This is the next subject.

Factory Structure and its Influence on Schedules

In our earlier discussion, it was pointed out that there are three basic kinds of work centers in a factory: gateway or first operation; secondary (fed by others); and assembly (including subassembly and final assembly). Fig. 2–8 shows how, in a particular factory, these kinds of work centers form a structure which is analogous to the familiar product structure.

Now consider how the scatter of work done early and late might look for these three kinds of work centers. (See Fig. 2–20.)

Again the warning: These properties of the work centers are shown as normal distributions for ease in thinking about them; we can be sure that they are not normal. But normal or not, their messages can be used in day-to-day factory operations. Let us see what they are trying to tell us.

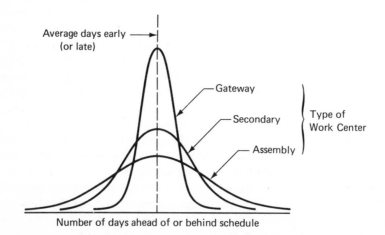

Fig. 2–20. General appearance of the distribution of early and late deliveries for three kinds of work centers.

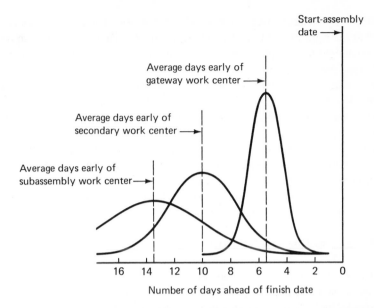

Fig. 2–21. General appearance of days early of parts deliveries from primary (gateway), secondary, and subassembly work centers that will assure the ability of assembly department to begin on time. Illustrative figures only.

As we discussed earlier, to be quite sure of being able to start the next stage of manufacture, we must wait until the rightmost tail of the distribution of the worst performing work center is virtually past. Also, to prevent this process from lasting forever, exception action will be necessary from time to time to truncate this tail. In this context, the worst performing work center is the one with the widest distribution. That is, it is the one adhering least closely to its schedule. In Fig. 2–20, the worst performing work center is obviously the assembly one.

Now let us visualize a model in which these three work centers feed final assembly, which is a common enough situation if the assembly center is considered to be supplying subassemblies to final assembly. Fig. 2–21 shows that the three feeder work centers will have to be working quite differently in order to supply matching parts to final assembly.

Specifically, the primary work center should deliver, on average, 5 days ahead of scheduled finish date; the secondary, 10 days; and the subassembly 13 or 14 days ahead. The figures are, of course, only illustrative.

Many practical questions arise around these concepts which will be dealt with later. For present purposes, it is sufficient to note that the interval which should be allowed the gateway work center (using the simplifying assumption that all parts across it are similar in work content) looks as if it should be about 9 days; the secondary work center, about 19 days; and the subassembly work center, about 27 days.

In a well-managed work center using these principles, the distributions are skewed to the right, toward the scheduled finish day. There are two main reasons: (1) Management by exception ensures that the right-hand tail of the distribution is cut off (i.e., that it does not go on forever); and (2) Some parts are typically being processed early as a legitimate and proper means of load leveling where this is possible, which accounts for the long left tail of the distribution.

It is worth re-emphasizing that, in most factories, the interval to be allowed to a member of a product family tree *depends a good deal more upon the characteristics of the factory than upon the characteristics of the product.* And since the factory's characteristics change constantly as overload, underload, or machine performance, for example, comes and goes, it is essential to keep tabs on the "vital signs" in ways we do not commonly do. These vital signs include work center balance, average days late, and priority index.

Keeping in Touch with the Real world

The explanations offered concerning Figures 2–20 and 2–21 must not be construed as some kind of hypothetical ideal situation or as a recommendation of what should happen if some particular system or algorithm is used. They are descriptions of what actually does happen, moment by moment, every day of the life of an operating factory.

One objective of our factory system must be to make these phenomena visible in ways that lead to effective action. When we measure, we can control. If we know average days late (or early) for our work centers, we can begin where we are and, with confidence and all safe speed, use our knowledge to balance production rates and shorten cycles. If we know the standard deviation of our departures from average days late, we have at least an estimate of how far we are departing from schedule sequence, and with this knowledge can zero in rapidly on the most promising improvement areas.

We are not inventing new systems. We are developing measurement tools that will reveal to us what our existing system is doing, so that we can then devise ways to do better.

SUMMARY: FUNDAMENTALS OF MANUFACTURING

Manufacturing's job is a continual iteration through the sequence: plan the work—work the plan—measure and replan—work the plan—and so on.

A good plan provides enough time and synchronization between the levels. Good plan execution consists of working the right number of hours (capacity-load balancing) and working the right hours (priority or sequence control). Planning must output two main documents to make good execution possible: a load summary and a sequence control list for each work center.

Factory loads are developed by picking apart the myriad of routing sheets collated for all orders in-work and posting their aged loads to time buckets in the load summaries. Reasonable accuracy in routings, including inspect, subcontract, etc. is essential if this process is to succeed. This accuracy is often not present but must be obtained.

Load leveling is a difficult, risky, and deceptive business in a multilevel factory and is probably impossible to do in advance of production. This book recommends that leveling decisions be left to shop management, and not be attempted by the computer.

A schedule must be created for each work center. It should be short and should have no dates on it. Its sequence can be governed simply by operation start date or by priority rules like critical ratio: start date is probably best.

The length of the STS can be governed by the demonstrated capacity of the work center. The input can thus be kept in lockstep with the output. Such a release rule also imposes a very healthful discipline upon the shop which assures that out of date or unwanted operations are kept to a minimum.

On-line systems are not usually a first step in improving manufacturing control and may in fact never be needed. Badly managed, they can delay production.

An STS shows what should be done, not what can be done. The system should display as much information as possible to enable Production Control to convert "should" into "can".

Critical work stations need special forms of loading and management and so do their feeders. Any work center running beyond 70% of its all-out capacity is doubtless critical.

Work centers typically cannot deliver exactly on the scheduled day but must be permitted a tolerance. This tolerance governs the manufacturing intervals required to produce. In the usual case where several work centers feed into assembly, there is an interdependence which is revealed by the numerical amount of this tolerance, a figure which can be developed and portrayed readily by the computer.

Work centers that work differing amounts late cast up a great deal of useless WIP.

Working as close as is practical to STS sequence can minimize WIP greatly by reducing useless mismatched parts. If work centers also work abreast (similar average days early) this useless WIP can be reduced still further and on-time assembly start probability improved dramatically.

Actual factory conditions will change the numerical values of these indicators but not their message or their importance.

Working the plan cannot be divorced from planning the work. And load-capacity control cannot be divorced from sequence control.

Being current to schedule, at the work center level, means delivering parts, on average, ahead of schedule.

Because of the structure of the factory, different work centers must work different amounts ahead of schedule, on average: primary (first-operation) work centers least, secondary and subassembly work centers most.

Manufacturing intervals depend more upon the characteristics of the factory and its structure than upon the characteristics of the product and its structure.

CASE STUDY: SCHEDULING TWO SMALL ORDERS

Two different components are to be made for stock. Component #1 is required in-stock on Day 564, while #2 is required in-stock on Day 575.

On command, the computer program has pulled the routings for these two parts, assigned order #1 to Part #1 and Order #2 to Part #2. Both parts are made by consecutive operations on work centers A, B, C, and D, but the operations are not in the same sequence for the two parts. When the computer program was finished scheduling them, the on-file records looked like this:

Order #1:

Oper. No.	Work Center	Start Date
1	A	561
2	B	562
3	D	563

Order #2:

Oper. No.	Work Center	Start Date
1	B	540
2	D	558
3	C	570

It would be good exercise for the reader to pause here and to write schedules for these two orders alone, through the four work centers involved. When the computer program did this, the results were:

Schedule: Work Center "A"

Start Date	Order No.	Op'n No.
561	1	1

Schedule: Work Center "B"

Start Date	Order No.	Op'n No.
540	2	1
562	1	2

Schedule: Work Center "C"

Start Date	Order No.	Op'n No.
570	2	3

Schedule: Work Center "D"

Start Date	Order No.	Op'n No.
558	2	2
563	1	3

Questions

1. The ship date for order #1 is 564, for order #2, 575. Which should start into work in the plant first? Why?

2. Despite its formal system, the factory actually works to an informal system, which calls for all the parts for March orders to be ready at the end of February, and so on. If Day 564 is end of March, what are some of the probable effects of this mode of operating upon delivery of these two orders?

3. What are some of the probable effects of this mode upon Work Center "B"?

Chapter 3

Finding Out Where You Are

MEASUREMENT

"An engineer is one who believes in measurement, knows how to measure, measures, and is directed by the results of those measurements, whether they fit his preconceptions or not."*

It is necessary to measure the right things in our program to control work in process. Unfortunately, much of the time we either do not measure or we measure the wrong things. An example of measuring the wrong things is using labor efficiency alone as a measure of a foreman's performance, when an equally important aspect of his performance is his adherence to schedule. Or we measure in the wrong place. For example, it is fairly easy to measure an assembly foreman's adherence to schedule, because he either does, or does not, ship on time. Yet probably 80% of his problems were created for him by people who will not be held accountable for them: planners, production men, feeder foremen, draftsmen, buyers. Or we do not measure at all. For example, our adherence to schedule in a feeder department, 14 weeks before order shipment, is fully as important as the labor efficiency in that department, because it controls on-time shipment *and* labor efficiency downstream from it. Yet few plants measure in any concrete, numerical terms this vital aspect of feeder performance.

THE NEED TO SET A BENCHMARK

We must know the point from which we began, if we expect to satisfy ourselves and our management that we are accomplishing something. The starting point for a cost improvement is invariably today's level of cost. Some new level is targeted, based upon new knowledge or other inputs. The investment necessary to progress from one cost level to the next is estimated and a decision made whether the project will pay back.

When the project is completed, the estimates are recycled to learn whether the objectives were reached, and also to determine what was learned during the project which could be fed back beneficially to still another level of improvement. We must measure, install programs, and remeasure to ensure that progress is being made and to make corrections if it is not.

---

*From a lecture delivered by Dr. Lillian Gilbreth to an AIIE meeting.

Managements are rightly skeptical of rosy promises of better deliveries, less idle time, and less WIP. How? How much? How soon? How costly? are legitimate questions. Later in our discussion we will deal with the detailed arithmetic of carrying costs and project justification. But now we want to explore the indicators that are available to us for measurement, day-to-day, of how well we are handling the details of our jobs.

It is assumed here that the reader has taken advantage of the self-test suggested in Chapter 1 and has decided that his firm can, indeed, get value from a program to improve control of WIP. Now it is necessary to use the principles of Chapter 2 as standards against which to measure the present performance of the factory.

Measuring Present Performance

We said earlier that manufacturing is a continuous repetition of the sequence: plan the work, work the plan. So an examination of these two activities, planning and execution, is the best place to begin our measurement. Such a test will enable us to identify where our main opportunities lie. If the plans are good but the execution could be better, we are beginning to zero in on the payoff area, viz., working the plan. If we find that capacity is not our main problem but that working out of sequence is, we are a step closer to our present objective, which is to find out where to spend our scarce time.

We strongly recommend that the person responsible for the WIP improvement program personally make the tests and checks described in this chapter. This is because (1) the measurements are not usually available from most factory systems, and (2) working directly with the numbers will give this responsible person a "feel" for his opportunities which can be had in no other way. It's a learning experience. Those who have studied statistics and similar subjects will testify that understanding the principles is quite easy; so is forgetting them. Actually working with the detailed arithmetic of the problems in a way the student hopes he will never have to in practice is the best way to fix principles and to understand how they apply, what to watch for, where the pitfalls are.

The Quality of the Plan

No amount of shop floor control or expediting will economically correct a wrong plan, so checking out the present plan is the place to start. Considering the two components of a good plan, enough time and synchronization, how do the plans stack up? Determine this by sampling orders in-process on the shop floor. (In this context, an *order* is a complete structure of a product or subassembly which has several levels and components.) Looking at the dates the planning system generated, was enough time provided to:

- perform the labor operations, including things like inspect, pick parts, cut stock?
- move from place to place?
- wait for nonlabor processes such as heat treat, dry paint?
- wait in queue?
- leave the plant for subcontract work and return?

Beware of arguments over whether "clean and deburr" should take 0.3 or 0.35 labor hours.

Lack of good labor standards, like poor forecasts, are often used as a smoke screen. Watch, instead, for these real problems:

- operations omitted or wrongly routed
- overhead operations ignored
- no recognition of crew size (a four-man job requires an elapsed time different from a similar one-man job)
- out-of-plant operations ignored
- shop practices such as overlap and splitting ignored
- route sheet outdated; part now made differently

The second principle calls for synchronization. This means the finish date of any given item must be the same as the start date of its parent item. If this is not true, the plan will have either *gaps* or *laps*. A gap occurs when the finish date of a lower level item is earlier than the start date of its parent, leaving a gap in time. A lap occurs when the finish date of the lower level item is later than the start date of its parent, which therefore cannot be started on schedule.

Gaps raise WIP because the item is made early. Laps raise WIP because matching parts have been made early. They also threaten the ship date because start of the parent item must await finish of its detail parts. If requirements were planned by MRP, gaps may exist because of lot sizing. As with ORP systems, this is a compromise between economy and investment. Only the user can say if it is an acceptable one. But regardless of the requirements planning method, *laps are unacceptable in any plan* except where deliberately provided because feeder parts are not needed until partway through assembly.

To test synchronization use the same procedure as was described above for "enough time." Go one level up and one level down from each item on the order. Identify the assembly calling for the item (up) and the assembly called by the item (down). Record the start and finish dates found. Tabulate the results as in Fig. 3–1.

A summary of the entire order of which Fig. 3–1 was a part showed that there were 59 total items. All 59 had enough time. But only 19 were synchronized. Of the remaining 40, 19 displayed laps, 21 displayed gaps. Fig. 3–1 is fairly obvious, but it does not follow that it is trivial. Most production problems, looked at with hindsight, are obvious. But missing a customer shipping date is never trivial. This plan will guarantee a missed ship date until and unless repaired by the informal system.

Symbol	Item	Date To		Days Of	
		Start	Fin.	Gap	Lap
M	Main assembly	380	390	–	–
R	Rotor	370	375	5	–
RA	Parts—rotor	370	375	–	5
RB	Other parts—rotor	365	370	–	–
S	Stator	372	380	–	–
SA	Frame	360	375	–	3
SB	Core	358	372	–	–
SBA	Parts—core	344	350	8	–

Fig. 3-1.   Analysis of the quality of a plan.

This can be seen at a glance by noting that the stator requires a frame; obviously it cannot be started until the frame is ready. Since the frame finish date is three days later than the stator start date (three days overlap), there is a potential late shipment of three days built into the plan. This three days can be recovered by:

● recognition of the problem in advance by experienced expediters, probably working out of assembly, who ignore the formal plan and set their own dates for the frame, or

● emergency overtime in the machine shop when it is discovered that the stator start date has arrived but the frame is not finished, or

● keeping our fingers crossed and ignoring the whole thing, hoping the slack built into the plan will be sufficient to bail us out. (This is known as "letting the shop sort it out.")

This is a fairly common problem in many scheduling systems. Where it exists it has usually existed for many years; the shop knows the dates are not trustworthy and that, to cover their flanks, they must check every item, every date, on every order and adjust, correct, expedite, or whatever is needed to replan the load. Without realizing it, the firm has gradually accumulated enough staff to plan every job at least twice, wrong both times: wrong in the first place when there was still time to do it right, wrong during actual production when it has become too late to do it right.

Until the promoters of any system intended to help the factory ship on time can demonstrate to their associates in the factory that the plan is worth following and can be followed, they should save their breath. The fact that these two simple principles of creating a sound plan—enough time and synchronization—may not have been identified in so many words by foremen and their staffs does not diminish their importance. These people are all too painfully aware of the impact upon them of plans that do not have enough time and synchronization.

If, in a factory, there is evidence that inadequate plans have been made and published for some time, it will pay back many times over to fix the problem (by working with the computer people and with whoever creates the plans) and to let the old, bad plans drain out of the system before launching with fanfare into the new.

A warning: Do not assume that, since the planning system is computerized, the likelihood of coordination or synchronization errors is small. Peculiar things happen within computer programs, particularly when lot sizing or other special case logic is embedded in them. In a set of programs of any complexity at all, it is not in the least amazing to find glaring errors emerging for the first time after the system has been in use for many years.

The final characteristic of a good plan is that it is presented to the user in a good way.

It is worth saying again that effective manufacturing requires continuous, exceedingly well-aimed control over two things: (1) load-capacity balancing (or capacity control); and (2) sequence control (or priority control).

One of the best ways to ensure that this important distinction is drawn is to publish the control documents on two separate reports. The titles of these reports are important because they start the user's thought processes down the right track. For load-capacity balancing, we like the title Load Summary. For sequence control, we like the title Sequence Control Report or List. The omission of the word *Schedule* is deliberate, even though the sequence control report is in fact an STS. By calling the STS a sequence control report we are forcefully drawing to the operating people's attention that it exists for one purpose only: to indicate the order, sequence, or priority of work. We are entitled to expect that one day the message will sink in: load problems are not fixed by manipulating the schedule, nor are sequencing problems addressed by changing the capacity.

Later we will see another reason for these statements. The load summary is input to a planning meeting which must not degenerate into a production meeting. It will degenerate if specific order numbers and part numbers appear on the load summary.

Beware of single dual-purpose documents called Scheduled Load or some other such title. They are neither fish nor fowl, and their use perpetuates the misunderstanding between sequence control and its tools and load control and its tools.

The actual printed appearance of a good load summary and a good sequence control report are shown in Chapter 2, Figs. 2–9 and 2–13. Note the qualifications that are stated in that section; but test your own factory's documentation against these models, which provide the *minimum* requirements. If a given plant's system also provides a good, dependable eligibility subsystem, or some other enhancement, this may be good or it may not, depending upon how well it is working. If it is not working well, consideration should be given to suppressing it for a time until load-capacity balancing and sequence control are working, because all else depends upon these.

Under this same heading of a "good presentation" of the plan, it will pay to do some role playing. The technique is simple. Ask yourself, "If I were the operator, what would or could I do with this sequence control list?"

We are going to ask the operator to work his way down through the list. Very well, at a desk and later at the work center, we must form a judgment or opinion of just how hard or easy this might be.

Watch not only for practical difficulties (such as the FILO effect discussed earlier) but for overlooked, ridiculous system features. For instance, correct sorting (sequencing) of the STS is essential. We once saw an STS that had been sorted according to an elegant priority setting rule. But operations that obviously would be done consecutively on the part were listed nonconsecutively on the STS. Naturally, no one in the shop paid the least attention to that sequence listing. It was 95% right but useless because of the 5% wrong. And it was an error that was repaired by ten minutes of computer program maintenance work. As has been wisely commented, the trouble with computers is that they do exactly as they are told.

The Quality of Plan Execution

Fig. 2–1 shows us that good plan execution consists of working the right number of hours and working the right hours: or load-capacity control and priority control, respectively.

Load and capacity

At this point, a digression is necessary to clarify the concepts of *load* and *capacity*. These terms tend to be used quite loosely, but they need to be carefully defined and properly understood.

Load is the amount of work to be performed in some period by some work center. It can be expressed in pieces, man-hours, machine-hours, square foot hours (more about this later), or other units suitable for the environment. In most shops, labor hours is the most workable unit. Load has very little to do with capacity, except that when it exceeds capacity we have a problem. Load is further subdivided into released load (or queue) and load-ahead: or eligible load and ineligible load (go or nogo), depending upon the degree of sophistication of the particular system. An important attribute of load for our purposes (that is, for the people running the factory day-to-day), is that *the size of the load can be controlled very little or not at all*. The opportunity to control the size of the load, by adjusting quantities to be built, orders to be taken, and so forth, has long since passed. We are now committed to carry the load that the earlier activities have generated. Short-term control of load can only mean shifting it in time: usually earlier, seldom later because of the overlap problems discussed earlier (see Chapter 2). The obvious exception is if the final shop-loading process develops an unexpected load peak which absolutely prevents all these commitments being met (this is dealt with under "Rescheduling" later.)

Capacity is the ability of a work center to carry load, expressed in the same units as the load (e.g., man-hours). Capacity can be expressed in many ways. For instance, a work center has a maximum technical capacity which is seven days per

week, three shifts per day, minus allowances for maintenance and other down-
times. Few plants are interested in, or attempt to use, this all-out capacity. Probably
the most realistic capacity measure is the recently demonstrated output of the work
center, be it 5% or 75% of the technical maximum. There are many good reasons for
using this definition of capacity. Some of these reasons are as follows:

1.   Unless some specific management action (such as changing the number
of shifts) is taken, the work center will probably continue to produce next week
about what it did last week, if the work is available.

2.   It is self-correcting. Capacity figures that are calculated and then placed
on computer files for use by programs (or people) are almost invariably out of date.

3.   It is a very convenient number for people or computers to use in
estimating the amount of overdues the work center is carrying, expressed in some
instantly understood unit such as "3½ weeks of overdues at current working rate."
Knowing this figure is crucially important in keeping work centers in balance, as we
shall see.

4.   It can be used to control the release of work by computerized systems, as
a means of controlling the queue at the work center. Because it is self-correcting,
the work center input can be opened up or dried up to keep in lockstep with the
actual accomplishment of the work center, without laborious human intervention.

Recently demonstrated capacity is most simply and usefully calculated as the
moving average of the past n periods of work reports. The value of n will depend
upon the nature of the plant: in medium to heavy job shops, it is frequently two to
five weeks or some agreed number of labor-unload cycles.

To summarize, capacity depends upon the physical facilities available and the
way they are staffed. Load depends upon the flow of business and the mix of work
generated by the numerous customer and stock orders passing through the plant.
And a better expression for the phrase "Controlling load and capacity" would be
"*Balancing* load to capacity." This is because, in the end, of course, all load must
eventually be completed and, therefore, there is a balance struck between load and
capacity. Our job in production and inventory control is to be sure that the balance is
struck economically, with minimum investment in machines, inventory, and wasted
labor. (Note well: P&IC has no control over the labor content of the job, but has
immense power over the *wasted* labor in the plant. P&IC people should have cost
improvement as a very real concern.)

Measuring how well we perform this balancing act, and a discussion of the
consequences of doing it well or poorly, is our next subject.

Balancing load to capacity

To get an idea of load control, take a suitable size sample of the week's labor
tickets from a work center as reported to the pay office, shop office, or other center.
For each ticket, record the number of days it is being reported earlier or later than its
scheduled day. Using squared paper or any method you like, plot the individual
samples on a graph which will look like Fig. 3–2.

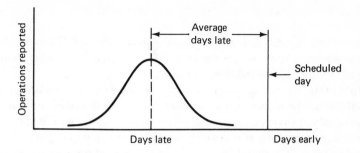

Fig. 3–2. Distribution of a sample of labor tickets about their scheduled day.

After enough points have been plotted, some sort of skewed distribution will emerge. (The distribution in Fig. 3–2 and those to follow will be represented as normal bell curves for simplicity and ease of understanding. In real life the distributions will not be normal.)

The purpose of this kind of work, of course, is to identify the most promising areas in which to work to improve plan execution. Naturally, if the plan has been found to be exceedingly bad, the execution will be found to be worse, and this exercise may have little payback. Here is still another of the ways in which clear segmentation of opportunity pays off: one need not even engage in this work if the plan is the culprit. Fix the plan first, then test execution.

If the distributions developed during this work seem very wide, priority control is a fruitful area. If their averages are very far behind scheduled day, or if their averages differ significantly work center to work center, load-capacity balancing offers potential.

Typically, in a factory that has not been subjected to this kind of scrutiny before, both sequence control and load-capacity balancing will be found to be in need of attention. But it will invariably be found that one problem outweighs the other here, while the reverse is true there. Since one cannot correct all problems at once (and indeed since all problems are not worth correcting), this kind of study begins at once to help the user apply his valuable time, talent, computer cost, and other resources to the areas in greatest need.

To some, our discussion of the necessity of setting benchmarks may seem a waste of time. Convinced readers of Chapter 1 and Chapter 2 may already be certain that they should press on at full speed to revise their computer programs to give the measurements described earlier, which are admittedly tedious done by hand. To them we can only wish all success; if they have the budget and authority to proceed this way, they should do so.

Other readers may feel more secure and certain if they test the principles by hand. They may have other people to convince and considerable amounts of money to request. Their care and caution must be respected, so long as a desperately needed WIP turn improvement project does not fall into what has aptly been called, ''paralysis by analysis.''

SUMMARY

To be sure of establishing high-payoff objectives for a WIP turn improvement program, we must know where we started from so that accomplishment can be monitored as work is done and funds are spent.

To do this, we can apply the principles of *synchronized production* (Chapter 2) directly to our own operation as we find it. We can determine plan quality and execution quality by comparing present performance with known criteria.

It is important that a plan not only *be good,* but that it *look good.* It should be presented to the user in sharply focussed, action-oriented form which draws a clear line between load-capacity balancing and sequence control.

Empathetic role-playing has a part: it pays to attempt to use each system output as the user must.

Load and *capacity* are two different things, and the differences must be understood and used during plan execution. *The entire procedure as described can be shortened, and the control system described in Chapter 2 set up at once if the user has the understanding, the confidence, the nearly-good-enough system, and the budget to do it.*

Chapter 4

Objective Setting

INTRODUCTION

In Chapter 2 we reviewed the fundamentals of manufacturing an assembled product. In particular, Fig. 2–1 shows, in highly condensed form, how to proceed directly and efficiently from general objectives to the specifics of serving a market effectively out of a manufacturing facility.

In Chapter 3 we saw how to evaluate our present performance by measuring it against the criteria of Chapter 2.

Now, in Chapter 4, we want to estimate realistically what improvement we should plan to get; that is, using the principles of Chapter 2, how can we estimate costs, benefits, and timing of a program that can be sold to our management—a program that demonstrates a powerful contribution to the business success of the firm? Starting at the point we have identified in Chapter 3, what improvement can we confidently forecast?

WHERE THE HARD-DOLLAR SAVINGS ARE FOUND

In what follows, we will explore a procedure that has been used and works well. Considering the differences among plant environments, it will not likely suit everyone exactly; but since it is based upon principles, it can safely be used as a point of departure.

We will estimate improvement potential under the following headings:

1. Delivery performance.
2. Labor efficiency.
3. WIP inventory level.
4. Parts and raw materials inventory levels.
5. Facilities utilization.
6. Managed costs.

Delivery Performance

Most sales or marketing departments keep statistics on the percentage of jobs, or dollars, or both that were shipped on time. The definition of *on time* can be expected to give trouble. On time with respect to what—the original promise, the changed promise that was made when the order was taken, the further change when the customer delayed approval, or just what promise? Since we are measuring manufacturing effectiveness, the best definition seems to be: the promise that was in effect at the time the factory began cutting material and applying labor. If a particular plant uses and is comfortable with some other definition of a promise, it should use it.

The next term whose definition will cause trouble is *late*. If a product is one day late in a cycle time of six months, little notice need usually be taken, unless of course that day caused the shipment to miss a boat, for example. A convenient index number that can be used is *dollar-days late*. By this measure, a million-dollar order shipped one day late is as late as a one hundred thousand dollar order shipped ten days late. Again, we should use a measure we are used to and with which we are comfortable.

However, since the fact that we are measuring sometimes causes some parts of the organization to become defensive—reluctant to accept the measurement—this may be a good time to change to something more acceptable. Dollar-days is objective and will often be acceptable to all. It has another advantage. It can be converted into a true index number, a single-figure tracking number that is easy to maintain.

We can compute an *equivalent days late* for each month's shipments. Consider a simple model of a plant that shipped three customer orders in some month, each costing $1,000. One of them was shipped ten days late to promise. The overall dollar-days of lateness for the factory for that month therefore was: 10 days times $1,000 or 10,000 dollar-days. However, the plant shipped a total of $3,000 cost of sales in the month. Therefore, the equivalent days late for that month was 10,000 dollar-days divided by $3,000, or 3.3 days. This single figure has no significance taken by itself, but it does have significance when compared with past months or with some objective.

Again, simple lateness may, under some circumstances, not tell the whole story, because lateness with one customer may be more serious than with another. But whatever measure is used should be simple, transparent, and acceptable to everyone, or it will fail. Elegant schemes for weighting customer importance, commercial advantage, size of billing, margin on the sale, and so on soon become so opaque and subjective that the people being measured will not accept them.

Labor Efficiency

Here again, sampling—probably classical work sampling (Waddell 1952)—is likely to be the simplest and quickest way to get an idea of labor efficiency. The industrial engineers in the plant can help with this and, in fact, can usually be found with a recent reading on the subject on their desks. We must answer the questions:

1. How much unproductive time is spent by operators in handling or searching for material, waiting for the next workpiece to be brought, talking to

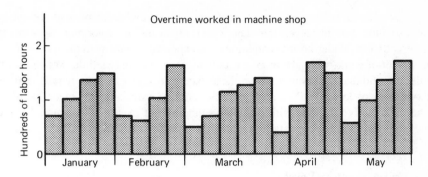

Fig. 4–1.   Bar graph of overtime worked by week.

materials handlers or expediters, and other similar activities symptomatic of unpredictable or disordered material flow?

2. How much emergency or unanticipated overtime is incurred each period? This is often a difficult figure to get, because we are so accustomed to our familiar situation of working overtime to make up shortages that we don't consider it emergency or unanticipated—just routine. Rules of thumb can help here; for example if overtime has to be worked on less than one week's notice, it is avoidable. Another useful tool of analysis is to record, for a few months, the rise and fall of overtime as the month-end comes and goes. (See Fig. 4–1.) An educated estimate can be made from such a record that some (probably large) part of the overtime represented by the periodic bulge is avoidable.

During this work, watch for other phenomena such as significantly higher overtime worked in the month prior to Christmas or prior to summer vacation. If this phenomenon exists, its cause and cure are outside the scope of this book but richly deserve attention.

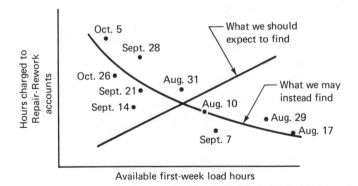

Fig. 4–2.   How to analyze whether excess cost accounts are being used as "cushion."

3. Do various excess cost allowances, such as rework, respond to volume as they should? For instance, the time spent repairing or reworking parts made incorrectly can, under normal conditions, be expected to vary with the load—if we have a lot of work, we make more errors than if we have only a little. Sometimes it will be found that the reverse is true: these excess costs *rise* as activity falls. This is a symptom of loose WIP control, usually resulting from attempts made to fill in what is actually idle time with plausible sounding but overdone "repairs." If the accounting system has the detail, as many have, plot this as in Fig. 4–2.

WIP Inventory Level

A very old formula states that WIP, in number of pieces, is equal to production rate multiplied by cycle time. This fact can be illustrated by two figures. First, consider a product being made at a rate of three per week, on a six-week cycle time, as in Fig. 4–3.

In this figure, notice that, once the production rate has been established, wherever you care to look along the time axis (e.g., a line drawn up through the middle of Week 8–9) you will encounter six units in production, ignoring the start point of each unit to avoid counting a unit twice. Now let us assume we find a way to manufacture this product on a three-week, rather than six-week, cycle. Further, suppose that we accomplished this cycle-time reduction while leaving the shipping rates and dates unchanged. Fig. 4–4 shows this transition. Fig. 4–4 carries on from the previous figure. Unit No. 11 was the last unit made on the old six-week cycle time. Unit No. 12 is made on the new three-week cycle time. Shipping rates and times have remained unchanged, but any line drawn vertically will now encounter only three, not six, units in-process.

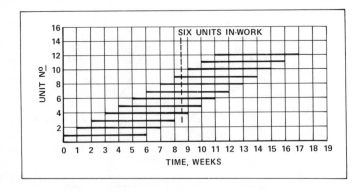

Fig. 4–3. Number of units in-process equals production rate multiplied by cycle time.

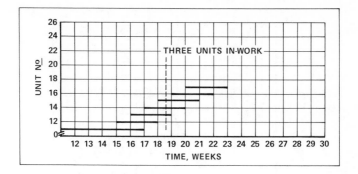

Fig. 4–4.   Halving the cycle time will halve the number of units in-work.

It is noticeable in Fig. 4–4 that, although no shipments are lost, nothing is started into production in Weeks 12, 13, or 14. This has profound implications during a cycle-time reduction program and can only be noted in passing here.

This discussion, however, is in units. We are interested in cost—the dollar level of WIP inventories. In the simplest case, one would say that, on the average, any unit is half-finished and, therefore, all units can be considered included in WIP at half their final cost.

But we don't usually have the simplest case. Factories making single-level assembled products from many parts on highly mechanized lines with little labor content incur all their parts costs at the start and add very little labor and overhead: any unit in-process is in the plant at nearly full cost. At the other end of the spectrum, plants that make complex, multilevel products may begin making hundreds of low-cost bits and pieces (like insulation, wood details, small steel parts) weeks or months before the significant elements of cost begin to accumulate: a randomly chosen unit in-process is likely to have accumulated much less than half of its ultimate cost.

So it is apparent that the formula for work in process in units must be modified somehow if we want work in process to be expressed in dollars. We can insert a factor which we can call S, the shape factor, to account for the differences in rate of cost buildup. And the formula is still pretty simple:

WIP $= SCR$ where
  $S =$ cost buildup shape factor, typically from 0.25 to 0.90
  $C =$ cycle time to make one of the product (days, weeks, etc.)
  $R =$ throughput rate, in cost dollars per day, week, etc. (must be the same interval as chosen for the cycle time C)

The shape factor S is likely to need careful study in a given environment. Accounting figures will often give it for expensive, long-cycle apparatus where it is

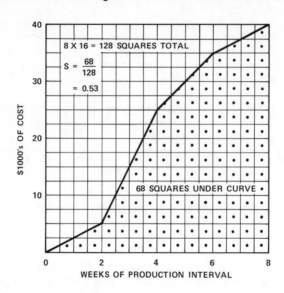

Fig. 4–5. Typical cost build up curve for one unit of work in process.

essential, at least once per month, to report costs accumulated to date. If these figures are available, it is easy to plot them on a piece of squared paper and arrive at S by counting the squares enclosed by the curve and then dividing this result by the total squares in the rectangle. Fig. 4–5 shows how this is done. If the numbers are unavailable from the accounting statements, it is necessary to identify the kind of product (high-cost input at the start, or at the end, or steadily through the production cycle) and create a synthetic cost buildup graph that satisfactorily describes your own product (Sirianni 1975, p. 73). To know whether you have succeeded in creating a satisfactory model, plug in your numbers, solve the formula, and compare the result with your reported WIP on the accounting statements. Example:

Factor $S = 0.65$ (estimated by the method of Fig. 4–5)
Factor $C = 8$ weeks (average cycle time, from analysis, observation, records, statements)
Factor $R = \$100,000$ per week (cost of shipments made, from accounting records or statements)

Therefore

WIP $= 0.65 \times 8 \times \$100,000$
$= \$520,000$ of WIP needed to support this level of production, on these cycle times, with this shape factor.
WIP $= 562,300$ (actual figure from accounting month-end inventory statement)

The conclusion from such an analysis would be that the model is reasonably good, since its result is within 8% of the accounting figure.

In the typical case where a plant has several important products with different values of S, C, and R, it is necessary to model each of them as just shown and sum the results.

Special cases exist, such as seasonal products or products being phased in or out. These can be analyzed by a capable practitioner in his own environment, using the principles just outlined (see also Sirianni 1980).

Having succeeded in developing figures for the WIP model which we can, with confidence, plug into the model to predict WIP to support any given level of production, we are ready to examine it for improvement possibilities. This can readily be done by studying each of the factors in turn. The shape factor (S) is governed by how soon the various labor and material inputs are charged to the job. If expensive items are charged early, the buildup graph bulges outward to the left, enclosing more area, leading to a high value of S and hence high WIP. If these inputs can be delayed without threat to the ship date, the bulge can be reduced, S will fall, and so will WIP. An excellent example of this technique was the engine in a locomotive plant. At one time, the engine was mounted in the locomotive at what seemed a suitable time, and assembly proceeded for several weeks. Then it was realized that a drilled steel plate would be a fully satisfactory substitute for the engine until it was time to pipe it up. This was done, and the engine—the most expensive single component of the locomotive—was scheduled in later. Furthermore, the assembly crews' efficiency increased because they had room to move about and somewhere to stand—a typical result of a properly run WIP reduction program.*

The cycle time (C) tends to be an exceedingly uncomfortable compromise between what Marketing would like it to be, which is what the factory occasionally actually achieves when the president gets interested in a particular order, and what the factory thinks it needs to do the work without disruptions like overtime and air-freight. Unfortunately, the misconception that providing a little more cycle time will assure better on-time performance is a myth that dies hard. And so cycle times tend to be very much on the long side rather than on the short side.

To some degree, cycle time can be legislated. That is to say, if we plan on a shorter cycle, we will deliver on a shorter cycle, often with no worsening of the on-time performance. But this process cannot be carried too far in any given plant without colliding violently with other things that impede the cycle-time reduction effort. These other things comprise the main subject matter of this text.

There are two ways to get shorter cycles:

1. By hardware technology.
2. By system technology.

---

*Our thanks to Dave Garwood for passing on this example.

As an example of hardware technology, a builder of large power transformers at one time used hot air to dry them prior to oil filling and electrical testing. As the transformers became larger, they became more complex, with more paper insulation (notorious for its affinity for atmospheric moisture) and more devious passages and remote corners. Hot air was simply blown in one opening and out another. Finally the firm found itself spending as long as 50 days performing this process, which had become less effective as unit size rose. A vapor-vacuum process was then devised that resulted in a much superior dryout in 2 to 3 days. A minimum of 45 days at nearly full WIP value was taken out of the production cycle of a $200,000 piece of apparatus.

As an example of system technology, a builder of steel fabrications, such as tanks, found its shop clogged with WIP at all times, despite which it could not meet customer dates. Machines were not overloaded, the work force was sufficient in quantity and quality, and production support (such as computer programs) was thought to be quite good. The manager heard of input-output control and felt that it held a potential for reducing his cycle times and his WIP. He called in the systems manager, production control manager, and shop superintendents and demanded that whatever needed doing, be done to assure that these goals be met. One of his comments was that he was tired of paying $20,000 per year for useless computer programs; a very sound attitude to take.

By close attention to synchronization of requirements, working to load summaries and schedules, making minor improvements to the computer programs (which really *were* quite good), training, and coaching, this manager's team achieved stunning results including over 50% WIP reduction; 10% to 15% better labor efficiency; a drop from an average 15 days late delivery to an average of 2 or 3 days late; and much improved efficiency in the following departments. The cycle times did, indeed, come down—from far over the nominal times which Marketing, with many misgivings, quoted, to somewhat below the nominal times, with recognizable scope for further reduction.

The production rate (R) is, in the short term, predetermined for the people who must produce—the factory. The opportunity to raise or lower R by adjusting selling rates is long since past. While management will occasionally agree to a reschedule, it is best to assume that R is a given—either fixed (steady production) or changing with business conditions. The far-seeing materials manager or P&IC practitioner will study the business and be able to point out that it would pay the firm to raise R for this product, lower it for that product; but such studies are outside the scope of our discussion.

We are left with S and C which we can alter to alter our WIP. Let us look first at C, the cycle time, which is the more powerful of the two in most practical cases.

WHERE THE WIP TURNOVER POTENTIAL LIES

This section might be subtitled ''Getting it all together.'' We have discussed the importance of, and the theory behind, synchronized production. We have warned that manufacturing cycle reduction alone, although it seems so enticingly simple from the WIP = SCR formula, can backfire and have disastrous results if prior attention has not been paid to planning the work flow and to load, capacity, and sequence control. Now we want to estimate the potential for turnover improvement through WIP inventory reduction which is available if we blend these two vital techniques: (1) load, capacity, and sequence control and (2) cycle time reduction.

Fig. 4–6 shows a model of a simple multilevel assembled product in the familiar "goes into" format. Each heavy bar is drawn to a time scale and shows the planned interval for the component. Each bar has a small normal distribution drawn beside it, intended to show the probability that the component will be completed by the time opposite it on the time scale. Recall that intervals must be longer than the bare time needed to do the job because it is not possible to control a job shop so tightly that the completion of any operation can be expected to occur at the exact minute it was planned. This, then, gives rise to some kind of probability distribution which suggests the likelihood that the component will be completed very early, about on time, very late, or somewhere in between. The small normal distributions shown on the chart are an expression of these probabilities.

Note that every component needed by M, the main assembly, is very likely to be completed in time for M to begin on schedule except for component A. For whatever reasons, the work center through which component A passes has a very wide distribution of its completion dates. On average, it completes its work somewhat ahead of schedule, but the rightmost (or top) tail of its distribution encroaches well into the start date for M. By inspection, perhaps 25% of

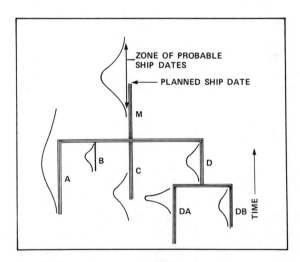

Fig. 4–6. How lateness and out-of-sequence working combine to determine how often the product is shipped on time.

components A might be late, and, therefore, 25% of the assemblies to be made in the final assembly work center cannot start on time. This final assembly work center may or may not be able to absorb this compression; but this is immaterial for the present discussion.

This model is drawn as if one product were involved, but it is a composite picture of what happens with a large number of jobs which do not coincide in time. It is created by normalizing many jobs, i.e., bringing them all to the same shipping date. The scheduled date of each reported event is subtracted from the reported date and the result used as one element of a standard distribution which uses the planned interval as an axis, or time base. In this way, the confusion created by the presence of many jobs with many dates in the production stream at the same time is cleared away, and we can see what we actually do and compare it directly with what we planned to do.

From this model, several important inferences can be drawn.

In the first place, as long as the trouble that A's work center seems to be having continues, a significant number of M work center's jobs will be started late. M's work center will, at all times, be working partly in an emergency expediting mode, using overtime to pick up the compression forced upon it by the poor performance of A's work center in adhering to sequence.

Adding manpower or overtime in A's work center may or may not help the situation: as the picture looks, it probably won't. A's work center, *on average,* is delivering ahead of schedule. If it could adhere better to sequence, its distribution would narrow and its encroachment upon the interval allowed to M would vanish. This is a priority problem, not a capacity one.

In addition, the work center through which component DA passes is apparently able to adhere very closely to schedule sequence. There is a very high probability it will deliver parts DA just about when needed, very little early and almost never late. It appears that the planning interval for DA is unnecessarily long. (In an actual factory, a punchpress shop might show this characteristic.)

And finally, it can be inferred that, typically, components B, C, and D will be completed before component A and will wait in WIP longer than most components A.

Recognizable Stages of WIP Reduction

From our model (Fig. 4–6) three recognizable stages of WIP inventory reduction can be described. The first stage is to identify and improve the performance of work centers (e.g., A's work center). The first concern is working to sequence; insufficient manpower may or may not be a problem. If the distribution of probable delivery dates can be made narrower and higher, it will no longer encroach on the assembly work center nor force the assembly work center to start late. Nor will it force some of the WIP of components B, C, and D to wait for matching parts.

Results to be expected from this stage are as follows:

- improved on-time shipment performance,
- reduced WIP because of reduced delay in matching components B, C, and D with late A's,
- increased inventory *if* it has been necessary to add manpower in A's work center to overcome the lateness problem.

The decreases and increases in WIP inventory may or may not offset each other. In this stage, there typically is little improvement in inventory levels but a dramatic improvement in on-time shipment.

The second stage is to bring all work centers up to the level of performance of the best, namely DA's work center. Here, enough product is made, and it is made close to the time wanted. If all work centers had distributions this high and narrow, very little WIP would be made ahead of schedule and all needed WIP would be available on schedule. This upgrading is done by controlling sequence very closely and maintaining a suitable average days late figure. This in turn depends heavily upon labor flexibility among work centers so that, as much as may be economical, the available labor follows the load peaks through the shop. It does not very often depend upon large infusions of extra labor. It may require temporary infusions of limited amounts of overtime in selected work centers.

Results to be expected from this stage are as follows:

- a significant fall in WIP inventory as more and more parts are made toward the end of their allowed intervals rather than being made toward the middle or start of their intervals. (Or earlier—see parts C.)
- a measurable improvement in labor efficiency as less and less material is on the floor at one time, less searching and waiting are needed at secondary and assembly work centers.
- a temporary drop in manpower required as WIP inventory falls. (Every piece of WIP inventory has its labor element. If we are going to reduce WIP, we are going to have to throttle-back, temporarily, on labor inputs.)

The third stage is to selectively reduce the production intervals allowed for the product and its parts. As commented earlier, this step can be legislated to some degree, because product intervals which have been in place for some years are, in most cases, much too long and it is safe to assume this is so and reduce them, across the board. However, this must be done with clear recognition of the fact that if we cut too deeply in this arbitrary fashion we will again encounter a situation such as shown for part A. Here, the late end tail of the distribution begins once more to encroach on the intervals provided for the next stage of assembly. It is better to examine individual production intervals allowed for the various branches of the product and compare them with the shop section's ability to deliver on time and in sequence. If there is a favorable comparison—as there is for the work center that makes part DA—then the interval for that part of the work can be reduced.

Results to be expected from this stage are as follows:

● a further very significant fall in WIP inventory as slack is removed from the product plan.

● a temporary loss of work for the early feeder departments (such as DB's work center) as new orders are started into work on the shorter cycles.

● continued increase in labor productivity as factory clutter continues to fall.

● the potential for reduction in managed costs; less expediting effort will be needed.

● possible degradation of on-time delivery performance if the process has been unintentionally carried too far in some areas. This is not inevitable—merely a possible outcome of an overzealous interval reduction.

● a significant competitive advantage will develop as manufacturing intervals fall and physical shop capacity rises. *A warning:* This time pickup can be lost if Parkinsonism creeps into upstream functions and the order processing or engineering intervals increase.

● a significant reduction in parts inventories, since we have eliminated time spent waiting for chronically late work centers to start, and we have also brought the plan start date closer to the plan finish date, eliminating slack in parts cycle time as well as WIP cycle time.

The Importance of Sequence

It is essential that WIP reduction be done in these three stages. It is tempting to try to reduce cycles first because the effect is so powerful; but getting the feeders in order is a precondition. The reason can be induced from Fig. 4–6. If the feeders are not delivering matched sets of parts to assembly, reducing cycle times will simply require more and more frantic expediting and will probably worsen delivery performance.

Recall, too, that delivering matched sets of parts requires *planning* as a first step. So planning is also a precondition to getting the feeders in order. And the experience of many factories is that planning is seldom in good enough order to support effective load-capacity balancing and priority control. The troops who get production out have enough to cope with in the ordinary exigencies of shop operation; they simply must not be loaded also with the responsibility for correcting a bad plan.

If these two preconditions have been satisfied—planning is in order, load-capacity control is in order—then cycle-time reduction can be undertaken. The most effective place to reduce cycles is, of course, where the cost is highest; that is, when the product is nearest the shipping door. This suggests a cycle-time reduction program which begins with final assembly and is worked back upstream. Such a program is also the easiest to control and to phase in, since there are fewer departments to monitor (often only one or two) and far fewer parts to control. (A little later in our discussion, we will recommend a feasible cycle-time reduction program.)

Parts and Raw Materials Inventory Levels

Our stocks of parts and materials can be significantly affected by our management of WIP.

Many factories quite typically start late, for many good and bad reasons. When a job is started late, its parts and raw materials wait that long before being released into production. The requirements planning system must believe the dates it is given; it has no other. If these dates are not adhered to, the better the requirements planning system we have, the higher our excess parts and raw materials inventory will be. Estimating how much money is thus tied up is fairly simple if one has a requirements planning system with an aged applications list. By computer or by hand, go through the applications (on a sampling basis if it is necessary to do it by hand—5% to 10% is a sufficient sample) and total the overdue dollars. A job overdue starting generally has a large percentage—90% to 95%—of its material on hand, and so accounts for a good deal of money. The total of these dollars, multiplied by the sampling ratio, is an estimate of the amount of parts and raw material inventories that are on hand because of habitual late starting. Sometimes we feel better if we take another sample later to confirm but the answer seldom differs much. Firms, like people, get set in their ways.

Facilities Utilization

Very few factories are loaded to the practical limit, or even very near it. Work sampling in any part of the plant will usually reveal that even key machines (critical work centers) are actually performing their assigned functions a surprisingly small percentage of their manned hours. ("Small" could be 75% in the case of an extremely expensive, high-production, numerically controlled machine, but can easily go as low as 15% in a heavy equipment assembly bay.)

In the case of individual machines, the unused machine-hours will usually be accounted for by waiting, handling, sorting, searching, and similar delays caused either by inadequate physical facilities (such as infrequent trucking) or by the confusion and uncertainty created by the presence of large volumes of WIP.

In the case of work centers limited by area (such as assembly bays), the unused area-time is invariably accounted for in large measure by a need to have several jobs on the go at once, so that labor can be swung back and forth as feeder parts become available. Alternatively, jobs are allocated a space and set up awaiting sufficient parts to warrant starting assembly. As a result, any given space in the bay is likely to be in actual use for manufacturing, as distinct from storage or waiting, only 15% to 20% of the manned time.

It is interesting to analyze this problem mathematically. If a given product requires any significant number of feeder parts, say 20 or 30, and the probability of each one's being available goes even as low as 96% to 98%, the probability of that job's being able to start on time falls surprisingly low. Having several jobs coming into a "go" state at the same time provides a hedge against running out of work one week and requiring double shifts the next. Every assembly foreman soon learns this, though he may know or care little about the mathematical laws driving the process. The entire thrust of the procedures outlined in this text is the elimination of these sources of uncertainty in the feeders; reducing the randomness of the material flow; eliminating most of the need for sorting, resequencing, finding, and expediting; and making it possible for the assembly departments to depend upon a flow of *matched* sets of parts. In this effort, we cannot hope for perfection but we are entitled to expect very large and noticeable improvements.

All these effects express themselves, ultimately, as reduced cycle time. In the simplest case of a factory making one item at a time, finishing one before beginning the next, it is obvious that halving the cycle time will double the physical capacity of the plant, assuming we can find the needed manpower. Of course, no factory falls into the simplest case, since we are constantly beginning new work and finishing old. The complexities of this process conceal from us the basic simplicity of the principle, which is: If cycle time and WIP can be reduced 10%, the physical capacity of the plant will increase. The increase will range from very marginal in heavily loaded critical work centers to a full 10% in the assembly bay where area-time is the limitation.

The natural instincts and reactions of the work force should be heeded in this connection. Nothing in our discussion suggests that we reduce WIP by reducing the amount of time the operators are allowed for their work; in fact, in one or two places we have suggested it may be insufficient to cover the extra work involved in, say, sorting through the inputs for the next job on the schedule. And yet, sooner or later, during a drive to improve WIP turnover, some operator (or perhaps union steward) will label the program a "speedup."

In this, he will be absolutely correct, far from the mind of the P&IC practitioner as such a thing may be. It is not the kind of speedup so hated and opposed by the union movement in general, whereby the standard times are progressively reduced. But it certainly is a speedup in the sense that the work moves faster, the discipline we demand of ourselves and the rest of the work force is tighter, and the whole operation is leaner—the WIP barnacles are gone.

Expansion of physical facilities is, of course, dear to the hearts of many a management. It is especially dear to the hearts of staff people who get to do interesting work like planning shop layouts, choosing machinery, and writing large and imposing appropriation requests. This is not to sneer at such activities, which sooner or later do become very necessary in every growing firm. But they are not always the answer to an apparent capacity problem. They may, in the memorable words of one manager, simply be a process of "expanding our inefficiencies." If the business is growing at a modest rate of, say, 5% to 10% real volume per year, it is probably a "cash cow" (The Boston Consulting Group 1968) and the need for additional capacity can be deferred for many years by improving the manufacturing systems rather than expanding the manufacturing plant. Individual machines and facilities, of course, will continue to wear out or be superseded by improved equipment which can be justified as cost reduction, but this is not expansion as such.

Alert managements, properly concerned with return on investment as much as with profits, recognize too that the first effect of a plant expansion is a sometimes terrifying fall in ROI. This is because plant expansion, by its nature, cannot generally be done in small increments. It is most unwise to incur all the disruption that an expansion entails for the sake of a 5% increase in capacity. An expansion is seldom for less than a 50% capacity increase, often more. But the completion of the expansion very seldom coincides neatly with a 50% increase in volume. There is a traumatic period during which the investment in the business has risen in a big jump, but the profits from the business have not increased, are increasing only gradually, or in some cases have fallen owing to business conditions.

By contrast, improvements in the manufacturing system can be incremental, and by their nature do tend to build up steadily over a period of months or years. This improvement may, of course, also require investment (in better programs and sometimes people) but the investment tends to be relatively small and followed almost at once by improvement in ROI instead of worsening of ROI.

Given a choice, a profitability-oriented management will exhaust all available resources to improve utilization of present capacity before augmenting it. Improvement of WIP turns is one of the most promising of the available resources.

Managed Costs

Managed costs can be defined as those which are fixed in the short range, but will rise or fall (usually in steps) if management decides to cause them to do so. Examples include numbers of foremen, ledger clerks, buyers, production control people, computer hours, heating fuel, and so on.

In firms with large WIP assets, the people part of managed cost tends to be large. Many planners, production control people, buyers, and shop clerks, for example, are needed to maintain control over the manufacture of items which are different from order to order, have many levels, are in the shop a long time, and are changing their identifications constantly.

A management decision to change the levels of these costs generally results from one of two things: (1) a profit crisis that requires immediate expense reduction regardless of problems so created, if the firm is to survive, or (2) a planned increase or decrease timed to match changes in business systems or changes in business volumes. This section deals with the latter.

These people costs are concentrated in two areas: production planning and plan execution. If planning is done poorly, execution can only be worse, because the plan has to be remade bit by bit on the factory floor long after the opportunity to do it well has passed. And planning does tend to be done poorly because it requires simply enormous amounts of arithmetic, posting, sorting, printing, and so on. In a firm of any size, it is impossible to do this well by hand, let alone change it when change is needed, as it invariably is.

This, of course, is where computers, MRP, and the rest of the mechanized tools come in. They can (although sadly they do not always) lift the oppressive burdens of sheer clerical data handling.

This is also where control of WIP comes in. For if the planning is done well, it becomes possible for execution to be done well. There is then a synergistic effect. Let us consider two possible scenarios:

1. Bad planning results in poor execution: it becomes necessary for large numbers of people to intervene during execution. This intervention can only be on an order by order, item by item basis—the familiar order-launch and expedite mode.

2. Good planning makes possible good execution.

Small numbers of people can view an overall job involving many, sometimes thousands, of parts. It is no longer necessary to intervene with each part; only with those that are creating trouble (i.e., the genuine emergencies that require legitimate expediting).

As an example of this consider a weekly planning meeting between Shop Supervision and Production Control. They use load summaries as inputs and agree on output rates for the forthcoming short period. They combine hundreds of individual decisions into a handful of decisions; one decision per work center instead of one per piece-part. And these few decisions do not even require reference to individual shop orders.

Accordingly, with good WIP control the factory manager can consider his managed costs in a different light. This different light is illustrated in Fig. 4–7, adapted from the circumstances of a particular firm. This firm had noted that its costs of planning and controlling production (Curve A) had been rising faster than overall costs of production. It designed and installed an integrated computerized production planning and control system.* After a learning-curve period of about two years, several retirements gave the opportunity to reduce managed cost by not replacing retirees. Curve A dropped slightly over a period of one to two years, then resumed its rise, but at a rate much below the rise in physical volume and far below its rate prior to installation of the new system.

As a check on the reliability of this indication, the firm plotted, on the same graph, a line (Curve B) of some managed costs deliberately chosen to be as

---

*Doing this kind of work in-house is no longer necessary and this sentence must not be construed as a recommendation that major integrated systems be designed from scratch.

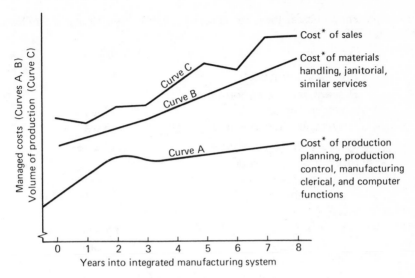

Fig. 4–7.   How different kinds of managed costs change with and without capable WIP management systems.

independent as possible of the production planning control system. It was found that these costs had tracked the rise in physical volume almost perfectly.

It is plain that good WIP control can lead to much improved managed cost control, and an alert management will see to it that this happens. It all begins with superior planning; and it ends with fewer, better people doing higher grade work and less of it.

DEVELOPING NUMBERS FOR THE OBJECTIVES

Alert managements will favor those programs which are proposed with objectives that are:

- numerical,
- credible,
- attainable,
- capable of being completed in a reasonable time,
- relevant to the needs of the business,
- worth much more than their cost.

For our present purposes, then, let us set up a model firm having the following attributes:

Annual sales at cost	$12M
Present delivery performance	
shipped on time	60%
average late of balance	3 weeks
Typical product cycle time	10 weeks
Present working mode	
critical work centers	2–3 shifts
most of the factory	1½–2 shifts
Inventories:	
Work in process	$1.8M
Finished parts	.5M
Raw materials	.2M
Finished goods	.6M
Total	$3.1M

Using these characteristics where appropriate, let us take the various general objectives and become specific with them. To do this, we will outline a process synthesized from several in my own experience. The following discussion is written as a narrative with a "cast of characters." The leading parts are played by "the manager" and "the analyst."

The student may well be puzzled by the shortcuts, estimating, and quick decisions which sprinkle the narrative. The experienced P&IC practitioner will recognize, however, the fact that this is how things are in industry. It is not always possible to obtain the information one would like upon which to base a decision. Even when it is available, its gathering and analysis are sometimes too costly. This is not meant to suggest that industrial managers are sloppy in their analyses. The successful ones have good minds and memories and long experience, and have thought a lot about their problems and opportunities through these years. Almost without conscious thought, they will identify and eliminate the irrelevant and non-significant data inputs and zero in on the "vital few" pieces of information. This process will not be analyzed or explained further, except to note that it accounts, in what follows, for what may seem at times like shooting from the hip, but is not. Another characteristic of the narrative is that, almost without exception, the manager takes the initiative in what is done. Successful projects for the improvement of WIP turns (or of any other facet of the business, for that matter) almost invariably begin, are pushed through, and end with the open, determined direction of the one in charge.

Delivery Performance Objectives

Examination of the working mode of the factory showed that it was in the expedite mode most of the time. Evidence of this included:

- feeder schedules written out by customer order number, with all parts for an order scheduled at one time;
- existence of a ship-for-sure list each month which had some relation to the original plan, but reflected mostly those jobs on which expediting had been most successful last month and/or those in which there was high management interest;
- parallel operation of a computerized system and an informal "black book" system based on shortage lists derived from the ship-for-sure list;
- shipment of 75% of the month's schedule in the last few days of each month;
- several other symptoms.

The manager personally analyzed the records of several customer orders that had gone late and came to the conclusion that his plant shipped late because it started late: even in the expedite mode, it was clear from the order records that the plant was able to start five to six weeks late and ship only two to three weeks late. This indicated that, even with disorderly production systems, the true cycle time for the product was not the ten weeks used for quotation purposes, but more like seven weeks.

The manager also studied the present status of one key work center that was chronically late, was pacing the production of the plant, and was very often, so he was told, not in a "go" condition because of shortages of material. At the time he checked this work center, it did indeed have a few "nogo's," but it had far more overdue orders for which material was available.

During this exercise, the manager learned that it was extremely difficult to determine, from the computer reports, exactly what the load on the work center was. The information simply was not reported in action-oriented form but required extensive manual analysis to develop a picture of the load. Shop supervision had never had good visibility of the load and had habitually undermanned for fear of being caught with surplus labor. Priorities were governed by the informal system, not by the computer reports. The manager checked the material received dates for the selected orders which had gone overdue: none of the material had been received late, and all of it had waited several weeks to be put into work.

At this point, the manager concluded his personal analysis, having formed the opinion that there was no particular reason he could not ship 90% to 95% of his orders on time. He was determined to limit his late deliveries to orders on which he had specific, serious quality (test) problems, engineering errors, and genuine parts and material shortages, none of which he felt could possibly account for 40% late shipments.

After consultation with staff people who knew the computer programs and understood his production problems, he developed a program for:

- upgrading the planning function so that synchronization was more reliable,

- upgrading the reported loads and sequence lists (schedules) so that information like average days late, current capacity, weeks of overdues was generated and displayed,

- upgrading the people so that they understood the principles of synchronized production and could generate their own local plans and projects for getting out of the expedite mode.

His objective was a 95% on-time shipment before year-end. Several small systems projects costing a few hundred to a few thousand dollars were required and were easily approved because the manager knew what he wanted, knew how it related to the business, and could explain exactly how the expected objective was to be reached. At this point, the manager asked Marketing several key questions about deliveries. First, could a dollar value be placed upon the improvement to 95% on-time shipment? After some thought, Marketing realized that a reasoned guess (which they refused to call an "estimate," saying the information base was too scant) could indeed be made. The reasoning went like this:

On two occasions in the past year, orders had been lost to competitors whose bids had been higher—4% in one case, 3% in the other. In both cases, the customers had selected a bidder whose on-time deliveries record was better and had so advised the losing bidders. In each case, the order would have been a welcome load addition and could have been handled without difficulty; in other words, the firm simply lost the profit on those two jobs. Industrial intelligence indicated that this same thing happened at other times when the firm did not directly hear the reason for the lost business.

Based on this extremely fragmentary evidence, Marketing was willing to make some guesses. They suggested that with a 90% to 95% on-time deliveries reputation, the firm might expect to receive 5% additional business at its normal margins, which were about 20% of selling price. Gross profit for a year might therefore increase by $150,000.

A small part of the firm's business involved penalty contracts, where the firm could and sometimes did lose some or most of its margin if the order went late. Penalties had cost $25,000 in the previous year. If Marketing could depend upon 95% on-time delivery, then conservatively $15,000 of that cost might be saved.

Marketing, with a 95% on-time reputation behind them, could be much more confident and aggressive in bidding in certain delivery sensitive market areas. Customers had demonstrated a willingness to pay a premium for delivery dependability which (again with extremely fragmentary information) seemed to be about 3%, at least. Marketing therefore suggested that, on about 10% of the firm's business, it might be possible to obtain 3% better margins, which would be $45,000.

From the commercial point of view, therefore, it seemed there was a potential of $210,000 if delivery performance could be improved to 95%. The manufacturing manager left the marketing department very much cheered up, even though the marketing manager's earnest warning not to use the numbers for anything which would later have to be proven was ringing in his ears. He realized that this would probably be his strongest project justification, even though it would have to be very conservatively stated.

Labor Efficiency Objectives

The plant had a large machine shop. Study of the overtime records indicated that very little overtime was worked in the first week of most months but that large amounts of overtime were typically worked in the third and fourth weeks. Overtime premiums, in fact, accounted for 8% of the labor bill. Once this graph was drawn (see Fig. 4–1), the group analyzing the situation (working under the direction of the manager) began to wonder how heavily loaded the first two weeks of the month were. Sympathetic questioning of the supervisors revealed that they had difficulty, most months, getting enough work for their men in the first and usually the second weeks. When it was pointed out that the schedules showed adequate work to be done on available material, the invariable reply was, "But Assembly isn't asking for it yet."

The group realized they had serious training and industrial relations problems: if overtime is part of the job, the resulting income is not given up easily; and overtime had become part of the job. After further study of the figures, and suitable consultations with IR and supervision, the analyst persuaded the manager that 50% of his overtime in the machine shop could be eliminated quite quickly, with another 25% to go after a few more months. These figures were extrapolated to other departments where appropriate, and a final objective was struck that 40% of overtime could be eliminated, for a saving of about 3% of the total plant labor bill. Since the product was about 13% labor and fringes, this amounted to 3% of 13% of $12M per year, or an objective saving of $46,800 per year.

The plant also had reports showing labor efficiency (i.e., ratio of standard hours to in-plant hours). These numbers tended to hover around 70%. Work sampling indicated that machine operators were spending at least 20% of their time searching for materials, consulting with production men, waiting for crane lifts, and other activities some of which could be attributed to disordered work places and unsequenced queues. The analyst assigned to the work estimated that an improvement of at least 10% in labor efficiency was easily attainable if the delays caused by poor production flow were reduced. He cross-checked this with other work he knew of, where he found that an improvement of 13% had been obtained. He also knew that the P&IC literature spoke quite often of 20% efficiency improvements. He reported these things to the manager, and again with IR and supervisory help developed a plan calling for an improvement of 5% in the first year, 5% in the second, or 5% of 13% of $12M or $78,000 saving per year rising to $156,000.

Knowing from experience how difficult it can be to get these kinds of savings without major delays and labor troubles, the manager targeted $78,000 but privately felt that the $156,000 was attainable and the target would be reviewed within a year.

Objectives for WIP Inventories:

The manager, while analyzing his delivery performance, had formed the opinion that he actually was delivering on a seven-week cycle, not the ten-week interval he and Marketing had thought. Yet parts of the plant, he knew, were working to the schedules provided by the computer programs and were building up WIP at times far in advance of this seven-week interval. He referred back to a Manufacturing Cycle Efficiency study he had done a few months previously and found that his MCE was from 20 to 25%.

He worked with the WIP = SCR formula, trying to develop an inventory objective from first principles, and found to his considerable dismay that his WIP should probably be closer to $1M than $1.8M.

He called for some of the new reports that were beginning to emerge from the computer. They showed his work centers to be working as much as 6 days ahead of schedule and as much as 40 days behind schedule. Making allowance for bad records which were in the process of being cleaned up, he felt, after some analysis, that probably 40% of his feeder WIP was useless at any point in time because it was waiting for something else to catch up. This, in turn, was about 40% of his total WIP.

Since this was very untried ground for him and for his supervision, he had some difficulty arriving at a target, and settled for an initial (4 months away) objective of eliminating half of 40% of 40% of his WIP, or $144,000. However, he determined to review this target extremely carefully as soon as he got a better feel for just how tightly he could run his ship. For instance, his priority indices were showing very wide spreads of labor reports about their scheduled day, and he was quite unsure how much this could be improved, and how fast. He had a pretty good conviction he could eliminate more than 15% ultimately.

With WIP in the various assembly areas he had less trouble. His industrial engineers already had been studying assembly delays and were able to show him figures which, with a little reworking, demonstrated that the assembly WIP on average was 75% idle. Over 50% was due to shortages, to the last minute insertion of other jobs ahead, or to similar situations symptomatic of poor planning and control. Because of the large amount of systems work, retraining, record purging, and correction which was in prospect, the manager realized he had better go a little slowly in the assembly departments and wait for definite signs of improvement in deliveries before he began his program of cycle-time reduction there. Nevertheless, he felt that he should aim to remove half of the control-related delay, or 50% of 50% of 60% of $1.8M, or $270,000.

Thus an initial objective for WIP reduction, to be reached in stages over a year, was $270,000 plus $144,000 or $414,000, 23% of his total WIP, more next year.

But before leaving this subject, the manager realistically estimated that, in his drive to bring all work centers more nearly abreast, he would *increase* his WIP temporarily by about 8% to 10% or $144,000 to $180,000. This created labor and other problems which he considered very severe, perhaps intolerable, and he determined to consult with his staff and his supervision to avoid some or all of this temporary bulge.

Now back again to the marketing department. How much, the manufacturing manager wondered, might reduced delivery intervals be worth? Did the firm ever lose business because of noncompetitive delivery intervals?

Since, of course, all firms do lose business from this cause at one time or another, the answer was no surprise. Business lost because of deliveries was in two main categories:

1. Regular industrial bids in which the customer's available time was very short.
2. "Breakdown" work in which the customer had experienced total failure of a critical apparatus and would pay a large premium for quick replacement.

Again warning that the figures were educated guesses, Marketing suggested the following:

Ability to deliver on shorter intervals would open up for them several jobs a year of a kind they were accustomed to declining to bid, or on which they bid high. There would be every reason to expect to get a normal market share of such business (if the reputation for dependable delivery had been established). This could account for an additional $1M per year of business at normal margins or an addition to gross margin of possibly $200,000.

If the plant could absorb a small number of breakdown jobs each year on even shorter intervals—say 50% to 75% of the new, already shortened normal—another $500,000 of business could quite easily be obtained. Engineering was brought into the discussion, because their intervals now became a very large part of the total interval. Engineering pointed out that many such jobs were the firm's own design originally in any case, and on some of them the engineering could be abbreviated greatly. If not too many all-new jobs were superimposed on regular work (and never more than one at a time), Engineering would undertake to contribute a full share to the interval reduction, through overtime, etc. For such extra efforts, Marketing felt it should be possible to get extra margin to the extent of another 10%. Margin on this additional $500,000 of business would, therefore, be $150,000.

Thus the total favorable dollar impact from the commercial effects of reduced intervals might be $350,000. Again, the warning from Marketing: Don't use such numbers in anything that will ever have to be proven! (It has been said that, the higher one goes in management, the greater is the importance of the decisions to be made and the less definite is the information upon which they must be made. This is illustrated by the unavoidable uncertainty of the Marketing people in supplying information of this kind. It's a form of forecasting even harder to do well than the forecasting we've been accustomed to complaining about for so many years.)

Objectives for Parts and Raw Materials

The computer system used by the firm had a requirements planning ability. It generated, once a week, a list of applications, pegged, dated, and aged, with planned receipts inserted as negative applications.

The production analyst wanted to form an opinion whether overdue applications were accounting for significant dollars of inventory. He picked off the top item on each page of the report—about 40 items—and recorded each one whose want date was past. This sample indicated that there might indeed be an overdue-applications opportunity, since 15% of the items were still open with past-due dates. Other reports in the system indicated that little or none of this could be accounted for by bad data in the system such as left-behind, unrelieved applications. This encouraged him to take another step. He matched his short list of overdues to the master ledger file transcript, picked off unit cost, extended and totalled the dollars, then multiplied this by the sampling ratio. This indicated that 40% of the material and parts inventories were in this condition of being available to use but not yet withdrawn. The analyst knew his sample was too small to make the 40% number reliable, but he also knew that this kind of hint could not be ignored.

A full-blown retrieval, using an available file retrieval program, was then done on the entire materials and parts ledger. The analyst asked the computer program to tell him how many dollars of material were applied, available, but past due. This was, of course, a 100% sample.

The answer was that over $70,000 worth of material was in this condition. The analyst then conferred with the manager and the materials supervisor.

A review of the figures indicated that probably 60% to 75% of these past-dues were for no particular identifiable cause (such as change in due date, quality hold, engineering errors) but were due simply to late starting, as the manager had previously noted. On the assumption that late starting could be reduced by at least 70% in the first year, a target was struck that materials and parts inventories could be made to fall 70% of 75% of $70,000, or $36,750. A target of $37,000 was included with those for WIP etc., with the subject brought forward for review in 8 months.

Objectives for Managed Costs

This manager, relatively new on his present job, had inherited a group of people called *planners* who sat in shop offices. He had initially been puzzled by this and now came back to the subject. He called for job descriptions of these people and he interviewed their supervisors. He realized that what had been bothering him was that, if a product has to be planned by people in the factory, while the work is going through, a key element was missing from his preproduction functions. The planners, it seemed, did things like:

- identify parts requirements to support assembly operations for the immediate forthcoming period.
- coordinate work orders for parts; establish dates for them; load the paper work and drawings out to work centers.
- identify shortages and take necessary action. Establish liaison with Purchasing, Stores, and so forth as necessary.

In other words, he had a crew of highly skilled expediters whose job was partly to correct faulty plans, partly to supply missing parts of plans, but mostly to write shortage lists and chase them down. The computer reports were used for miscellaneous purposes such as checking off completed work, acting as a master cross-reference book of current production, and so on. Their dates could not be trusted.

The manager felt that this talent could be better used, and he set about, with the aid of his supervision, to determine how. Reasoned estimates of the true expediting requirements were made. These were based on the assumption that the preplanning could be made 95% accurate or better as to synchronization, completeness, and so forth. Four good people were found to be surplus to requirements under such conditions. The best of these was selected to strengthen the preplanning function and to work with the production analyst and computer system people to upgrade the system. One was about to retire and was not replaced. All were aptitude tested.

One was placed elsewhere in the company, and one was given extensive assistance in finding suitable work outside the company. All this took time, was done fairly and openly, and the reductions were carefully timed to coincide with the diminishing need for expediting.

During review of the manpower plans left by his predecessor, the manager found that another planner was to have been hired in the following year. He cancelled this requirement.

Total targeted managed cost reduction therefore was: three person-equivalents of cost eliminated, one avoided, total four, at salary plus benefit cost.

The production analyst checked with Data Processing about run costs of the new programs and reports. Prior to the program changes he had been assured that the enhancements would cost little or nothing, since they were minor changes to the internal program logic whose total run time was likely to be a few seconds a week. However, several reports the system once had to support its expedite mode had been pruned, and the schedules, since they were now used as queue control, were about 10% as thick as they once were. He found that there were indeed some savings here—about $2,000 per year in printing time, paper, decollating, mailing, and ancillary costs. Not much, but in the right direction. Furthermore, he enjoyed being told that the new letter size reports were a godsend to the people who had to use them and once had had to struggle with 15 inch wide sheets.

The manager knew that labor flexibility would cost him something, but he wasn't sure how much. In the early days of a similar program in another firm, he had experienced a slowdown and one walkout because he had tried to install too much too soon without understanding the consequences to his people's overtime pay, their willingness to work shifts occasionally, and, ultimately, to the size of staff he needed—there had been some unexpected layoffs. He never had quite satisfied himself whether it was the aftermath of these troubles or the inability of his people to be equally effective in two or three jobs, which had offset some of his hoped for productivity gains.

The manager dispatched his industrial engineer into the only area in the factory which was already using a good deal of labor flexibility—the machine shop—with instructions to find out what it cost, in lost efficiency and learning curve effects, to transfer a qualified operator from a machine where he had been for some months to another machine on which he was also qualified but which he had not worked recently.

He was told that the cost of refresher training on the second machine was about equivalent to the loss of 25% of the first day's production, 10% of the second, and thereafter became unmeasurable.

After consultation with his supervision, he made a rough estimate that this effect might cost him $20,000 in lost productivity the first year, then $10,000 the second year, and staying stable there from the second year onward. This figure would have to be monitored, because no one had much idea just how many transfers a year would be needed.

Objectives for Facilities Utilization

The company owned land, buildings, machinery, and equipment whose original cost had been about $6M but whose book value had depreciated to about $2M. Over several years its sales volume had risen from about $4M to the present $12M; but inflation meant that, in real (uninflated) dollars the output had gone from $4M to about $7M. The manager looked at his key areas with his staff (manufacturing and industrial engineers, production head, and superintendents) to try to estimate their ultimate capacity. The shop seemed busy and was always full of product. But this group knew from experience that whether times were good or not so good, this seemed always to be the case; the amount of product in the shop was not a good gauge of how nearly the shop was working to capacity. Furthermore, doubling (say) the factory capacity would now probably cost closer to $20M than the $6M for which it had been bought over many years, again thanks to inflation.

The group identified the following major facilities and estimated their needs for expansion:

Plant level

1. The casting stores was overcrowded; identification and handling were giving trouble and the overflow in the yard sometimes had to be found under the snow. There was little question that something had to be done soon. However, a lighted, unheated steel building without any cranes but with some racking would serve the purpose at minor cost. No other stores were seriously crowded.

2. The main assembly bay was chronically crowded and partly finished units sometimes had to be sealed up and stored in the yard. On the other hand, a third shift had never been started because of the lack of supervisory personnel and a policy which frowned on three-shift operation. This policy had not been reviewed for many years, and someone felt it had been set when the plant was used for munitions work and it was unwise to have women workers coming and going at night.

3. The machine shop was working a full two shifts, and at times it was necessary to subcontract some turning. Fortunately, in the last decade some excellent small machine shops had sprung up in the district, able to give quite good service on short notice, although their prices were higher than the factory's direct cost and the manager didn't like to lose his overhead pickup.

Machinery and equipment level

1. Several machines in the machine shop were due for replacement because of age and obsolescence. They would require no more space but would more than double the shop's capacity for shafts, one of the key feeder items. They were being bought as cost reductions.

2. The increasing size of the units was forcing the management to consider replacing the existing test pit with two, a large and a small, along with test equipment which, with any prudence at all, would have to be much larger than needed for today's products. This same increasing unit size would soon call for a rail spur to be built into the same end of the building. There simply was no room. However, there was 100 meters of yard between the roller door and the back fence.

3. Work centers in general, with only a few exceptions, had little or no facility for organizing their incoming or outgoing work. WIP was often piled loose on the floor or lowered by the crane in stacking trays which made it extremely probable that the item wanted was on the bottom. Even in low-overhead areas like the machine shop, vertical space was almost all wasted.

4. A new protective process for the product developed by Engineering would replace a long sequence of repeated dips and bakes with a one-step vacuum-impregnation-and-cure. This would get rid of two tanks and one oven and reduce cycle time by three to five days. It could be tended by one man rather than three.

5. There were five clearly recognizable critical work centers, one in each of the five major feeder departments. These machines worked two to two and one-half shifts including overtime, and inability to synchronize their outputs was a constant planning problem and a worse execution one. In each case, however, alternatives were known that would increase capacity by from 50% to 300%. In two of the five cases these improvements were accompanied by productivity improvement more than sufficient to justify the machines on that basis alone.

Looking at the firm's five-year plan, the manager noted that, based upon increased volume, the management had protected $7M for major plant expansion in the third year, winding up with $2M more in the fourth year. The manager pondered these facts and realized that selective capacity increases, most of which would pay for themselves in productivity, would get him out of the worst of his problems. The one exception was the assembly bay, where there wasn't much question he was running out of room.

He also noted, however, that his WIP target called for a reduction of 15% in assembly cycle times in the first year, and that the major expansion was slated for the third year. By third year, he felt, he could cut another 15% out of his assembly cycles, and the assembly bay would no longer be crowded, even in the face of production increases. This left the problem of the test pits and the rail spur. The spur actually required no more room so he set it aside. Looking at the assembly bay, he realized that a great deal of fixed test equipment was bolted down at the end of it. Product flow was such that the casting stores was in the next bay, on the other side of the wall. The fixed test equipment could just as well be there as taking up space under the crane; the test panels and jacks could face into the assembly bay and form part of the wall. Instead of moving some of his castings into the unheated shed, he could move them all in there, free up high-grade inside space for the test gear, and clear the 4,000 square feet of space he needed for the new pits and have a little extra besides. There would be some extra cost because parts of the new shed would now have to be heated and a small office built.

By now, the factory management group were convinced that as much as 50% additional capacity could be obtained by a combination of facilities replacement (most of which was justified by cost reduction); minor rearrangement; construction of a small storage shed fitted with new racking; purchase of one new short-turning electric lift truck; technological progress (shorter impregnation and curing cycle); and, most important of all, a planned, phased-in reduction of 30% in the product cycle time, hopefully rising close to 50% before the third year of the five-year financial plan.

The group recognized that added skilled labor would be needed, as would more supervision and services. But these things would be needed in a new facility anyway, and would be more easily managed in a geographically more compact, better organized, less cluttered space.

Now the manager was faced with quantifying these benefits. How long could a major new facilities construction project be deferred? What would be the dollar value of the deferral? He decided to quantify the benefits by assigning a present value to the deferral of investment in new buildings. He chose a cost-of-capital of 9% which he felt would understate the benefits rather than overstate them. Looking at the market forecasts and at the many numbers he had gathered over several weeks, he felt it quite in order to suggest that major expansion could be deferred out of the third and fourth years and into at least the sixth year out—a three-year deferral. So he wanted to know the present value of several large amounts of money (Skrotzki 1945, p. 333).

	Present Value of Cost of Project If Begun	
	In 3 yrs.	In 6 yrs.
Major expansion—$7M today's money	$5.4M	$4.2M
Project completion—$2M (1 year later)	1.4M	1.1M
Totals	$6.8M	$5.3M

The deferral from the third year to the sixth year could save the firm $6.8M−$5.3M = $1.5M (present value) one-time cost. This suggested that any one-time cost needed to assure this deferral which was appreciably less than $1.5M was very attractive.

The manager could not see anything he might need which could be more than a small fraction of this $1.5M (computer program changes, a storage shed, charges for a consultant, miscellaneous racks and shelving). He was satisfied, therefore, with this part of the analysis and confident that he had a strong piece of project justification.

THE COSTS OF THE PROGRAM

The credibility of any proposal to management increases with the care with which costs are identified. We have discussed at some length the costs which will fall and the benefits (such as on-time deliveries) which will be obtained when WIP is brought under tighter control. To get these benefits, we must pay out money. These costs can be expected to be in several areas.

The System

Systems analyst. A systems analyst or coordinator must exist in the organization. Depending upon firm size, this may or may not be one person or several people. But some identified person(s) in the firm must be assigned full responsibility for the system: he must be made to *feel that he owns it.* His main jobs are maintaining systems integrity, solving operating problems, identifying areas for improvement. Only under exceptional circumstances should he be a data processing person or programmer, because *the system is not the computer programs.* He should be a person who will be sorely missed where he now is. The broader his background in various departments, but particularly manufacturing, the better.

Consultant.   The help of a consultant is invaluable in the early stages. He may be from inside or outside the company (but outside the department), with a good reputation which should be checked out before he is retained. Time spent on calls to his clients is a good investment. He will cost more than inside people cost, per day. This, again, is money well spent. A good consultant can put his finger on your best areas for improvement and upon the worst threats to success, sometimes in a few minutes, always in a few days. Your own people aren't stupid; they just don't have the consultant's breadth of experience and the confidence that comes with it. Furthermore, in nearly every consultive episode, there comes the time that the consultant must take one or more managers aside and tell them, *"You* are part of the problem. Unless you are willing to do this, this, and that, forget the whole project.'' This is medicine which is very necessary to swallow but which management is unlikely to receive from its own staff.

Computer hardware and software.   You may need entire new programs or enhancements to old ones. The cost can vary from a few hundred dollars to scores of thousands. If you decide to buy, audit every package for its ability to produce the outputs we have described (such as load summaries showing average days late) or its amenability to tailoring to provide these pieces of information. Who will do the tailoring? What will it cost?

Run costs may change, up or down, and hardware may be inappropriate. In the day of minis and micros, the emphasis is swinging back to where it always should have been, which is to define the problem and needed outputs first, then find machinery that will do this. Increasingly software houses are developing packages which can run on anything from a $50,000 mini to a $4M mainframe, or by time sharing.

Training

It is hard to overemphasize the need for training. But, just as with stock-replenishing systems, there are two questions: How much? and When? When is training needed? is the more important question. Too soon means fadeout before implementation; too late means frustration because troubles have already begun. Training is at several levels:

1.   General manager and plant management must be trained. It's best to do this by use of proposals based upon financial requirements. The proposer must have a command of the financial, business language well enough to attract the manager's attention, generate respect and credibility. From there on, the manager, who is one because he can do this, will train himself by probing, questioning, defining, identifying potential problems, prioritizing, and judging. Perhaps the best and first thing to do is ask management for money, because (a) without a budget, you have no program, and (b) faced with a demand for money, the manager will be enthusiastically responsive or completely unresponsive. Beware the lukewarm go ahead.

2. Supervision must be trained in new ways. The first step is to train them out of the old ways (such as leveling load by allowing overdues to fluctuate). This may be a difficult assignment, because this is a hard-bitten crew who have suffered many disappointments, had their hopes raised and dashed many times. "The last time he helped me, I nearly got fired," is an attitude one man once voiced and others would echo. Train them we must.

3. Operators must be trained in their new ways, such as the simple need to stick to schedule sequence. This should be done with, or preferably by, supervision, because there are some delicate questions to be fielded. We're trying to cut down overtime: don't dodge the issue. We're trying to get people out of their comfortable rut in which they report, every day of the year, to a place called "Joe's lathe." There has to be something in it for them. "One thing I'll say for your _____ _____ system," an operator once grudgingly remarked, "there's at least someplace to lift and lay things." Work hard to find more such advantages for the operators and emphasize them at every opportunity. This is a place to show good faith by following up on what should have been done long ago, such as perhaps providing a rack in which part-finished, flat fabrications can be stored vertically, where the next one needed isn't on the bottom, and where the operator can get a grab on one as easily as any other. And if an operator makes a suggestion for improvement, use it if you can: $200 for a file cabinet to store shop prints beside the gas-cutting machines may be the best small investment ever made. Make sure he gets a cut of the savings, too.

4. Operators will need training, or upgrading, in a second or third job. Depending on the environment, this may be as simple as on-the-job training, working beside an experienced person, or as complex as sending him to night school (or day school one day a week at company expense) to learn or upgrade a trade such as pressure-vessel welding.

5. The systems man may need various degrees of upgrading, from full-scale schooling at night or during the day, to help in covering conventions and seminars, to books, and so forth. See that he gets it. *But see that each investment results in something*—something definite, job related, and helpful to the company. Do not have people wandering off to a two-day seminar as a reward for three months of good behavior.

Facilities

Improvement to plant and office facilities is seldom big or expensive, but if ignored when funding is requested, returns to haunt the organization with constant minor embarrassment.

As commented often, material storage at each work station should be surveyed and any shortcomings fixed. Use vertical space by employing racking. Some firms use color coding for segregating by date. Make sure the lathe operator is not, in reality, a materials handler who does some lathe work.

Typically the storage of papers such as shop prints and templates can be improved. These things should be near the work centers, safely and conveniently stored, protected against dust, oil, sparks, or other environmental hazard.

Be sure any system that calls for reporting back (such as labor completion) is supported by equipment (some form of terminal) which makes the reporting possible without imposing an unforeseen load on some clerical function whose people were never consulted in advance. It happens.

Review materials handling equipment and ensure that, insofar as possible, routes, schedules, and equipment will support on-time production as well as merely getting parts from here to there at some time convenient to the trucker. Look over the possibilities of line rearrangement or installation of inexpensive gravity conveyors to eliminate as much as 100% of the handling cost and time. Conveyors are underutilized in job shops; we mistakenly assume they're for factories that make thousands of items or products a day.

Labor Costs

Labor flexibility has a cost. No one can be 100% effective in more than a very few jobs—at times only one. Few numerical guidelines can be suggested because situations vary so much from plant to plant. The costs of labor flexibility are not typically large (sometimes as high as 5% of the total labor bill) but if ignored lead to embarrassment and disappointment. The improvements in labor efficiency, which are a feature of better WIP systems, far more than offset this cost.

There may be added elements of work in what we are asking the operators to do. They have to be more concerned with sequence and finding the right "next job" than they were before. Whether the shop is incentive or not, allowance must be made for this extra administrative work: it's a cost.

The occasional setup is lost as the work center's output storage area fills up and the operator then stops reaching out into the future of the schedule to combine jobs. Again, the magnitude of this problem has to be determined or estimated in the individual plant. However, we can comment in passing that this loss, always viewed with foreboding and forecast blackly by opponents of change as likely to be extremely large, has never yet in our experience resulted in cost changes large enough to measure. Here is what probably happens: There is, indeed, some lost cost resulting from lost setups; however, it is offset by the setups we recover because we no longer have to break into jobs in order to get one or two of some part for an emergency in assembly. On setups, we probably come out ahead because breaking into a running job means *two* lost setups—one to do the emergency job, one to get back on the interrupted one. It also means another first-piece inspection and risk of scrap.

Inventory

As commented earlier, one of the first results of using information like average days late is that the shop works hard to bring the very late work centers up closer to the current ones. It's instinctive, and it's a sound instinct. *But it raises inventory*. The effect lasts just about long enough to create panic in the financial circles of the plant, unless they have been warned ahead of time. Because one or two months of a determined program of bringing work centers abreast "breaks the log jam" in assembly and the firm rapidly begins reducing its inventory in the very best way there is; it begins shipping on time. Upper management can accept and forgive a lot of things as long as those things are not surprises.

To Summarize

The management and the P&IC practitioner owe it to each other to analyze every major new program for its impact, good and bad, so that a balanced view can be taken and a correct priority can be set. In this connection the two mottoes embedded in the management style of one major firm (Northern Telecom of Toronto, Canada) are worth quoting and noting for permanent reference:

1. We do what we say we will do.
2. No surprises of any kind at any time.

Tabulated Summary of Figures

We can summarize by tabulating costs and benefits for the first years of the program. See Table 4–1.

Investment Deferral Elements

The present worth of the investment deferral made possible by such a program is $1.5M, if money costs 9% per year.

Discussion of the Numbers

There are as many ways of viewing funding requests as there are companies (Anthony 1960, p. 531; Buffa 1961, p. 122). Some firms still use the accounting method, averaging savings and depreciation over, say, a 10-year period and calculating a rate of return. Increasingly it is being found that 10 years is too long; technology doesn't hold still and such long-range forecasts are of little use.

Other firms use discounted cash flow, a more modern approach that brings the flow of expenditures and earnings to a common base, namely, their present value. This recognizes the importance of time in the flow of money; for instance, if I can earn 10% on my money by investing it, a promise of $100 to be paid one year from now is worth only $100/1.1 or $91 to me right now.

The cash flow figures shown on the cost-benefits summary are a very rudimentary illustration of the discounted cash flow (DCF) method. Typically, however, the management will have to bring into the analysis other factors— depreciation and taxation as a minimum.

Table 4–1

Cost Elements in $1,000's	Year in Effect		
	1st	2nd	3rd
Increased WIP: 15% of $150 for 3 mo.	6	—	—
Lost productivity (switching jobs)	20	10	10
Computer program changes	20	5	1
Racks for casting stores & m/c shop	10	2	1
Lift truck	15	—	—
Part-time system function	15	15	15
Consulting fees	10	5	2
Training (hourly & salaried)	25	10	5
Minor office improvements	5	2	—
Terminal equipment rental	5	5	5
Totals by year	131	54	38

Saving Elements in $1,000's

	1st	2nd	3rd
WIP carrying cost			
unsynchronized WIP, 15% of $144	10	20	22
cycle-time WIP, 15% of $270	5	20	41
Overtime reduction	20	40	47
Labor efficiency improvement	40	70	78
Reassignment of planners	20	40	60
Parts inventory, 15% of $37	2	5	6
Totals by year	97	195	254
Net cash flow by year	−34	141	216
Cumulative cash flow	−34	106	322
Present worth of net cash Flow by year, @15%[1]	−34	92	243
Present worth of all cash Flow 1st 3 years is $301			

Commercial Advantages in $1,000's	Year in Effect		
	1st	2nd	3rd
Commercial benefits from 95% on-time shipments capability and reputation	50	100	210
Margins on additional business available through reduced intervals	—	100	350
Totals by year	50	200	560

[1]Skrotzki and Vopat. 1945. Applied energy conversion. New York: McGraw-Hill. p. 333.

A refinement of DCF calls for calculating present value at two discount rates, one just low enough to show a positive result, the other just high enough to show a negative result, interpolating between them, and finding the effective rate of return of the project; that is, the discount rate which just brings the present values to zero.

Most computer and calculator manufacturers provide financial program packages to do this kind of work. It is essential to select one, the results from which your firm's financial people will agree to use. Many strong feelings are held on these matters, and it is essential to be in step with your own firm.

The example was carried out only three years. Your firm's policy may call for some other period. However, in a fast changing world, a project that does not pay back and begin to earn profit before the second year is often open to suspicion. We must, as well, bear in mind the adage from systems work, "A project scheduled to last more than six months lasts forever." Your overall project should be clearly turning around and beginning to pay back its cost in well under six months; be sure you have measurement devices in place to ensure that you know when this begins to happen and how much is flowing back in.

It invariably pays to break a big program up into smaller ones which can be more easily visualized, tend to get faster approval from management, and can be more readily checked for their results before a decision is made to proceed into another phase. For example, a major WIP improvement project could be logically subdivided as follows:

- Ship on time
- Reduce unsynchronization WIP
- Reduce overall cycle times

Control, progress, and momentum can thus be vastly improved.

The graph of cash flows, Fig. 4–8, is a useful tool that some managements like. It shows just where the project is expected to begin paying back. Of course, it does not discount the cash flows, although it could be redrawn in discounted form. It pays, in any sales presentation (which a request for funds truly is, make no mistake), to intersperse relevant, illustrative, attention-getting, easily understood charts of this kind.

The part of the benefits summary dealing with commercial advantages resulting from a WIP improvement program is kept separate. Reasons for this include: (1) Projects like this should pay for themselves within the walls of the factory, and usually can. (2) Departments other than Manufacturing control the marketing activities; Manufacturing should not be dependent upon them for proving the benefits when the job is done. (3) It is generally extremely difficult to prove that many, or any, of those things happened in the marketplace which our educated guesses suggested might happen. Management, in passing upon and approving a funding request containing such a listing of commercial advantages, will be, in effect, considering them as "gravy."

It is essential, however, to obtain, and show that you have obtained, the agreement of Marketing that such figures are reasonable.

The investment deferral advantages can be shown in many ways. Again,

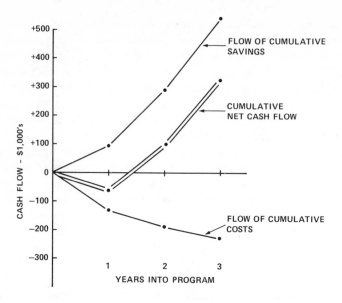

Fig. 4–8.   Cash flows of cost and savings based on present business levels, commercial considerations excluded.

dollar figures generated from such deferral estimates should probably not be drawn into direct project justification, since the WIP project will have ample justification. Further, such calculations lead to much futile discussion at times, because of the uncertain nature of the cost of capital (Cool and Reece 1978, p. 28). It is best to leave such a benefit out of the direct project justification, bringing it into the proposal as an important fringe benefit. In calculating the present worth of future money, these are some of the alternative discount rates that have been used from time to time:

1.   Bank interest rate at which the firm can obtain short-term working capital.
2.   The firm's most recent ROI figure.
3.   The firm's planned objective ROI figure.
4.   Arbitrary percentages based upon whether or not the firm is over some objective level of investment.

What cost of capital is used is a matter of local management policy. The first alternative raises the fewest arguments. The second and third are sometimes used together, the higher one being selected for such analyses. The final one is not recommended, since it is usually designed for other purposes and tends to be much too low or to vary in large irrational steps which distort the picture we are trying to develop.

WIP Carrying Cost

One of the key numbers in any presentation is the carrying cost, or owning cost, of WIP inventory. This is another symptom of the neglect to which WIP has been subjected over the years: one frequently sees discussions of the carrying cost of ledger inventories, seldom indeed of WIP.

Yet its carrying cost is significant. To take a very simple view, one could say that if we didn't have to house it, we could dispense with some of our most costly buildings, cranes, and so on.

Figure 4–9 shows a calculation form used by one firm. For some business purposes, the total 21% carrying cost is used. For others, the so-called *tangible* cost (carrying cost excluding Line 2, "Opportunity Cost") is used. The reader is warned that this carrying cost calculation is no better, no worse than those usually applied to ledger inventories. It can quite correctly be argued that, if we reduce inventories by $1.00 we will nowhere be able to find a saving of $ .21. Nevertheless, if we permit inventories to rise on account of this, we will assuredly, some time later, find ourselves paying 21% more (or even 30% or 35% if we have had to build new buildings to house it). In the examples of this section, a modest 15% carrying cost has been used. The choice has been arbitrary and has been made in order to deliberately understate the savings available from WIP control. Most firms are willing to use much higher figures.

Explanation of the form

WIP investment (average).   This is the average of the 12 months prior to the date of the calculation. If some known anomaly exists, e.g., the startup of an important new product, it may be necessary to adjust this.

Carrying cost—expenses incurred.   In each line, a knowledgeable (not necessarily precise) estimate is made of the percentage of this cost which is caused by the existence of WIP inventory. This will range from rather low (supervision may spend 5% of their time making decisions about where to put WIP, how to man cranes, etc.) to rather high (crane drivers, obviously, are there to handle WIP—their percentage may be 70% to 90%). In between will come accounts like Other Losses, some of which are caused by rework, refinishing, and remaking lost or damaged WIP.

In the case of depreciation and rental, estimate the portion of the facility occupied by WIP and enter that under "Cost Chargeable To WIP."

Hourly vacation and holidays covers only the portions of the other lines which involve hourly labor, such as idle time. Lines n through p are provided for expenses which may be of interest to specific firms. For example, some firms have evidence that idle time accounts are affected by WIP.

Opportunity cost.   This is the cost of capital. As commented earlier, it can be one of several alternatives. We favor the firm's ROI objective, the bank cost of borrowed money, or the firm's current ROI performance, whichever is the highest. It must be kept up to date as these conditions change, which they do, frequently.

Carrying Cost of WIP Inventory

Calculated By _____ Calculation Date _____

A. WIP Investment (Average)

$1,000's

B. Carrying Cost

	Annual (Prior 12 Mo.)		
	Total $1,000's	% Chargeable To WIP	Cost Chargeable To WIP
1. Expenses incurred			
a. Supervision			
b. Supv. staff			
c. Prod. con.			
d. Crane & elevator			
e. Material handlers			
f. Idle time			
g. Vac. & hol.			
h. Computer support			
i. Other losses			
j. Main stores			
k. Plt. transp.			
l. Depr. & rent			
m. Maint. L&B			
n.			
o.			
p.			
2. Opportunity cost			
3. Total annual cost			

C. Carrying Cost Rate $= \dfrac{B3}{A}$

Fig. 4–9.   Work in process inventory carrying cost calculation form.

SUMMARY: OBJECTIVE SETTING

WIP turn improvement results in hard-dollar savings which can be estimated with considerable confidence. They come from such things as improved efficiency of labor and higher profits owing to better shipping performance and faster cycles.

WIP inventory levels depend upon cycle times. A full factory does not necessarily mean a heavy load, nor does a tidy factory with little WIP mean business is slack; the facts are usually the reverse.

There is a formula for WIP investment which reveals the contributors to investment. The main contributor is time.

It is essential to do prework before reducing WIP and also to reduce WIP in stages timed correctly. Prework involves getting a sound plan: sequencing calls for getting feeders in order before assembly.

Facilities utilization and investment deferral are important but little noticed elements of savings which arise from higher WIP turns.

Program credibility comes from sound cost and benefit numbers, conservatively estimated and supported. Despite the difficulty of measurement, it is feasible and defensible to estimate benefits arising from on-time shipments and other market considerations.

Shop labor and supervision play a key part. Since less labor will be needed after the program is installed (and markedly less during its installation), Industrial Relations has a part to play.

Managed costs can be made to fall because there will be less need for expediting, emergency overtime, and so forth. Costs-in-prospect which can be avoided are legitimate justification for savings estimates.

Money will be needed to pay for system improvements and for the services of a good manufacturing systems analyst. A consultant may also be needed. Hardware and software may need upgrading. Training is a cost and must extend from the general manager downward. Facilities may require improvement. Labor costs will rise and fall at recognizable stages of the project; they must be forecast. Similarly with inventory; it may go up before it goes down.

It is essential to boil down for management review and approval the costs, benefits, and timing of the program. A cash flow graph is useful. Use this stage of project preparation to ask for money and get management commitment.

CASE STUDY: THE COST OF CAPITAL

The text points out that the cost of capital is not some definite figure which can be calculated from accounting or other data. In one firm, it was found that these costs of capital were in use:

1. Corporately, divisions were charged 3% of the book value of their assets employed up to the level they had forecast in the prior year's financial plan. If they exceeded this level, the charge became 12% on the excess.

2. Divisions within the company required a figure for "I", the carrying cost of ledger inventory of finished goods, parts, etc. Some divisions used as low as 12%, arguing that bank interest plus a few minor expenses like computer runs would be the only factors which would change if inventory levels changed. Other divisions used as high as 35%, arguing that their ledger stocks were subject to a lot of obsolescence, their warehouses were nearly full after many years of doing business, and that a factor was needed in the EOQ formula which would tend to set order quantities on the low rather than the high side.

3. Divisions with large WIP investment sometimes did not even consider a

WIP carrying cost, arguing, "It's all good, sold inventory. You have to have it. You'll have it whether it costs 5% per year or 50% per year. What difference does a specific figure make?"

4. Profitable divisions tended to put a high value on their inventory carrying cost because their performance indicated that they could earn as much as 20% on assets after-tax. One such division required the materials manager to submit an appropriation request each year for any increases in inventory levels he foresaw. Such an appropriation request had to be justified exactly as any other investment— to support higher sales, to support change of mix, to improve customer service, etc.

Question

Critique each of these ways of approaching the cost of capital. Would you favor one of them for WIP? Why? Do you disagree strongly with one of them? Why?

CASE STUDY: "ALL OUR FACTORY INVENTORY IS IN WIP"

Background

A certain company makes a light industrial product. This product has only 2 to 3 levels of assembly, and relatively few of the parts are actually made in the factory. That is, most of the work is subassembly and assembly from bought-out parts. Customers do not specify very much nor do they have many options—the product is made and sold as designed. There are over thirty basic products with some variety in each: typically several voltages are offered, and the customer can obtain vandal-proofing options, for example.

Situation

The accounting statements show the following (in $1,000's):

	Inventory	Cost of Sales
Work in Process	$1,766	
Raw Material	—	
Parts	—	
Shipping Stocks	$ 428	$20/day
Totals	$2,294	

Factory personnel consider their typical manufacturing cycle to be 20 working days, or about one month. Parts are ordered by a once-monthly MRP system augmented by a once-per-week shop-loading system which gives the last-minute sequencing of items to be made.

The operations manager feels his WIP inventory is too high and has asked an in-company specialist to assist in identifying means of improving it.

Questions:

1. Is the WIP inventory "too high"? Why, or why not?

2. The accounting statement indicates there are no parts or raw materials in stock. Is this likely to be true?

3. On being questioned, the materials manager says that most material is input at the start of the 20-day cycle, and that labor cost is only about 10% of total product cost. From this information, estimate the dollar value of WIP needed to support this operation.

4. Is there a significant difference between your calculation from #3 above and the $1,766 shown on the inventory statement? What might account for it?

5. In light of what you have found in Steps 1 to 4, what would you suggest as the next steps in the turnover improvement project?

Chapter 5

Reaching the Goals

PRECONDITIONS

The Plan Has to Be Good

Refer again to Fig. 2–1 and note that a sound plan has four attributes: (1) No unplanned laps or gaps, (2) Each item finish date matches its parent start date, (3) Enough (but not too much) time is provided to do the required work and make the necessary moves. (4) All elements of work are accounted for and recorded in the plan. So are all supporting requirements such as tooling, prints of drawings, and process specifications. It is essential to get as far along the path to manufacturing resource planning as is practical.

The plan must not be overloaded or be wrenched around unnecessarily by Management, by sales people, or by anyone else. Part of the "goodness" of the plan is that it be "doable" and *stable*. This does not mean cast in concrete, never to be changed; it *does* mean remaining unchanged until all resources have been exhausted to avoid a change. It also means having an information system that can show us enough about the consequences of the change that they can be evaluated and management given a set of options, with costs and benefits, for making the change.

The System Must Work

Any system (man, computer, or combined) that has been in place for any length of time has its known errors. It also has some unknown errors that come to the surface when an earnest attempt is made to use it as a formal system. It will pay to canvass the system users to ask them for their own lists of errors in the system which they know how to look after, and get the errors fixed.

It pays, also, to audit the key functions of the existing system. Does the change system function properly? Are all adjustments to dates, when needed, tracked down to the lowest levels and the loads and schedules revised to suit? Do labor and material applications unload properly when completions are entered into the system? Do *all* labor and material transactions pass through the system—or is it bypassed in emergencies, leaving a litter of incorrect inventory records, misstated loads, and wrongly applied costs behind? These are merely a few thought starters: where systems are concerned, Murphy's law is an unfailing guide; whatever can go wrong, will. Your own system needs a thorough checkout before being made the basis of a *formal* system.

The People Must Be Prepared

Earlier, we touched on the need for training and explained at some length how we could enable management to train themselves, simply by submitting a request for funds.

Training which is more time consuming and in a way more demanding, is also required among the operating supervisors, their staff support, and the hourly operators themselves. It is not possible to install a truly effective WIP turn improvement program without instilling in all who will be concerned the principles of synchronized production. They must be trained to plan the week's production using the load summaries. Only when everyone in the operation, including the truckers and handlers, truly understands what we are trying to do will results be as good as is possible.

This is a test of the people who are guiding the effort, because they must develop and present training materials suitable to the level of the organization being addressed.

Training for training's sake is a waste of time. The objective of training is to change behavior. It is not gathering a group together and giving a lecture. Training has happened when the group, at the end of a session, have identified something they can and will do differently when they return. Even the word *training* should probably be avoided. Instead, hold workshops and ensure that each participant is committed to do some one or two things, however minor, which will be different from his prior practice and will move the organization a little in the right direction.

Some firms hold production workshops for a day or two. At the end, each participant is asked to submit a document like Fig.5–1, which identifies clearly some one, two, or three things he feels (and the group or leader has agreed) he should do to get one step closer to synchronized WIP flow. Sometimes these actions are exceedingly simple (like moving a filing cabinet to an accessible location). Sometimes they are more complex and require skilled work (such as having a computer program revised). Sometimes they are nothing more than New Year's resolutions—in which a foreman undertakes to get his priority index below 15 by month-end. But every participant in a workshop should submit one or more proposals. For motivational reasons, the leader will want to follow up, help, encourage, and recognize accomplishment.

Realistic Objectives

Objectives must be structured so that they are appropriate to the person and his level in the organization. It is very difficult for a subforeman or an operator to relate his work directly to return on investment. Many of us are

Production Workshops
Production Improvement Projects

#	Who	Will Do What	With What Results,	and When	Measured By	Comment
1.						
2.						
3.						

Date _____

Fig. 5–1.   Production workshop docket form.

quite startled when we first hear that our hour by hour decisions have important asset management overtones.

The Means-Ends Chain is an effective method of illustrating to an employee the consequences of his individual effort. Look at Fig. 5–2 which is a partial means-ends chain, or cause-effect tree, showing the hierarchy of reasons why "We cannot ship on time." At the top level, it doesn't look as though there is much in it for the clerk in the fabrication shop; but at the bottom levels it should be quite apparent that if he does his job, ensuring the schedules move promptly to the work centers and the unload reports move promptly to the unload system, he can have considerable effect upon the end result.

To be called an objective in this kind of business, something must be numerical and measurable. Information like average days late and priority index are numerical and make measurement simple. One of our main failings in industry is to measure the wrong things, then be puzzled and disappointed by the results.

Example 1

A firm making electronic components of the same general type but varying greatly in size had certain cost problems. A consultant was called in. He found that setup costs were higher than they should be and that there was a great deal of scrap. He soon learned that the production people habitually broke into long runs of a certain size product to introduce a smaller one, then swung back to the larger to complete the run. Since a line changeover and a certain amount of startup scrap was involved each time, he inquired why this should

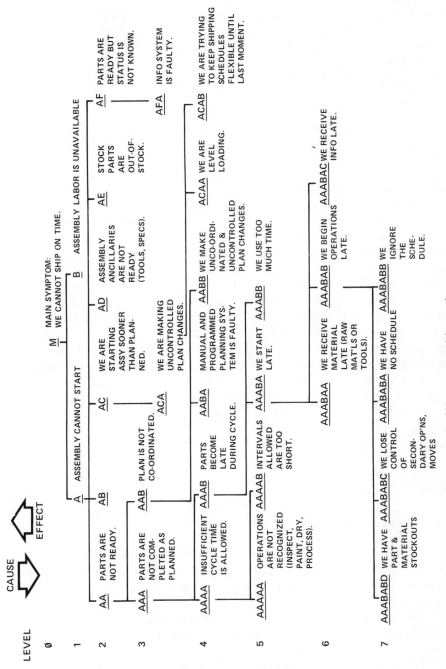

Fig. 5-2. Opportunity analysis matrix: We cannot ship on time.

be done. He was told that it was to "keep the PPOH up." PPOH, he found, was parts per operator hour, a measurement the superintendent set great store by. Since the line ran much more slowly on large units than on small, a long run of large units pulled down the PPOH. This was a glaring example of measuring the wrong thing and causing poor results by the measurement.

Example 2

It is characteristic of factories that some figure called *departmental efficiency* is steadily monitored. Usually, this is a ratio between standard hours, or number of parts, and the attendance time (in-plant time) of the work force. Because this is fairly easy to measure, it receives much attention. Obviously, efficiency should and must be measured; but not at the expense of all other measurement. Shipping on time between cost centers is at least equally important but is almost never measured because measurement is so difficult. This is like looking under the street light for the dollar we lost in the dark alley, because the light is so much better. The search for high efficiency, pressed too far, leads in some undesirable directions, such as combining too many setups and thereby disrupting the schedule; or picking easy, long-running jobs whether in sequence or not. We need to recall, more often, Drucker's distinction: Efficiency is doing the thing right, while effectiveness is doing the right thing. It is possible to be quite effective without necessarily being extremely efficient; but efficiency without effectiveness is wheel spinning. Getting a high labor efficiency at the expense of missed shipments is efficiency without effectiveness.

It is essential to divide a program like WIP improvement into small, manageable pieces, each with a termination date. Even ongoing objectives— like lower priority index—should be restated as improvement is made, so that visible progress can be recorded and attributed to the right people. A PERT chart can be a big help.

USING THE PLAN

Looking Ahead

A plan, by definition, is a description of the future. MRP has had such stunning results because it is an orderly method of looking at the future—dim though the visibility sometimes is—instead of assuming that the future will be like the past.

WIP turnover improvement depends critically upon the ability of shop supervision and production controllers in particular to look ahead and plan ahead.

The computer reports such as the load summary and sequence listing which are recommended in this book are part of a plan. The final, most important part is done a few days or weeks ahead, using the load summaries and sequence lists as inputs.

A Plan for the Week

The load summary is the input to the foreman's final planning process for deploying his men over the short run. Using it, he can determine, work center by work center, which machines he should be leaving idle for a couple of days and on which machines he should be working overtime. In his new, probably unfamiliar role as an asset manager, he allows himself to have a limited, planned amount of WIP created in advance of a peak load, so that the peak, when it arrives, just cleans it out. He does not allow himself the luxury of a large, unsequenced input queue from which he can select jobs which suit him or which happen to be atop the pile.

He uses the information provided by the computer to aid him in decision making. He does not permit the computer to take over. For instance, the visible peak may be one week beyond the computer's "ideal reporting rate" calculation horizon. When this sort of thing occurs (as it does, constantly), a decision is required on how it shall be handled.

Embedded in this commonplace observation is a principle of WIP control often overlooked: *a decision is required*. The commonest way of handling load fluctuations in a job shop is to let the overdues fluctuate. This isn't a decision; it's avoiding the problem. Its consequences are disastrous; and the tragedy is that the disaster is so familiar we think it's part of the scenery. Evidence of the disaster includes continuous expediting, low labor efficiency, missed shipments, high inventories—both of WIP and ledger items.

To get into a different mode, then, requires a decision. Broadly, the decisions required can range across a broad spectrum. For example we can do nothing. A *decision* to do nothing is not a cop-out and is often correct, so long as consequences are judged to be a low threat to production, efficiency, and on-time shipment.

Another alternative is to work more or less than the ideal working rate in order to absorb a peak or cushion a drop. Working temporarily at a higher rate requires other decisions involving labor availability through overtime or borrowing personnel from less loaded work centers with interchangeable skills; material availability from stores stock (which MRP probably won't make available earlier than planned) or from other work centers (which may simply move the raw material problem upstream or involve juggling other overloads); and so forth.

Another solution is to let the load flow as forecast on the load summary and plan to handle it with capacity which can be made available (e.g., by going to a second shift). In many ways, this is the ideal solution since it has the least rippling effect on other parts of the system. It can be used if the skills are available and are underloaded at the time of the forecast overload. Its limitations typically are statistical (two interchangeable skills are overloaded at the same time), contractual (limits to overtime or shift working on short notice are in the contract), or administrative (we can't run a properly serviced second shift for only one or two work centers).

To get a feel for this kind of planning, let us look at Fig. 5–3 which is a load summary for a portion of a machine shop. This, by the way, is not a simulation and is the kind of thing supervision will have to cope with in the early days of a WIP improvement program.

Let us imagine ourselves as foreman or production controller having just received this report some Monday morning. It is now time for the weekly load-planning meeting. To simplify our example, let us assume that these three work centers are all we have in the department, and our job is to man them the best way.

As a foreman, one would study the sheet and note the following:

1. Work Center B is in a good deal of trouble. It is reporting work 25.2 days late on average, with a great deal of the work being done 27 days earlier and later than average. Thus it is delivering parts all the way from on time or early to 2½ and more months late. It would require 13.5 weeks just to work through the overdues and the first four-weeks load we now have—by which time, of course, a great deal more would be overdue. Its 3-week moving average of work reported is only 22 hours; the computer program suggests 116 hours would be more appropriate. As a foreman, too, we would note that the work center is spending more time (39 hours) on unscheduled work than it is on scheduled work (34 hours). However, there is one ray of light—the work center is raising its demonstrated capacity, because it completed 34 scheduled hours last week, compared with the 3-week moving average of 22 hours. However, there is no question that the work center is in serious capacity trouble which is not being corrected fast enough.

2. Work Center A is much closer to current than the other two—only 2.5 weeks overdue, only 3.7 average days late. The priority index could be improved, but as long as matching parts from other work centers are being delivered so late, this won't even be noticed. So it seems that Work Center A is working too far ahead; it should be slowed-down until others catch up. Perhaps the men running it can pitch in on Work Center B on the night shift for a week or on overtime—whichever will do the most good and is more practical.

3. Work Center C is midway between A and B so far as currency (being current) is concerned. At the moment, there is little call for it to attempt to get current. However, note that, even if the decision were made that overdues were to be held at 92 hours, the current working rate of 14 hours would cause a buildup of overdues, because the first few weeks show loads of 14, 33, 11, and 17 hours. The overdue increase rate shows steady positive values except for Week no. 2, no. 9, and no. 10.

CBR= 28 IBR= 38 ODUE+4 WEEKS   LOAD SUMMARY FOR WORK CENTER A
LBR=   8 DLW= 38 S&C= 30 WOD= 2.5 PRIORITY INDEX=   11.98   60 IN. BER
                                       AVERAGE DAYS LATE   3.7

TYPE HRS	OVER DUE	020	025	030	033	038	043	048	053	058	063	FUT	TOTAL EXCL FUT
MI NOMI	71	1	1	10	69	31	3	1	1	6		12	194
TOTAL	71	1	1	10	69	31	3	1	1	6		12	194
OVIR		27-	27-	19-	41	3	25-	27-	27-	22-	28-		

CBR= 22 IBR= 116 ODUE+4 WEEKS   LOAD SUMMARY FOR WORK CENTER B
LBR= 39 DLW= 73 S&C= 34 WOD=13.5 PRIORITY INDEX=   27.17   80 100 MM
                                       AVERAGE DAYS LATE   25.2

TYPE HRS	OVER DUE	020	025	030	033	038	043	048	053	058	063	FUT	TOTAL EXCL FUT
MI NOMI	297	83	43	8	30	38	37	55	37	19	4	23	651
TOTAL	297	83	43	8	30	38	37	55	37	19	4	23	651
OVIR		61	21	14-	8	16	15	33	15	3-	18-		

CBR= 14 IBR= 42 ODUE+4 WEEKS   LOAD SUMMARY FOR WORK CENTER C
LBR=   1 DLW= 18 S&C= 17 WOD= 6.6 PRIORITY INDEX=   15.83   LAYOUT TAB
                                       AVERAGE DAYS LATE   10.4

TYPE HRS	OVER DUE	020	025	030	033	038	043	048	053	058	063	FUT	TOTAL EXCL FUT
MI NOMI	92	14	33	11	17	33	24	44	26	13	3	18	310
TOTAL	92	14	33	11	17	33	24	44	26	13	3	18	310
OVIR		19	3-	3	19	10	30	12	1-	11-			

Fig. 5-3.   Load summary for a factory with three work centers.

Note that last week the work center reported more standard hours than its recent average: a good trend. Possibly a very small amount of overtime or other extra labor in Work Center C would prevent it from going farther behind, which is a sufficient objective for just now.

As a foreman, one would have endless alternatives to consider; but the decisions made have to be quick and "not-wrong." There is no such thing in this arena as an unquestionably right decision.

One logical decision would be to stop work entirely on Work Center A this week, and put its staff on second shift on Work Center B, if the skills are interchangeable. Any shop supervisor will know, of course, that, having so decided, he will have emergency work which needs doing on Work Center A on the first morning it is not manned. While embarrassing, this kind of problem is not insurmountable by capable supervision which has played its cards carefully.

Supervision, of course, will be acutely aware that decisions on staffing and hours to be worked by some work centers are critically dependent upon the performance of other work centers. If this work center is a secondary one such as a brake or a drill, or an assembly one, it must depend upon reliable sources of supply from other work centers, from the store rooms, and from vendors.

This emphasizes again that secondary and assembly work centers can, in general, do little better than the functions feeding them. For instance, if Work Center C is dependent for some of its flow of parts upon Work Center B, a decision to work overtime to bring C more current might be quite meaningless until and unless B's performance is improved considerably. The most likely result would be the manufacture of still more unwanted parts by C, a severe deterioration in C's priority index, and very little accomplished to support assembly operations.

A corollary to this, by the way, is that it gives still more urgency to the need for getting feeders in order (working the right number of the right hours) before extending the WIP improvement work to assembly departments. And it highlights that, even within feeders, there is a sequence in which improvement should be undertaken; that is, primaries first, secondaries second, subassemblies third.

Supervision would have to look for guidance elsewhere, too. How late on average is the firm as a whole? (Refer to Fig. 5–4.) Is this department a severe or minor part of the problem? Does there seem to be a need to speed up or slow down the output of the department? What does this suggest to the shop supervisor for the medium term? Is his load, on the whole, rising, falling, or staying stable? For this, he needs to look at a computer or manual record of what his 10-week load has been doing recently. Figure 5–5 suggests that his load is rising fairly steadily; the steps he has just decided upon will help him get his work centers abreast, but won't meet this rising load. What to do?

Perhaps other areas in the plant, which have some of their men on loan, have seen their peak come and go and can return the personnel. Possibly some of the load, if it is expected to be temporary, can be subcontracted. But perhaps, sometime in the next 6 to 10 weeks, he is going to pass the limit of his ability to use overtime, borrowing, and other expedients. He may need a second shift, or start up and man

```
REPORT # 4.9.15B              - LOAD SUMMARY BY COST CENTRE

         PAGE    1                                      DAY  020


CBR=   356 IBR=   492 CDUE+4 WEEKS       LOAD SUMMARY FOR COST CENTRE   100
LBR=    31 OLW=   363 SCC=  332 WOD= 1.5 PRIORITY INDEX=   6.68
                                         AVERAGE DAYS LATE   1.9
TYPE  OVER  020   025   030   033   038   043   048   053   058   063   FUT   TOTAL
HRS   DUE                                                                     EXCL FUT

MI    519   325   624   178   323   228   168   167   194   107    26   269   2859
NOMI
TOTAL 519   325   624   178   323   228   168   167   194   107    26   269   2859
OVIR        31-  268  178-       33- 128- 188- 189- 162- 249- 330-


CBR=   388 IBR=   449 CDUE+4 WEEKS       LOAD SUMMARY FOR COST CENTRE   200
LBR=    78 OLW=   525 SCC=  447 WOD= 1.6 PRIORITY INDEX=   5.20
                                         AVERAGE DAYS LATE   4.2
TYPE  OVER  020   025   030   033   038   043   048   053   058   063   FUT   TOTAL
HRS   DUE                                                                     EXCL FUT

MI    604   411   343   180   258   256   377   691  1092    39    66   224   4317
NOMI
TOTAL 604   411   343   180   258   256   377   691  1092    39    66   224   4317
OVIR        23    45- 208- 130- 132-  11-  303   704  349- 322-


CBR=   453 IBR=   711 UDUE+4 WEEKS       LOAD SUMMARY FOR COST CENTRE   300
LBR=     0 OLW=   412 SCC=  412 WOD= 2.8 PRIORITY INDEX=   9.46
                                         AVERAGE DAYS LATE   1.4
TYPE  OVER  020   025   030   033   038   043   048   053   058   063   FUT   TOTAL
HRS   DUE                                                                     EXCL FUT

MI   1261   643   398   255   289   183   159   279    53    35    69   309   3624
NOMI
TOTAL 1261  643   398   255   289   183   159   279    53    35    69   309   3624
OVIR       190    55- 198- 164- 270- 294- 174- 400- 418- 384-
```

Fig. 5-4. Summarized load summaries for several departments.

135

Date of Review	Total 10-week Load Hours
305	765
310	772
315	798
320	828
325 (today)	850
330	

Fig. 5–5. Running record of total 10-week hour loading for a department as shown on weekly load summaries.

older machines which are less efficient. This may call for a personnel requisition. Or it may call for personnel upgrading, whereby manufacturing processes, no longer as labor intensive as they once were, can make available good men to be retrained on other machines.

In this way, the load summaries can be used to provide input to a high-quality shop management decision-making process. The "what if's" have been explored very briefly and will be carried no further, in hope that it will be understood how powerful a tool good information can be in the hands of the decision makers.

However, the end result of the process, so far as the immediate future is concerned, is that the foreman and his controllers have decided upon a target rate of reporting standard hours for each of the three work centers for the following week, and the foreman has a plan to obtain the right kind and quantity of labor, either within his own department or elsewhere. This makes it possible to check, daily, on the actual rate of reporting, so that it can be compared with the planned rate.

If this process results in the development of a need beyond the foreman's power to fill (load too high or low to be handled, for instance), the foreman must kick the problem upstairs to his boss. If something is going to slip, he must say so. (Remember—no surprises!)

The output of such a short-range planning meeting is usually some kind of follow-up sheet (see Fig. 5–6). This is an essential feature of WIP control. Work in process cannot be controlled from the front office, but has to use a lot of what has been called "management by shoeleather"—constant follow-up and daily course corrections. The man on the machine should have access to, and be visited by, his immediate supervisor many times a day. He, too, must know the target and how we're doing toward it.

Input-Output Control Sheet
Work Center B. Week of 020

Target Daily Output   **14 Hrs.**
Target Issued Std. Hrs   **8 Minimum**
Target Hours This Week   **70**

Day	Reported Std. Hrs.	Issued Std. Hrs.	Cumulative Reported	
			Hours	% of Target
Opening	—	8	—	—
Monday	12	13	12	86
Tuesday	18	14	30	107
Wednesday	11	10	41	98
Thursday	12	14	53	95
Friday	13	13	66	94
Closing	—	6	—	—

Fig. 5–6.   An input-outout control sheet.

A Plan for the Day

The plan for the day consists of just two things: (1) a statement of the target standard hours (working the right number of hours), and (2) a list of what comes first, second, etc. (working the right hours).

The load summary seldom needs to go to the operator on the floor; the STS, in some form, does. The operator must know what comes next, understand that it is important that he do what comes next, and understand, too, that if he is prevented from doing it he must so advise his boss.

Recall the thumbnail job descriptions for foreman and Production Control. Production Control ensures that the schedule matures as scheduled; the foreman ensures that available work is done in sequence, on time, and with good efficiency.

Production Control's main job is one of close-in eligibility testing. There are many ways of doing this. Some firms have elegant on-line systems that can be called upon to display the status of any item at any time. The cost of such systems is diminishing rapidly and more and more firms can afford them. However, in the more typical operating modes, Production Control must depend upon "go" and "nogo" lists produced every day or week by the computer programs. Such lists are much like a schedule and, in fact, might just as well be on schedule format. The report title of course is different, tending to be something like Ineligible Operations Next 5 Days. They can be generated by work center for maximum effectiveness.

Two problems tend to plague nogo lists.

1. If we begin checking too far out, of course, we find virtually everything is ineligible. But if we don't check early enough, the opportunity to correct problems is lost. So where is the right horizon for eligibility testing? Depending upon the firm and its sources, this will be highly variable. Failing a concrete answer, we suggest that you don't check out too far; perhaps no farther than one and one-half of the intervals between computer cycles, plus critical items known as such to the controllers.

2. Do we have the programs test eligibility on work which is scheduled for this week—or only on the queue ahead, overdues first? If we will consider our real problem—which is to work through our total load, overdues and all, in priority sequence—the answer, quite apparently, is that elegibility should be checked out to the horizon as measured in hours of work, overdue or not. A numerical example will help. Consider Fig. 5–3 again. There, work center B has an average working rate of 22 hours and is 13.5 weeks overdue. Let us assume the computer cycles are twice a week—Tuesday and Friday nights. It might be thought logical to have the system check eligibility on operations accounting for 2×22, or 44 hours of work, since shop management has made a decision to increase the working rate and we don't want to run out of eligible work to support this decision. This 44 hours would be accumulated beginning with the earliest operation open and ending when 44 hours has been passed.

Some readers may be puzzled by the reemergence of what they might consider to be the shortage list, or expediter's shortlist. Perhaps we're just reinventing "order–launch and expedite," after all!

But we are not. There are profound differences between working with a nogo list and working in the expedite mode. These differences include the following:

1. The expedite mode starts with the making of a shortage list; this nogo list mode ends with it. In this mode, the people, working with the system, have done all they can—perhaps 95% of what needs doing—to assure an orderly supply of material to the next stage of manufacturing. Nogo lists are true exception lists, covering the 5%.

2. Nogo lists tend to be small because they are aimed at the work center level, showing nogo's over a few days only, and they are exception reports, as already noted. Problems are metered out in small, manageable bundles.

3. Many things which get onto a shortage list would not make it to a nogo list. This is because the process of checking begins so much earlier. If the steel shear operator cannot make a piece on his schedule because of shortage, he will not be able to cross it off his STS. Since his STS gets turned back in for action on

falldowns of this kind, action to recover from the problem begins long before it shows up as a shortage at assembly.

4. The formal system, working with accurate records (which should sound familiar, somehow!), can pinpoint true nogo's and bring them to the user at low cost, without the user's having to do the grubby bull-work of listing, checking, and chasing. In order-launch systems, the records are so bad that the machine cannot do this dependably; the user must generate his own information, at high cost.

Converting the Plan for the Day into the Day's Output

Working to schedule sequence is a very easy principle to get people to accept. Of course, they say, we should always work in schedule sequence, and whenever we can, we do. But then they usually present an extremely long list of why they often cannot. It is not possible to work in exact schedule sequence, we may be told, because:

- the material doesn't come to us in that sequence.
- the expediters are always around contradicting the schedule.
- our suppliers are unreliable. They often do not ship on time.
- tooling is often not available or is found to need maintenance when it is pulled for the job.
- we can't pull the same material from stores a half-dozen times in the same week: we shear all the ⅜ plate we can see on the schedule at one time.
- we must save setups.
- we can't take the schedule seriously—that top item has been there for months. There's an error in the program.

And, of course, all of these reasons and more are true at times. And if we let their presence drive us away from a principle, force us to give up when we know better, we're in the wrong job.

In the section on checking out our present performance, the penalties associated with *not* working to schedule sequence are demonstrated in specific, numerical terms. For present purposes, let us refer to Fig. 2–1, look one more step to the right of "working the right hours" and note the two key components of this principle. We have to ensure that eligible work arrives and then do it in schedule sequence.

A schedule is a model of what we plan to have happen in the factory in the future—sometimes only a few days or hours in the future. Therefore, until the moment arrives when the schedule says something should happen, it can say only that: it *should* happen. Only unfolding events will dictate what *can* happen. Work which is scheduled to be done *and can be done* is "eligible" or "go" work. Any which is scheduled but cannot be done because of parts shortages or for whatever other reason, is "ineligible" or "nogo." This is a useful distinction because it leads directly to a set of clear cut responsibilities for Production Control and Supervision.

Assuming that the plan is workable, the job of Production Control is to ensure that ineligible work becomes eligible, on-time, while Supervision's job is to see that eligible work is done efficiently and in sequence.

These thumbnail job descriptions contrast starkly with the situation in some plants—thankfully diminishing in number—in which Production Control avoids the issue by commenting that, "It's on order—I told them that long ago," while Supervision neglects its important jobs by racing from feeder to feeder with shortage lists.

It is tempting at this point to go back to the list given earlier of reasons for not working in sequence and offer profound advice on overcoming each obstacle. But they are symptoms, not problems. The presence of large volumes of such problems indicates that the organization does not have a stable, formal, workable plan; or a simple, transparent, dependable system for executing it; or some of both. For instance, if suppliers are undependable, how many change notices have they had recently? For instance, if gas-cutting templates aren't ready, have we taken any pains to train, for example, our draftsmen or industrial engineers to ensure that they too are in series with a production path and must produce on time? For instance, if a work center persistently produces out of sequence, have we tried to find out what it needs by way of racks or pigeon-holes for in and out materials—or do we just let FILO govern all that? Certainly, there will be supplier falldowns, computer problems, and blizzards. Emergencies like these will call for expediting. But expediting to meet emergencies is not the same as operating a factory in the expedite mode.

Requirements for Working to Sequence

These are the requirements for working in schedule sequence at the work center level:

1. Work must enter the work center's queue in schedule sequence. Compromises are inevitable, because batching is usually essential in a job shop; for instance, it is not practical to have the fork truck bring pieces one at a time in most cases. Nevertheless, the principle must not be lost sight of. If a batch coming in is half a day's work, it must not be buried or covered by the following load; it must remain accessible to those working tomorrow morning instead of being dug out of the bottom of the pile by an expediter next week. It is hard to overemphasize the importance of this single, simple, very destructive phenomenon: later work gets laid atop earlier work. It must not happen if the schedule is to be kept.

2. The operator must have a responsibility for working to sequence and must have a method of discharging it. This method involves providing him with a list (his copy of the STS) and sufficient physical facilities that the search for the top item on the STS does not become frustrating. Given a reasonable amount of accessible storage at the input queue, a vast majority of operators will take a responsible interest in working in sequence.

3. Work must leave the work center in schedule sequence, for reasons exactly the same as those just discussed.

4. Input and output queues must be kept small, otherwise the problem of adhering to sequence quickly becomes insuperable.

Inhibiting Factors

Many times a day, of course, the ''next item'' on the operator's STS is not to be found. He has discharged his obligation if he has attempted to find it, notified his supervisor or Production Control of the problem, and has then gone on with the first item he can find. He must, then, keep checking incoming work for the missed items. This suggests various subsystems for cooperation among operators, Supervision, and Production Control which will not be gone into further here; they are better evolved in a local environment.

Many work centers have practical difficulties in working to sequence. Consider a steel plate shear in a true job shop, for instance. If ⅜″ plate items appear in four different places in this morning's STS, it is obviously ridiculous to pull the ⅜″ plate four times in one morning. Yet the shear is at the start of a long, complex, synchronized plan; if we depart from sequence at this point, the situation will become rapidly worse as secondary operation work centers attempt to do their work in sequence.

This kind of practical problem usually has to be solved in a very pragmatic way, with some sort of rule of thumb. One rule is this: Combine setups as far out into the future as you like, so long as you (1) do not starve the secondary work centers of currently needed work which is at the tops of their STS's, and (2) do retain all such production at the out-rack or queue of the work center which produced it, until it can be released downstream *on schedule* instead of *when produced*.

The commonest—and often quite violent—objection to this rule is that we don't have room at the shear, say, for all this held-over work. That is often true; and when it is true, then that is the message. If the shear hasn't room for it, then probably no one else has. We may find that we have, for years, been forcing the problem underground rather than solving it. It can often be noticed that we will save an hour of setup by creating a situation which will require four hours of expediting—really resequencing—to fix later on. The sad delusion under which we labor is that setups cost us money while expediting somehow does not.

Using the Human Resource

In shops where the heaviest stress in the past has been upon labor efficiency, operators have been held responsible mainly for *working on something* (almost anything!), while someone else worries about the schedule. But we must not neglect to use a key resource like the intelligence of the operators. Most operators enjoy and will take an interest in having influence over the on-time performance of the plant, and they are in a situation where this influence is very powerful. At a secondary work center, for instance, the operator is the one most able to filter and resequence work which will, inevitably, come to him randomized to some extent from his feeders. We must not underestimate the potent effect of having the *entire work force*—not just the manager and one or two of the superintendents, perhaps—aware of, and working actively toward adherence to, a correct principle.

Another key person in the operation is the material handler. He must be trained to recognize that, by so simple a thing as his choice of where to lay something down, he can have a powerful effect (good or bad) upon the performance of the plant.

In the end, of course, the responsibility for assuring improved schedule adherence will come back upon the plant management. And this means that plant management must be both knowledgeable and credible. If we strongly encourage operators to work in sequence, we must provide the paper, tools, and physical facilities (such as racks, bins), and training to enable them to respond. If we insist on improved sequencing out of the shear, we must not complain if the odd setup is not saved.

If the shop is on incentive or piecework, credibility also requires that we provide time allowance for administrative work like checking the input queue for the next item on the STS, so that we are not solving our problems at the operators' personal expense.

Measuring Our Performance

We can control what we can measure. Our measurements for sequential working are shown on the example load summaries studied earlier (see Fig. 2–9).

The reader may wonder why a piece of *schedule* information should appear on a *load* document like the load summary, when our discussion has emphasized the vital differences between load control and priority control. The reason is a practical one: we have, on one piece of paper, all the inputs needed for the weekly and daily planning meeting which will be described later. In addition, the unload data stream through the computer programs is usually best intercepted where the unload-reload function is happening. A particular factory might wish to display the information elsewhere, and should do what is comfortable for it. There are two measures shown here: average days late and priority index.

Average days late is just that: the difference between a given labor report's scheduled day and reported day, summed with all other labor reports for the work center and averaged. If the number is zero, we are, on average, working on and reporting today operations which were scheduled to be reported today. If it is negative, we are working ahead of schedule. If positive, behind schedule.

But averages can be dangerous. We need warning of a condition in which the work center is on time on average, but only by virtue of the fact that it works far ahead of, and behind, sequence. As commented elsewhere, work centers vary greatly in their ability to adhere to sequence, depending upon everything from the sources upon which they must depend (the more sources, the less adherence to schedule) to the personalities of the people working in them (some people like a steady, dictated routine while others will go out of their way to do it differently).

Since the interval which a work center must be allowed to do its work depends upon its ability to stay in sequence, and since intervals are so important to us for so many reasons, we must become very interested in how far ahead of and behind schedule the work center operated in generating its average days late. This can be recognized as a problem of deviations and standard deviations. The labor reports will have a distribution about their average, as portrayed in Figs. 2–15 and 2–16. We can apply statistical analysis to these deviations and arrive at their standard deviation, which is, of course, a direct measure of the width of the report distributions.

Statistical purists will object that we have no idea of the shape of the distributions and can probably be sure of only one thing: they are not "normal." In this they are absolutely right. However, once again the model maker's maxim can be applied: A model need not be true to life to be useful. The usefulness of a standard deviation applied to a nonnormal distribution lies in the fact that when the situation is under good control, the standard deviation will be small; when it is not under control, the standard deviation will be large. And so the standard deviation, whether the curve be normal or not, gives us the right indication of what direction to take, and will continue doing so no matter how it varies.

A small or large deviation is relative and depends upon the kind of work center and the limits which the shop management, using purely empirical means, learns to live within. As will be dealt with at length later, the best way to use these measures of adherence to schedule is to produce them, view them for a time, then begin to use them as indicators of areas of difficulty. An ABC analysis of the average days late and of the priority indices will quickly point out the areas in the shop most in need of help in getting on schedule and keeping in sequence.

Working the Plan: Dispatching

Disptaching is one of the key functions in any WIP control system. Dispatchers must have alert minds and genuine interest in, and understanding of, what they are doing. Resilience and good judgment are essential, because dispatchers are subjected to many pressures from many people, from operators to foremen.

Dispatching is the point at which planning finally ends and shop floor control begins. So let us sketch out what these key people are responsible for doing. In the first place they must issue to the shop the manufacturing requisitions for those operations which are next in priority on the schedule and are eligible to "go."

They must also keep such tallies as are necessary to ensure that the total of dispatched work does not exceed an agreed level. Usually this level has been set during the weekly planning meeting. This level must not be confused with the *rate* at which work is being done: they are directly related but are not the same. The agreed level typically is enough to keep the work center busy over some practical reporting interval, such as one-half shift, which implies the operator will report for reload twice per shift; or a shift and a half, which would carry the work station through one evening turn when no staff services may be available. If this agreed level is exceeded, priority keeping will degenerate because there will be a certain amount of picking and choosing resulting in unsequential working. If the agreed level is not reached, there will be lost motion several times a shift when the administrative work of unloading-reloading has to be repeated.

Dispatchers must ensure that requests for reload are subjected to the rule: *no reload without an unload.* If ten standard hours have been reported, about ten new hours should be issued.

They are also responsible for monitoring and reporting on danger signals such as operations left behind. Dispatchers should work from the STS, dispatching only go operations. If there are remnants of an earlier reload still not checked off as complete, dispatchers are entitled to ask why before reloading. The reason, of course, is that it is quite possible for a work center to be working at about the right rate but on the *wrong* jobs. *Even a job due today is the wrong job if an earlier job remains unreported* without good reason. They should take prompt action to get late new arrivals into the work center queue ahead of whatever may most recently have been loaded-out to it. Late new arrivals generally come from one of two sources:

- operations that are late and were nogo until now,
- operations on orders which were released on short intervals and arrive overdue. (Discussed elsewhere is the overall rationale behind this class of overdues.)

The objective here, of course, is to begin promptly the process of catching up the time that has been lost on this branch of the order. Another dispatcher function is to monitor system performance and report on improvements which may be necessary. Such improvements can range from changes in the computer sorting sequence and headings, to office arrangement and equipment.

Dispatchers must also monitor day by day progress toward the week's objective number of hours worked and report significant departures. In this regard, the dispatcher is part of the foreman's sensor system, since he or she will be the first to know when one of two undesirable situations arises: (1) The work center is not meeting its cumulative production commitment for the week, (2) The work center is exceeding its commitment and is going to run out of work released from the computer files or build up useless WIP or both.

Finally, dispatchers must periodically audit the issued standard hours to ensure that the backlog at the work station is not becoming too large or too small. Little errors in reporting and in arithmetic accumulate in this figure and it needs purging every few days. The best time is the moment the new STS is received. Any item recorded as issued off the old STS but still outstanding on the new STS must obviously be in backlog.

On-line, Real-time Systems

In reviewing the subject of shop floor control, it is irresistible to think what a fine thing an on-line system would be. And it is true that such systems strongly support two of the three characteristics of good information (i.e., it is timely, accessible, and accurate.) A good on-line, real-time system can be timely—up to the second—and very accessible.

However, we sometimes overlook the fact that *we are always on-line, real-time*. Before work can begin on anything, someone must learn that it could begin—that parts, machinery, men, drawings, and so forth were all ready at the same moment. Whoever made this determination was on-line, real-time, whether he had a computer or not. Thus, the question is not, "Should we be on-line, real-time?" but, "How can we improve our on-line, real-time system?" Maybe improvement needs terminals and CRT's. Chances are it doesn't.

Firms that do not have on-line, real-time systems for control in manufacturing should not consider installing them as a first step in WIP turnover improvement. Several reasons can be cited for this injunction:

1. If the factory is operating in an expedite mode, an OLRT (on-line, real-time) system will be a powerful incentive to continue and to strengthen that mode. Expediters will use the OLRT system as a convenient source of information to replan the bad plan and to generate shortage lists more easily than before. The OLRT system's basic purpose—to provide short, crisp, action instructions exactly when needed, based upon a sound plan and good information—will be undermined.

2. The design of OLRT systems for shop floor control is by no means perfected. For instance, ingrained thinking in terms of "lists" of things to be done can actually cause the factory to slow down because it is in an eligibility-testing, OLRT mode (Gue 1976, p. 117).

3. The condition of the data base in WIP tends to be even worse than the condition of the data base in parts or raw materials ledgers. Record accuracy is precisely as important to WIP management by a formal system as to parts management by MRP. A firm that has not looked at its record accuracy in WIP in this light can be sure that it has the usual large number of inaccurate records. These will include labor operations still outstanding for orders shipped long ago; rerouted operations not taken off the original work center's STS; stale operations for jobs that have been rescheduled; operations dated incorrectly because some parts of the writeup are wrong or omitted; or laps and gaps in the schedule. Superimposing an OLRT system on such a data base merely augments chaos with confusion and increases the rate at which confusion is generated.

Firms that do have OLRT systems for WIP control will be well advised to review the planning behind the operations of the shop to ensure that it is satisfactory by the criteria dealt with earlier; that is, audit the accuracy of the data base and determine what the OLRT system is really being used for. Some such systems are little more than expensive toys that help perpetuate the order–launch and expedite mode. Some such systems have been installed, have become expensive disasters, and have been removed. Some, alas, have become expensive disasters and are still in use. This may be partly because removal would entail too much loss of face, and partly because "complex systems are beyond human capacity to evaluate" (Gall 1975, p. 131). Such systems tend to take on an existence of their own, independent of the people who are paying for them. This is because their workings are so mysterious and their useful parts become embedded in so many phases of the operation, that their owners are quite simply afraid of excising the cancer for fear of destroying something vital.

Firms that have gone through a WIP turnover improvement project will generally acknowledge that their biggest payoffs came from doing the simple things better. Such firms, after getting planning in order, getting feeders working abreast, and reducing cycle times, may then be looking for ways to improve still further by speeding up the information cycle times; and this is where the OLRT system is potentially a very great help.

Again, *a warning:* It is enticing to have the computer system make many of the decisions which can and should be made by people, but, especially in the beginning, the OLRT system should be an *information* system, not a decision-making system. Presenting good information rapidly and conveniently to operating managers is such a big step forward and is so much quicker to install and cheaper to buy than more glamorous systems, that the first step into OLRT should be limited only to this. Furthermore, complex systems that work almost always evolve from simple systems that worked, while systems that were complex at the start frequently never work at all, ever.

Overcoming Load Fall-off

Figure 5–7 shows how a plant's load of customer orders falls off as it looks farther into the future. But of course, in an ongoing business, the future load always looks like the curve in Figure 5–7. When we check again the following period, the point at which we "fall off the cliff" has usually moved outward in time by the same amount we have moved. (See Fig. 5–8.) This is complicated by the effect of factory cycle times. If the sales department is promising ten-week deliveries and the product cycle time is eight weeks, then obviously the primary feeders are going to get at most only two weeks warning of incoming firm business, while the assembly department may get eight or nine. (See Fig. 5–9.)

In businesses of any complexity which have MRP, the load fall-off effect can be reduced markedly by the use of planned and firm-planned orders, which call for the manufacture of parts called for by planning bills. These orders are released into the manufacturing stream as they fall within lead time. Such orders for stock, distinct from customer orders, ought to be as good as any other kind of order for planning shop load-capacity control and priority-sequence control. And, indeed, in factories that make highly standard products on demand lead times much shorter

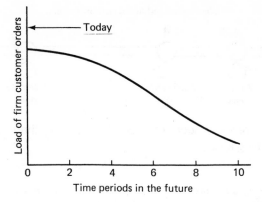

Fig. 5–7.   Fall-off of customer orders.

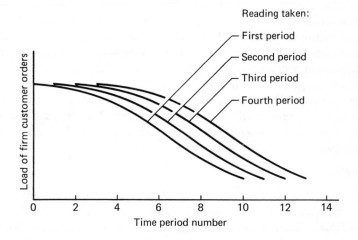

Fig. 5–8.   Migration of the load fall-off effect through time.

than manufacturing lead times, they are the *only* orders they ever see; customer orders are either nonexistent or penetrate only into the assembly departments. Manufacturers of power tools, appliances, and automobiles tend to be in this category. However, there is a very large group of industries which is between the extremes of wholly standard, never custom-building, and wholly nonstandard, seldom building for stock. One survey showed that 11% of firms with APICS members built to stock, 17% to order, and 72% *to both customer order and stock* (Greene, ed. 1970, pp. 30–36).

For this 72% of firms, there is great variation in the dependability of the forecast, and the dependability and stability of the planned and even the released

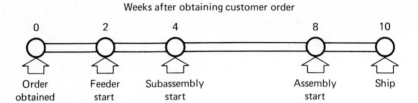

Fig. 5-9. How primary feeders have less notice than assembly work centers of oncoming load.

load. Undesirable as this may be, it has to be lived with until it can be corrected. We cannot afford to wait until matters like this are all tidied up before improving WIP turns. "If all objections were to be overcome in advance, nothing would ever be undertaken" (Winston Churchill).

However, the absence or undependability of the planned portion of the load is a powerful disincentive to shop supervision in their efforts to staff properly. The firm, customer-order portion of their load summaries shows a fall-off. They can all remember instances in the past when that is exactly what happened. Very probably they were caught with surplus labor. They may want, for obvious reasons, to hedge on the low side—to keep that backlog visible.

Overcoming this problem comes partly from training, partly from improving the information system, partly from employing labor flexiblity, and partly from a clear management understanding of the problem accompanied by a certain amount of management tolerance for the occasional error in staffing.

Training

Training refers to the need to ensure that supervision clearly understands the simple, but often overlooked, ideas just discussed. They must understand, for example, that primary work centers get much less notice of firm loads than do assembly departments, and they need not feel there is anything wrong with the system when it happens. Training in responding nimbly to load shifts, using the list of labor skills to gain flexibility, is also necessary. And perhaps as much as anything else, supervision must be trained to recognize that level loads at most of the work centers in a typical facotry are impossible. Managers—including foremen—are, in no small measure, employed to *manage change*. If there were no change, there would be few problems requiring any management attention at all.

Information system

An improved information system is important. If the plan is good, is displayed to the right people at the right time with the right action indicators (such as priority index), the system user will make staffing decisions with a confidence which the factory foreman typically does not have today, in many plants. One output from the information system which addresses this load fall-off problem directly is a simple tracking figure. A computer program module (or a manual tally in small plants) can total the firm customer-order hours of load which are in the system period by period. The variation in this figure is advance warning of needs for staff adjustments, borrowing, overtime, and so on. These variations can be dubbed a measure of load "acceleration," since the principle is precisely analogous to the mechanical concept of the same name. The load is building up or falling off at the rate of so many hours per week per week.

Using Fig. 5–10, a shop manager (from foreman upward) might note that his load appears to be building up at a rate of 20 standard hours per week for each week which passes (if he took a reading after three weeks); or 40 (Weeks 3–5); or 14 (Weeks 5–8). Each of these figures would suggest some kind of action to him. If he had chosen to extrapolate the first figure, 20 hours/week/week, he might have estimated that, after 8 weeks, he would be requiring 8 × 20, or 160 standard hours more output, each week. This would have suggested a need to staff up, by perhaps three or four men (preferably, by borrowing temporarily). In the example, if he had made this decision and stuck with it, he would have been prepared to handle a load which, by Week eight, would have been 140 hours/week more than the 310 hours per week he began with—only a few hours off target.

This, it can be seen, is very analogous to the problem of tracking customer demand for finished goods. The demand is "independent" because it is a direct reflection back into the factory, via bill explosions and MRP, of what is happening in the marketplace. It brings with it exactly the same problems of uncertainty in forecasting which all independent demand tracking systems bring; but such a technique will give at least some light on the load ahead.

If this acceleration figure is supplied by hand, it can be done by estimating a best-fit line as has been done in Fig. 5–10. If it is supplied by computer program, several algorithms suggest themselves and the best of them will be the simplest. There are many booby traps. For instance, fictitious variations can result from ridiculous and irrelevant circumstances, such as the absence of a key person in a

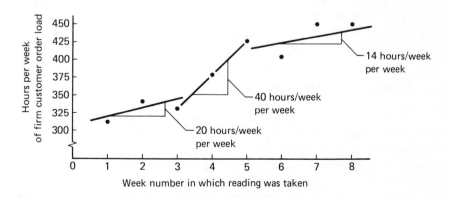

Fig. 5–10.   Tracking acceleration of firm load.

customer service or order entry function, where work piles up for a day or a week. But dim light is better than no light, and it is necessary to do what we can with what we have.

Later we will discuss the important subject of forecasting loads which are beyond the lookout horizon of the load summaries we are discussing here.

Labor flexibility

Labor flexibility, properly employed, reduces greatly the foreman's fear of being caught with surplus labor. It must be provided for legally, contractually, and as a matter of company policy surrounding such things as the labor rates which will be paid to the multiskilled manpower.

Management understanding

Management must clearly understand the following points:

● Various parts of the factory have various degrees of tolerance for plan changes. If plan changes are made on short notice, feeders may have no notice or negative notice (they are already launched on the wrong course). Time fences need to be respected or the consequences accepted without blaming supervision for a situation beyond their control.

● Staffing to a forecast is even more of a guessing game than the forecast itself. It has been explained how mix change within a dead-level billing load can cause feeder load changes of three to one and more. The management which recognizes this kind of phenomenon will also recognize that human beings can and will guess wrong at times. It's a tradeoff of a type which management is there to deal with effectively; it involves budgeting for and accepting a certain bearable amount of cost which results from simply running out of work for people to do. This cost will have various forms depending upon the industry. It will range from payment for time not worked, to payment at too high a labor grade, and all points between.

Nor should this cost be considered as a cost of installing WIP control. It is a cost we have always had, which WIP control will enable us to reduce, and which WIP control hopefully will force us to recognize, deal with openly and fairly, without prejudice to either supervision or their hourly people.

Overall Measurement: the Superintendent's Job

So far, we have spoken of measurement of work center performance as if the work centers operated independently, which of course they do not. At some level of management close to the shop itself, which may be the foreman, superintendent, or manager level depending upon plant size, it is necessary to take an overall view of the performance of the factory and to direct its elements toward a unified goal.

That unified goal is probably best visualized by looking at Fig. 5–11. The factory manager's unified goal is to ship most of his product on time, at low labor

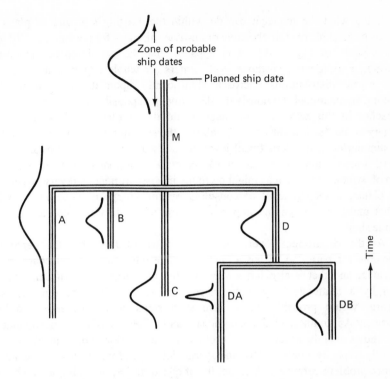

Fig. 5–11. Model of an assembled multilevel product production plan, showing the probability that any given component will be completed at the time shown.

cost, out of a small inventory. His means to this end are to move the "zone of probable ship dates" earlier in time, so that some acceptable percentage—such as 95%—of orders go out on time, instead of perhaps 50% as shown in Fig. 5–11; and to shorten the overall interval for the product by shortening any feeder intervals which it may be possible and wise to shorten.

The intervals we are talking about here are the true shop intervals as portrayed by the small probability curves*, not the planned intervals as shown by the heavy bars. These planned intervals can be shortened too, of course, but that is another phase of the WIP turn improvement project. For present purposes we are

---

*Note that the small curves do not represent *intervals* but the *distribution of lateness* of deliveries around their average. However a broad distribution (large standard deviation) of deliveries has the same effect as a lengthening of the shop interval for that part of the product. Therefore, in what follows, we will use the widths of these distributions as deputies or substitutes for true shop intervals.

considering what the manager can do within the existing structure of plans and intervals to meet his overall objective of on-time shipment from a smaller WIP base. From a study of Fig. 5–11, it is apparent that he can improve his on-time performance by identifying those work centers (or whole departments, in a large plant) whose distributions encroach significantly upon the interval for final assembly. In the model, obviously the department responsible for components "A" encroaches in this way. The manager would detect this by checking the load summary at the department level. Recall that the system must provide consolidated load summaries at the department level in plants of any size. For instance, there must be a load summary for each work center; a consolidated load summary for a group of work centers such as might be found in a department; and very possibly, in large plants, a second level of consolidation for groups of departments which together make up a large and important section of the factory, such as the entire machine shop.

At the department level, the manager would find that the department responsible for parts "A"* has a later "average days late" than Departments B through D, and that it also has a very much wider distribution of deliveries, as shown by a relatively very high priority index. His first operating decision, therefore, would probably be to take such steps as are necessary to bring Department A into line with the other departments. Because of high priority index in A, he knows exactly which kind of problem he has—priority or sequence control, not likely capacity control. His managerial job, therefore, is to get the mixed-sequence problem corrected. A partial list of questions he, or his foreman, could be expected to ask, would be as follows:

1. Is the STS too long—is there picking and choosing of jobs going on?
2. Is the department plagued by poor deliveries from some supplier (such as a foundry), by stores shortages, by tool unavailability or unserviceability?
3. Are the input storage facilities (racks etc.) suitable for ensuring that the top job on the STS can be moved into work easily, even if it may not have come to the department in the right sequence?
4. Is there a particular work center in the department which is much worse than the others and is dragging down the departmental performance? (There always is!)
5. What is the eligiblity testing system and is it working OK for this department?

This questioning process can be extended indefinitely, and its application to the particular plant environment will be left to the imagination of the reader.

---

*The expression "the department responsible for parts 'A' " is cumbersome. Henceforward, "A," "B," etc. will be referred to as if they were departments rather than product components.

Having given the necessary emphasis to what seems to be the main problem, unsequential working in Department A, the manager might well turn his attention to Department C, where it seems the plant is building a good deal of unwanted WIP. It is running well ahead of schedule. The parts it makes are somewhere in the plant, causing clutter, confusion, added handling and managing while they are waiting idle for product from Departments A, B, and D to catch up. The manager would detect this by noting that the average days late for Department C has a large negative value, while the priority index seems to be close to the values typical of the rest of the plant.

This, the manager would recognize, is a capacity problem. Except that in this case it is a problem of *excess,* not *insufficient,* capacity. His questioning process in this case could well go along these lines:

1. Is there a good reason for C's running so far ahead of schedule? Is it, perhaps, the result of a well-laid plan by the foreman to head off a peak he sees a few weeks away on his load summaries? If so, there may be no cause for concern, so long as we are not going overboard with the process and so long as we are managing Department C's out-queue in such a way that the excess is not creating storage problems in Department M.

2. If there is no good reason for being so far ahead of schedule, what can be done to slow down C's production for a few days or weeks? Noting that a temporary addition to Department A's capacity would help it get out of trouble (even though A's problem is basically a priority, not a capacity, one), the manager might well ask if any of C's manpower has skills which could be effectively used in A.

3. If neither of the above possiblities seems open and recognizing that we cannot indefinitely permit C to work farther and farther ahead, what options do we have, within the labor contract, to stop production in C (or parts of C) for, say, one day per week for a month? If, for example, this is a chronic condition, could we have some of C's operators spend one day per week learning A's or M's skills?

Again, the extension of this questioning process will be left to the reader. In all cases, however, the output signals from a well-functioning system based upon good plans enables shop management to pinpoint, quickly and accurately,

- what the problem is (capacity-load control or sequence control),
- where the problem is (by department and by cost center),
- therefore, using local knowledge of plant, product, and labor, what the most promising avenues of improvement appear to be.

Example

Let us review some typical numbers that might be generated by an information system such as we have described and ask ourselves what, as shop superintendents, we might do to direct our foremen for the following short period. In this model of a factory—much reduced in size for simplicity and clarity, and limited to the department level with no work center detail—we have: Feeder work centers F1, F2, F3, F4, all feeding into Assembly work center A1. We have just been presented with the outputs from the weekend computer run. They show the following picture (limited to a discussion of weeks overdue and priority index only).

Work Center	Weeks Overdue	Priority Index
F1	2.0	6
F2	1.9	11
F3	1.0	4
F4	3.2	5
A1	4.0	8

From these figures it is apparent that cost centers should be carrying more load; but not the same amount for everyone. In priority order, they need to carry more load in sequence A1, F4, F1, F2, F3. However, A1 should be left alone until its feeders can serve it better. Among the feeders, F4 is worst, F3 best. If we have management time and energy, overtime resources, and so forth for *one* drive this week, it should be in F4, preferably by borrowing men from F3.

Schedule adherence is quite bad in F2 and A1. Again, leave assembly A1 alone until feeders are in order. What is driving F2 so far off schedule? We need to swing Production Control attention over to it (maybe temporarily assigning F3's production man this week to F2 to help) to identify the problem.

So this week's decision is to staff up in F4 to bring it abreast, preferably by borrowing from F3, and to get back in sequence in F2. Next week will bring a different problem.

Tolerances and Trigger Events

Every control system involves comparison of some result with some standard. The wall thermostat, if set to 21° C, is expected to close the circuit which calls for heat when the temperature falls to perhaps 20½° C, and reopen it when its anticipator heater has brought its temperature back to 21½° C. If room temperature wanders between these limits, no action is expected from the thermostat and none is needed.

Measurement of this kind is needed if we expect to control our deliveries and our work in process to acceptable levels. Most of us are painfully aware of the measurement which says: You failed to ship on time (again); but we are not provided by our factory systems with signals which warn us that this is likely to happen, far enough in advance to do something useful about it.

However, signals such as average days late, weeks overdue, priority index, go and nogo, are such measurements. As has been commented, perfect reliability in delivering on time between work centers is uneconomic in most factories, which is to say that the cost of doing it is prohibitive. So we have to have a tolerance or band within which we can be comfortable in working. How is this band determined? How do we know, for instance, what a "good" priority index is? Because if we do not know, there will be a great deal of organizational lost-motion during which we will fret over imaginary problems while overlooking serious ones.

With our present state of knowledge, the answers to these questions are arrived at very much by trial and error, usually with a good admixture of arbitrary decision. Nevertheless, there are principles that we can use to guide the trials and keep the arbitrary decision leaning in the right direction.

In *principle,* we have seen that the cycle time through any one work center is governed more by its ability to stay in sequence than anything else. We have also seen that part deliveries from a work center are scattered through the interval provided to that work center, the distribution being very likely skewed right (i.e., with its peak later than midway through the interval). The *corollary* is that acceptable values of average days late will be negative (indicating the work center is completing work, on average, ahead of schedule); and that the numerical value should be between one-quarter and one-half of the work center's total interval.

In *principle,* we have seen that the priority index is a measure of the width of the distribution of labor reports about their average days late, and that a small priority index is very desirable to reduce WIP and improve chances of delivering matching parts to the next work center. We have also seen that primary, secondary, and assembly work centers have progressively more difficulty keeping in sequence because of the randomizing of arrivals which is constantly taking place. A *corollary* of these principles is that priority index can be expected to be small for primary work centers and much larger for secondary and assembly work centers. A guide to the numerical values of priority index can be found by comparing it with the average production interval allowed across the work center. More than two-thirds of all deliveries from the work center will occur within plus or minus one priority index; 95% or more within plus or minus two priority indices. If the average interval allowed across the work center is much less than four times the priority index, one or the other has to be changed: the interval lengthened or the priority index reduced. Practical experience is that it is far more useful to concentrate on reducing the priority index (managing to keep better in sequence) than to increase the allowed interval.

In *principle,* we have seen that ideally all work centers should be working abreast, that is, all the same degree late or early to their schedules. This will bring matched sets of parts up to assembly and will prevent the manufacture of idle WIP. However, we have also seen that, as a practical matter, to handle peaks visible in the future or for other good reasons, we may plan to work temporarily above or below the rate which would make this happen.

The *corollary* of this principle and this practical need is that having all work centers in the plant working perfectly abreast is ideal, but only a point of departure. Work centers operating with little variation in load visible within their load summary horizons should be adhering to an agreed plant ideal average days late.

Work centers preparing to meet a peak visible within their load center horizons should be working ahead (averaging deliveries earlier than their mates) in order to absorb the peak when it comes so as to fall back (ideally) no further than the plant-wide ideal. Work centers that can see a definite valley in load within their horizons should not drop behind the plant ideal average days late but should be preparing to work short time when the valley arrives.

Two useful guides to this performance are *ideal booking rate* (short term) and *total 10-week load* (medium term). Obviously the actual numbers decided upon are so much a part of the personality of an individual plant that little specific guidance can be given in this area; however, suffice it to say that experience indicates overwhelmingly that merely working to an ideal booking rate is generally far superior to what the plant may have been doing in the past, and can usually be a first-cut at the right number. Adding the intelligence of factory Supervision and Production Control to this at a later date will result in another giant step forward in on-time deliveries.

In *principle*, we have seen that the weeks overdue of a given work center can be used, in combination with average days late and current booking rate, to estimate the quality of execution of the plan. It is possible, of course, to have an acceptable average days late and good priority index yet have much too much overdue: we're working the right hours but not the right number of hours. Assuming that the stale and unwanted records have been cleaned out of the work center schedule, this condition shows we have a capacity problem: we're not carrying the load. Only some of the needed parts will arrive at assembly matched with others. Again, ideal booking rate is a guide to this. The *corollary*, therefore, is that all work centers should be running with similar weeks of overdue figures. If they are not, either housecleaning of the files or rebalancing the labor force (probably both) are needed.

The management of a particular plant is the only group who can feel their way toward a set of measurements which is helpful and suitable for them. And "feeling their way" is very much what has to be done. No one will ever know what the "right" figures are. Nevertheless it is generally quite possible to identify unacceptable figures. In summary, the specific tolerances for the various signals can be developed only in a specific plant. Guidelines however can be found, and it is *essential* that the operating people (especially Supervision and Production Control) have an agreement on what constitutes an out-of-control condition at the work center, cost center, and budget center levels. This will permit them, in their weekly planning meetings and during their day-to-day operations, to concentrate on the A items in the system: those work centers which critically need attention.

CYCLE-TIME REDUCTION: A LAST STEP

Why This Step Should be Last

Reduction of cycle times has a potent effect upon inventories. The inventory formula, $WIP = SCR$, where C is the cycle time, makes this exceedingly clear. But reducing cycle times as a first step is a little like the office worker who decides to run in the marathon. He'd better get into condition first, or he won't survive the first mile.

Factories which are in the order–launch and expedite mode are already using all the time they have—often more—to identify and overcome their shortages. Reducing the available time may have some effect, but the benefit will be small compared with the costs in emergency overtime, emergency procurement, and simple wear-and-tear upon valuable people.

Factories that are intelligently using high-quality resource-planning methods may not, despite this, fully recognize or take advantage of the principles of synchronized production. The managers of many such plants are genuinely unsure just why it is they need 250 hours of manned, factory time (elapsed time on all paths) to manufacture a product which has only 50 standard hours of labor in it. Some of these managers—even the best of them—have tried arbitrary interval reductions and have suffered serious setbacks in missed shipments and other problems.

In the light of what has gone before, particularly the explanations surrounding Fig. 5–11, let us begin at the shipping door and identify the conditions which will permit a reduction of cycle time.

Assembly operations can be completed in time for on-schedule shipment if (1) assembly begins on time, (2) skills and area-time capacity are available, (3) assembly can proceed without delays for parts which interrupt the process, (4) there are no manufacturing delays (e.g., undue waiting for customer inspection, correction of engineering errors).

The problem of nonmanufacturing delays is a subject of another book and can be omitted from this discussion. In general, there is nothing Production Planning, or Supervision, or Production Control can do about it, in the short term.

The problems of skills and area-time capacity, while hypothetically real, are not generally serious. In fact many assembly departments, over the years, drift in the direction of manning for the peaks, because so much last-minute pressure comes upon them each month. This means in turn that availability of men is not usually their problem. And since cycle-time reduction will free up area-time capacity, this does not inhibit shipment either. This causes us to focus our attention on the problems of whether or not assembly begins on time and on delays resulting from missing parts. Both problems are really one and the same; the flow of parts. This will hardly come as news to any assembly foreman. Given the parts, he can generally ship OK.

Having the parts needed to start on time and to continue assembly in an orderly way has two sides to it:

1. Presence of matched sets of parts required for the next job to begin,
2. Absence of anything else.

Oversimplified though such a view may seem, these two conditions are all that are required to make it feasible to reduce assembly cycle times. Obviously, life cannot be as simple as this, and to the extent it is more complicated we lose out on our potential to reduce cycle times. But before dismissing such a goal as unattainable, let us look once more, only briefly, at an automobile assembly plant. This is *precisely* what happens on the assembly line: The exact number of the exact parts required arrives at the exact time they are needed, wait for no more than a very few seconds, and then enter into an assembly which is created in very little more than the labor-machine cycle time. Again, while it is impractical for a job shop to reach this level of synchronized production, it cannot be dismissed as impossible and it is worth spending considerable effort to approach it. This is because WIP in the assembly department has reached its maximum value, and any reduction in cycle time here has a large favorable effect on inventory turnover. Cycle time reduction in assembly, then, depends upon an orderly flow of matched sets of parts, which immediately forces us to turn our attention back upstream to the feeders. How do we know we are ready for this last step: reducing product cycle times? What do we look for?

Recognizing when we're ready for cycle-time reduction

Earlier, a scenario was sketched which had a shop superintendent or plant manager continually reviewing his departments and work centers and giving them guidance upon how much early or late to schedule they should be working, how manpower should be deployed, and so forth, which is load and capacity control. He was also monitoring the various priority indices in light of what he considers (from experience and analysis) to be a livable deviation from schedule, which is priority or sequence control. Let us look back briefly at Fig. 5–11 and imagine that the above management process has been going on for some time and that the factory team has succeeded in improving the picture very much indeed. It's not perfect, but it is much better. Perhaps now the picture looks like Fig. 5–12.

In this figure, the heavy bars still represent the plan, while the little standard deviations still represent the actual performance of the shop.

Work Center A is now just about as good as B and D, which haven't changed much. Work Center C has been slowed down a little so that it is not so far ahead of schedule and is adhering to schedule sequence better. Work Center D has also been slowed down a little and its sequencing improved, while DB has been brought more into line with DA, which always was the star performer. Since D is an assembly work center itself, its improved performance had to come from better performance from either DA or DB—probably DB.

By this time, the flow of matched parts (and the absence of unwanted parts, like the piles of material C was once making so far ahead of schedule) has enabled main assembly Work Center M to start much closer to its nominal (scheduled) start date in many more cases. It can work steadily without inter-

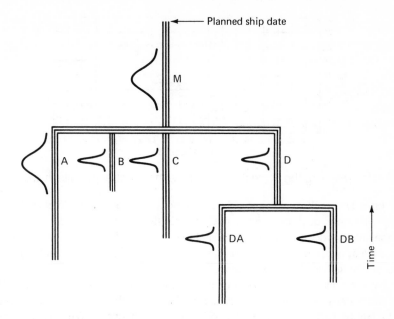

Fig. 5-12.   Model of an assembled, multilevel product that can be shipped on time.

ruption on a few jobs (instead of intermittently with constant interruption on a lot of jobs). Its average delivery date has moved in toward the center of the planned interval, and its distribution is much narrower. It ships only a few of its jobs late.

This is the stage of the WIP turns improvement project which was described earlier in which on-time shipments have improved markedly, labor efficiency is on its way up, and WIP has fallen part of the way toward the objective.

Planning for Cycle-Time Reduction

At this stage we can consider a planned—and quite large—reduction in cycle time. The planning, however, must be good; it's production *cycle* which is to be reduced, not *production,* in terms of product out the door. And yet, to reduce inventory, production must be reduced somewhere. This seeming contradiction has to be understood thoroughly and its implications managed carefully. To understand this phenomenon, let us refer to Fig. 5-13.

Now let us think of the units as products passing through the final assembly department.

For whatever collection of reasons, we have over the years become accustomed to having six units in-work to support a delivery rate of one unit per

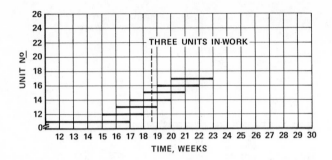

Fig. 5–13. Halving the cycle time will halve the number of units in-work.

week on a six-week cycle time. Now assume we have found a means of completing assembly in three weeks, not six. As the figure shows, if we put that decision into work at a single point in time, we will find that, for a period of three weeks, we need start *nothing at all* into final assembly. Shipping rates will continue undisturbed at one per week.

Now let us trace back upstream into the feeders to find what the effect upon them must be. For simplicity we will assume that every feeder provides one assembly part and also works on a six-weeks cycle. We can then refer again to Fig. 5–13, considering it as a feeder instead of final assembly.

Initially, let us ask what such a feeder must do to react to what has happened in assembly, without attempting a cycle-time reduction of its own. Quite apparently, it need not provide any assembly inputs at all for the three weeks during which the assembly department was starting nothing into production. The most economical way to do this is to halt feeder inputs *exactly six weeks ahead of the planned halt in assembly starts*. This will dry up the parts flow at the exact point in time at which assembly requires no parts. This halt in feeder inputs should also last for three weeks, since the feeder finish must keep in step with assembly start; therefore, the flow of feeder parts must start up again three weeks after it has stopped.

If we were to decide that the feeder cycle time should also be cut to three weeks and attempt to make that change at the same time, we would have to halt feeder inputs for *six weeks:* three weeks to synchronize with assembly restart and three more weeks to account for its own change in cycle times.

If this feeder has feeders (as most do, in factories of any size), this process has to be cascaded back upstream to the gateway work centers.

The example is deliberately oversimplified to illustrate the principle. It should not under any circumstances be taken as a suggestion of a practical way to proceed. It is an illustration of a principle which cannot be ignored without disastrous consequences. In particular, notice that a decision to reduce cycle time by three weeks must be stated rather carefully: is it to be three weeks in assembly only, or distributed along the feeder chain, or just what?

Bringing the Model Closer to Real Life

We have conveniently ignored several constraints. Among them:

1. The flow of product through the factory will never (except in a machine-paced production line plant designed to do exactly this) correspond neatly with the product structure chart, as we have implied. In a typical case, the feeder just examined feeds not only assembly but perhaps other subassembly work centers. The time relationships are not neat and clean and the feeder shutdown and startup cannot be clear-cut.

2. The assembly department is usually dealing with a variety of finished goods having many different cycle times. There is seldom opportunity to do the job as simply as by merely stopping the process of starting up new jobs for some fixed period of time.

3. The ordinary exigencies of business make a complete shutdown of some or any feeders a very unlikely course ever to be followed. There are always short-cycle jobs, repairs, rework, forgotten items, errors, castings delivered late, and so on.

Accordingly, for these and other reasons which will occur to the experienced shop person, cycle-time reduction will tend to be a gradual process rather than a step function. The simplified example, however, was studied in order to make plain a principle which can easily be obscured by the everyday complexities of factory life.

A Principle of Cycle-Time Reduction

If manufacturing cycle times are to be reduced without reducing shipping rates, inputs to all manufacturing activities except shipping must be reduced or stopped for a period which is related to the cycle-time reduction. The farther away from shipping (in terms of cycle time) is any given part of a factory, the longer this reduction or halt must last.

Corollary No. 1 to the Principle

The longer the cycle time of the product, the longer will be the reduction or halt in production of the primary work centers to satisfy the given percent reduction in cycle.

Corollary No. 2 to the Principle

Correctly planned, the cycle-time reduction effect will be felt first (and most) in the earliest feeders, last (and least) in the work center immediately before shipping.

Corollary No. 3 to the Principle

During the reduction in cycle time, less labor is required per week to get the same shipping rates. If this is not planned for, severe labor disturbances and high idle labor costs can be anticipated. In the extreme, the entire labor portion of the expected WIP inventory reduction can be irretrievably wasted and severe damage to labor relations and supervisory morale can result.

This must not prevent our getting reduced cycle times, but also must not be permitted to happen and thereby becloud and discredit our results. If this factor is understood and allowed for, however, the WIP reduction program can be synchronized with vacations; people with applicable skills can be moved temporarily to assembly departments to raise their shipping rates; large companies can take advantage of the flexibility they have by moving junior or low-skilled feeder people temporarily into other divisions or departments, where they can be productively used. In short, carefully planned, the job can be a creative and productive exercise in the imaginative use of temporarily surplus people; and people are, in the end, the only real asset we have.

Mechanics of Cycle-Time Reduction

Now that we know the theory of the thing and the major pitfalls to avoid, we can plan for success without unpleasant surprises along the way or regrets at the end.

This process requires a thorough understanding of the relationship between the structure of the firm's products and the structure of the manufacturing facilities. Whatever must be manufactured to satisfy the order must be routed through a factory which is created precisely for it and for nothing else (such as an automobile assembly plant set up for a certain family of products), or else through those parts of a job shop factory which can make the needed parts.

Over a period of time, a job shop develops facilities, product flows, stores areas, etc. which approximately match the requirements of the most frequently made products. Fig. 5–14 shows how this structure has evolved in a particular case.

If some important aspect of the product is changed—such as its size, fundamental design, or sales volume—severe strains can be set up between the factory structure, which usually can change only slowly, and the product structure, which can and does change rapidly. This is because, when product structure changes, plant structure must also change—for better or worse, economically or wastefully, smoothly or disastrously. But change it must.

Change in cycle times of important products is just such an "important aspect." The planning models must be shortened up, and this effect will penetrate into the shop in the form of temporarily decreased labor requirements, different for different parts of the factory depending upon which parts of the product structure are served by those parts of the factory. Further, some or all parts of the shop will require less labor permanently because of improved efficiency. Further, the factory

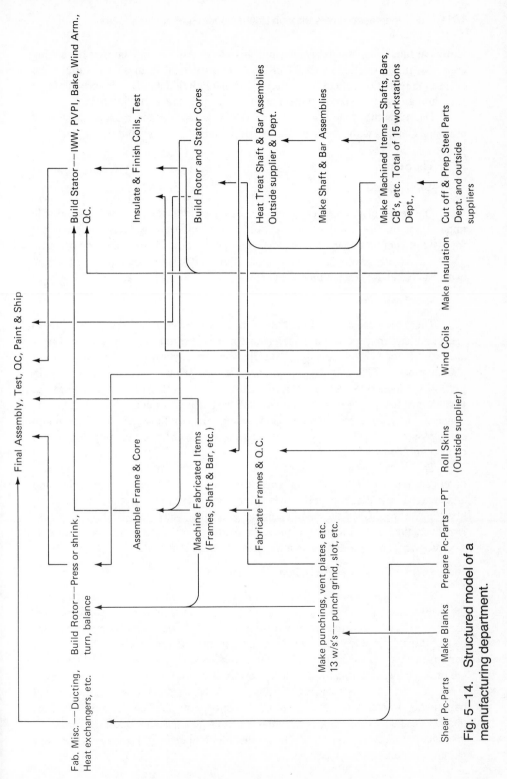

Fig. 5-14. Structured model of a manufacturing department.

163

will have much increased capacity; but this effect will be very uneven depending upon how fully loaded individual facilties were prior to the change. And further, the cycle-time reduction cannot be carried so far that individual orders or parts for them pass through on cycles so short that they become unmanageably "lumpy."

The steps that follow will help the P&IC practitioner to manage these very profound changes without unnecessary disruption to the factory and its people.

The Steps

Select the Scope

The scope of the project should be sufficient to make a definite, measurable impact upon the firm's turn rates. Candidates are families of products which account for a significant part of the factory load most of the time. They should be products under sufficiently good planning and control that a decision to reduce their planned cycle can be reliably transmitted to the factory's load summaries and schedules.

Select a Method

There are basically two methods. The first can be termed *cold-turkey* (all at once). All current production must have its intervals compressed by a definite ratio (such as .8 for a 20% reduction) and all new orders must be fed in on the new planning model. This will result in abrupt reduction (in places, cessation) of work in parts of the feeders. Large numbers of change notices will go to the factory and to Purchasing. It tends to have a traumatic effect, but it gets quick results if it can be managed. It will require computer help, using a one-shot program to do the initial compression; such programs often do not work well and leave lingering residues of cleanup problems.

The second method is called *phase-in*. Existing orders are left alone. New orders are fed in on the new plan. This results in minimum disturbance to the shop and vendors, but defers payoff and may provide opportunity to generate unrecognized idle time. Since the results appear gradually, they may be hard to track. However, this method requires no system disturbance such as a one-shot compression program, and this alone may make it the preferred method.

Select a Cycle-Time Reduction Objective

At this stage, the connection must be made between the product structure and the factory structure. The factory, by now, has been brought to the condition shown in Fig. 5–12, where there is clearly recognizable usable slack time along the various paths. But this usable slack can be quantified only if the priority indices of the various factory work centers are compared with the intervals allowed for the parts of the products which pass through those work centers. In Fig. 5–12, this comparison is implied, because the standard distribution widths are much less than the interval bar lengths. In concept, this is simple: in practice, not so simple. The complexities include the fact that (1) a given component typically, passes through several, not just one, work center; and (2) no one product interval model represents all the work passing over a given work center.

Nevertheless, given the visibility that the system provides, judgmental selections can be made of suitable starting places and objectives. Let us discuss some of the guidelines for this judgmental process.

Final assembly is perhaps the best place to begin. One of the preconditions to cycle-time reduction was that feeders are working abreast and delivering, on average, sufficiently far in advance* that the probability of having all parts ready for assembly at the same time has risen far above 90%. Product cost has risen to its maximum value at this stage, and thus the financial benefit is greatest. There are relatively few work centers to control and monitor. We should certainly begin where the risks are least and the benefits most; usually, this is assembly.

Estimating the reduction potential is done by applying the WIP = SCR formula to the assembly portion of the production cycle only. Example: An assembly department ships a product at a rate (R) of \$500,000 per month. Assembly cycle time (C) is 15 working days. Labor and overhead applied at assembly account for 10% of total cost, therefore 90% of final cost has accumulated before assembly begins.

Shape factor can be approximated as the average between 90% and 100% of cost, or 0.95. It is hardly worthwhile to be more precise than this. Accordingly, the assembly department's WIP, based on 20 working days/month, is:

$$\begin{aligned} \text{WIP} &= S \times C \times R \\ &= 0.95 \times \tfrac{15}{20} \times \$500,000 \\ &= \$356,250** \end{aligned}$$

During the earlier part of the work, the assembly department's distribution of deliveries around the scheduled day narrowed down and more and more deliveries fell within the planned interval. The factory management must now decide how much of the usable slack can be removed. This decision, again, is made by reviewing indicators such as priority index, on-time deliveries, and average days late (which by now has become days early in all areas of the plant, for reasons explained earlier). Assembly, however, by its nature, has relatively few orders to process per period. As a result, the days-late and priority index indicators are less dependable. Being statistical measures, they require numbers to chew on, and if the numbers are few and scattered, averages and deviations tend to become rather coarse measures. It is necessary to lean heavily on a management judgment, based upon product delivery performance and feeder performance, to arrive at a manageable interval reduction.

---

*The expression "sufficiently far in advance" is not to be misinterpreted to suggest that we have, by a complex, circuitous route, arrived back at a mode in which we are staging parts for assembly. It is worthwhile to review Fig. 5–12 at this point, before proceeding.

**This calculation can yield, at best, only an approximation. The use of six significant figures does not imply any precision whatever but merely provides the reader with a number he can check to see exactly where it came from.

If it is decided to reduce the cycle time by four days, the WIP reduction to be expected is $^4/_{15}$ of \$356,250 or \$95,000.

Feeders to assembly are the next logical opportunity. It is necessary to decide which one(s). Highest probability of success will come if feeders are chosen which:

- have a high dollar throughput,
- have improved markedly in their average days late and their priority indices during the earlier part of the project,
- are not critical, or bottleneck, facilities whose loads are already planned in detail to use all available slack time.

The yield from feeder WIP reduction can be estimated in the same manner as for assembly, except that more accounting department help may be needed to get numbers like R.

Plan how to use the freed-up labor hours

In the process of setting an objective for cycle-time reduction, the departments and work centers which will be temporarily unloaded will have been identified. The skills that will be temporarily surplus will therefore be known. The timing of the dip in labor requirements is, again, a place where the product structure must be matched to the factory structure and viewed in the light of the "principle of cycle-time reduction" as stated on p. 161. For example, review Fig. 5–12 once more and let us assign some numbers to it for illustration.

We can construct a model which assumes a ship day (shop calendar) of Day 300 for the product, and trace back through the dating process to establish start and finish dates for each component. For simplicity we will look only at the M-D-DA path. And we will do the model twice: once on its original interval of 35 days, once on the revised interval of 20 days. The labor content remains the same in both cases, of course. What we need to know is the impact (drop) upon the load in the department which manufactures DA. (Note again the simplifying assumption that the product structure and the factory structure are the same, and that Component DA is interchangeable with Department DA for purposes of discussion and illustration.)

Figure 5–15 summarizes what scheduled start and finish dates would emerge from this process for the two different intervals. Note that, to meet the same shipping day, component DA would have to start on Day 265 for the 35-day model, but not until Day 280 for the 20-day model: the 15-day reduction in cycle time has shown up as a 15-day delay in start date, as would be expected.

Now let us say that the customer's order due to be shipped Day 300 has been selected as the first order to be fed into the planning system on the shortened, 20-day cycle. Deliveries of one unit per week have been maintained up to now, and must continue.

Figure 5–16 is a diagram of the load and how it arrives in, and leaves, Department DA. Up until the change in cycle time, one unit was started, one completed, each week, and two were always in-work.

| | | Product Schedule If Built Upon | | | | | |
| | | Old Cycle = 35 Days | | | New Cycle = 20 Days | | |
Part	Labor Hours	Cycle	Start Day	Finish Day	Cycle	Start Day	Finish Day
M	10	15	285	300	10	290	300
D	5	10	275	285	5	285	290
DA	24	10	265	275	5	280	285

Fig. 5–15. Scheduled start and finish dates of all components on the critical path of a simple assembled product.

However, when the first order on the new, 20-day cycle was fed in, two things happened: (1) The next component DA was not needed in subassembly Department D for two weeks after it would normally have been needed, because two weeks had been taken out of the M-D path; (2) That same next Component DA did not need to be started until three weeks after it would normally have been started, because one week (which had to be added to the above two weeks) was taken out of its interval.

From this model, the hours which have to be worked in Department DA can be computed. Prior to the change, the shop had to work at an average rate of 12 hours per week on each of two Components DA, for a total of 24 hours per week.

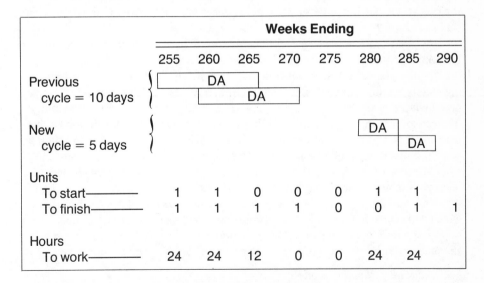

| | Weeks Ending | | | | | | | |
	255	260	265	270	275	280	285	290
Previous cycle = 10 days	DA	DA						
New cycle = 5 days						DA	DA	
Units To start———	1	1	0	0	0	1	1	
To finish———	1	1	1	1	0	0	1	1
Hours To work———	24	24	12	0	0	24	24	

Fig. 5–16. Effect of a change in product cycle time upon the standard-hours loads in a department feeding the product at level two.

After the change, the shop has to work at an average rate of 24 hours per week on *one* Component DA, which is still 24 hours per week, as might be expected, since the output rate has remained unchanged at one unit per week.

But *during* the change, Department DA's load tapered off from 24 hours per week, to 12, to zero, zero, then went back up to 24.

The loads in other departments involved in the manufacture of this product will see their loads dip in similar fashion as the cycle-time reduction is instituted. But the dips will come at different times depending upon how far away from final assembly, as a percentage of total cycle time, they are located.

We have gone through this model rather completely to illustrate the principle involved. In practice, no factory would attempt to pick apart its loadings in this detailed way in order to forecast the impact and timing of the cycle change. It was previously commented that the typical factory makes many products, some quite dissimilar, and many of them on different cycles. Any factory will have emergency, repair, short-cycle, and delayed work to do which will destroy the simplicity of the above model. But the model, nevertheless, displays accurately what happens, even though the aggregate effect is not as clear-cut. We will next take a practical factory look at how this job of quantifying the reduction in labor can be undertaken.

Review Fig. 5–14, which is a structured model of a manufacturing department, and note the level numbers along the right-hand side. These level numbers are good guides to when the dip in labor requirements will strike the particular shop section. The lower the level number, the earlier the impact will be felt and the longer it will last. To understand why, refer again to the model of Fig. 5–15 and, as practice, use the same technique to estimate the depth and duration of load fall-off for Department D. It will be found to be later starting, and shorter in duration, than for DA.

A plant or P&IC manager will know about how much of each component of his product is labor and material. From this and from the component's position in the structure, he can estimate when, and by how much, the load in the corresponding factory section will drop if he feeds in 10%, 50%, or 100% of new orders on the new, reduced cycle times. From his knowledge of his work force and its flexibility, its vacation, retirement, contractual provisions for temporary layoff, and other degrees of freedom, he can construct a plan which will get him onto his shorter cycle manufacturing mode as soon as is legal, contractual, affordable, and humane.

At this time, during this sensitive process, the load summaries are the manager's main tool in managing. They will give him several weeks of warning of the exact size and timing of the dips in manpower, work center by work center, which will enable him to confirm or to adjust the rough-cut plan just described.

It is worth repeating that, if the cycle-time reduction can by synchronized with an upturn in business, many of these problems will vanish or will be minimized.

Adjust the Planning Models

Every schedule and load system uses some kind of model upon which to schedule the factory. It may be detailed and elaborate, tallying labor hours, efficiency allowances, queue times, move times, setup times, batching and crew sizing. Or it may be primitive, showing only a number of days of interval for a given component. Regardless of its detail, it will contain arbitrary allowances of some sort, such as material move times. It is these which must be shortened. Labor standard hours, obviously, cannot be; nor can process times such as drying paint or heat treating.

Decide upon an implementation schedule

In the light of what has gone before, it is apparent that this is very much a local set of decisions, involving how rapidly the organization can digest the change. Bear in mind that there are rates of change that a given organization *cannot manage;* it is essential to develop a feel for what they are, and to stay below them.

Implement the new cycle times

This will generally involve simply piping the new models into the scheduling system.

Monitor results and correct course as necessary

If what has gone before has been thoroughly understood, no elaboration of this step is required.

Cycle-Time Reduction: A Final Word

The explanations offered previously have been much more in the interests of providing a clear understanding of the principles at work when we reduce cycle times, than in the interests of providing a set of cookbook rules for doing the job.

The simplest of all ways to reduce cycle times is simply to reduce them. If it is done gradually, *after* the feeders are working in synchronism, problems can be kept small. When handling the project in such a rough-and-ready fashion, however, it can be fatal not to recognize and allow for phenomena such as the drop in labor requirements and the timing of the drop. Unrecognized, these phenomena will scuttle the naive manager's program.

And sooner or later, of course, even the knowledgeable manager reaches the point where he is quite sure there is more cycle-time reduction potential but is not sure where it is: he dare not reduce a path which is full of irreducible natural processes such as baking or impregnation. At that point, he must begin the more detailed search for potential which has been explained above.

REACHING THE GOALS: SUMMARY

Preconditions include a good plan, a system that works, people who are prepared by training and practice, existence of objectives and schedules for reaching them. *Using the plan* calls for a disciplined periodic (often weekly) meeting among Supervision and Production Control (and others as required) to agree on a method of handling the load for the coming week and correcting problems which may have shown up last week. The load summaries (work center and department level) are the inputs. An input-output plan and a short-term schedule are the outputs. The Dispatcher is the key person and dispatching the key procedure: *no reload without an unload*. On-line, real-time systems may or may not help a lot. *A manager has to direct the work*. Knowledgeable, patient, determined follow-through by the man in charge is essential. His job is to view the overall set of signals he's getting from the system in order that he can (1) keep departments working in step (keep the load balanced), (2) detect and act upon danger signals such as unbalanced and unsequential working, and (3) provide management level assistance to his subordinates to solve problems they recognize they cannot handle. Work center queues can be controlled by pacing the release of work to the working pace of the work center as recently demonstrated by its rate of labor reporting. Continuous measurement and replanning is essential, with the computer doing the computation demanded by measuring and little or no decision making, and shop supervision doing no computing but all of the decision making.

Shop production control's job is to make the schedule mature properly, that is, to make ineligible work *go*. Shop supervision's job is to see that eligible work is done efficiently and on time. A set of *tolerances or trigger events* must be developed by operating people so that time is not wasted trying to determine if they are or are not in difficulty. This is very much an evolutionary process, beginning where the factory may find itself when it starts the WIP turn improvement program.

Cycle-time reduction is a powerful last step in WIP turn improvement, but is very dependent upon improvements in feeder performance. It is not a simple task and demands good planning and careful execution. Central to this planning and execution is recognition that production must be slowed or stopped selectively in parts of the plant, and that labor redeployment is necessary if the benefits are not to be frittered away.

CASE STUDY: THE SUPERINTENDENT'S VIEW

A certain factory uses Load Summaries similar to those described in Chapter 2. Some of the information from some of the load summaries is tabulated below:

	Weeks Overdue	Average Days Late	Priority Index
Entire Factory	3.2	22	11
Department "M"	5.0	31	19
Work Center "MA"	5.0	31	19
Department "A"	4.7	35	9
Work Center "AA"	6.2	12	14
Work Center "AB"	3.3	− 5	5
Department "B"	2.1	5	7
Work Center "BA"	0.1	− 5	3
Work Center "BB"	3.7	29	18

In the above, Department "M" is the main assembly department: "A" and "B" are feeders.

In the text we are told that, with allowable exceptions, work centers must be running abreast even though they may not be current, and that failure to do this is a major cause of high WIP and missed shipments.

Questions

1. Consider yourself the superintendent of such a factory. Identify your major opportunities for delivery performance and WIP turnover improvement.

2. Having identified the improvement areas, what specific steps would you take to get these improvements?

3. In any such project, you will find that some of your personnel will respond well to new ideas and new ways of doing things, while others—young or old—are set in their ways, seeing either no need or no possibility of change. Suggest a program for overcoming such people-problems

CASE STUDY: INPUT-OUTPUT CONTROL IN A FABRICATING SHOP

Background

A large steel fabricating shop, employing over 100 operators, was engaged in building heavy parts for large apparatus. Order quantities were typically one or two, with each product requiring as much as twenty weeks to complete and consisting of up to five levels of assembly.

The shop manager was being criticized for chronic late deliveries and very large work in process inventory. He heard a seminar speaker on the subject of input-output control. He felt that there was enough potential in input-output control that if he were to use it he could get better deliveries and could also smoke out other problems which were plaguing the factory operation.

The Project

The existing computerized production scheduling system was thoroughly checked to ensure that it was producing schedules and load summaries that were properly coordinated and reflected the way the product was actually being made. Several flaws were found and corrected and several improvements (such as computerizing the calculation of weeks overdue, current working rate, etc.) were made.

Finally, satisfied that the system had good outputs, the supervisory organization installed I/O control using a weekly plan similar to Fig. 5–5. The emphasis was on manning to the right levels as required by the load summaries and working to schedule sequence. A clerk was assigned the job of unloading and reloading and ensuring that agreed amounts of work were continually available.

Results

After about twelve weeks, late shipments began to drop markedly and in six months were down by 60%. During this time, work in process also fell steadily and at the end of the project (one year later) stood at 48% of what it had been. Labor efficiency was up by varying amounts in the various departments, averaging about 13%.

Comment

These results were better than had been expected, and some of them were unexpected: for instance it had been felt that there might be some degrading of labor efficiency. The increase that occurred instead was a pleasant surprise. Interestingly, the WIP reduction came about without any reduction in the cycle times built into the computer's model from which it did its dating.

Questions

1.   If planned cycle times were not reduced, why did WIP go down?

2.   Referring to Chapter 5, identify the stage of WIP control improvement in which this firm found itself at the end of the project. Do you think there is room for further improvement in on-time shipment, WIP reduction, labor efficiency, or such? Where is the further potential? How much more potential do you think there is (only a little, a lot)?

3.   Why did labor efficiency rise? If it rose without a definite plan to make it do so, what would you, as the factory manager, do to capitalize on this lesson?

4.   If you were the factory manager, what would you plan to do next to build further on this accomplishment?

Chapter 6

How to Handle the Problems

Winston Churchill is supposed to have said, while reflecting on the Gallipoli military disaster of World War I, "We won't make *those* mistakes again." Then, as an afterthought, "We'll probably make a different set."

While recognizing that every factory management group is capable of making "a different set" of mistakes, we will explore here some of the problems which everyone can expect to encounter and which flow directly from the principles upon which the control of WIP is based.

INVENTORY MAY GO UP BEFORE IT GOES DOWN

Any WIP control upgrading program will have as its core objectives improving service (better deliveries) and increased turnover (same business with less inventory, or more business with the same inventory).

Be prepared for inventory to go up before it goes down. Once the mechanism of how this happens is understood, it can be lived with, minimized, or avoided. But unrecognized, it will come as a disagreeable shock that can undermine both program and personal credibility.

Working the right number of hours and working the right hours brings sharply into focus the fact that some factory work centers habitually work out of sequence and late, while others are not as bad. Somehow, the objective of improving customer service rises to the top of any set of objectives, which is just about as it should be. Instinctively, or as a matter of careful intent, or both, any factory management, presented for the first time with the work center imbalance its improved WIP control system portrays, will concentrate on improving the performance of the late work centers. This means providing enough man-hours to make them less late; analyzing and overcoming the eligibility and other problems that drive them out of sequence; training, coaching, and in other ways reducing the threat that these late work centers will drive the entire factory late.

Everything just mentioned will affect inventories one way or another. Stock parts inventories will increase because the factory works to date sequence, which it may have done less well before. Intervals the ledger-keepers thought were 12 weeks collapse to 2 weeks. The pool of parts orders issued based on 12-week lead times is rapidly drained—straight into inventory.

The catching-up process impacts customers' orders too. Putting more man-hours through a work center can result in only one thing: increased inventory, *unless the man hours are obtained by slowing down or even stopping production* from other work centers which are not running as late.

Nearly finished WIP inventory will fall because of fewer assembly shortages. That is, if we ship more of the product on time, there will, very simply, be less of it in the assembly shop at any moment.

Parts inventory will fall because there will be fewer failures to start on time. Since the requirements planning system brings parts into stock to meet planned start dates, this can have a very significant favorable effect upon parts inventories. In a factory chronically running late, parts inventories are, of course, inflated by the days of supply corresponding to the general lateness of the factory.

Overall WIP inventory accounted for by the cycle time over which the product is made will rise if the new system forces the factory to start on time (as it should) and the cycle times have not yet been adjusted (as they may not have been in this initial stage). This is because, operating in an expedite mode, a factory may think its interval is six weeks, when in fact it typically does not start until three weeks before ship date, ships one week late, for a true cycle time of four weeks. There may have been a conscious—and wise—decision not to adjust cycle times as a first step. True cycle times will then revert to six, not four, weeks, and WIP will rise as a result.

On the other hand, usually at a later stage in startup, overall WIP inventory will drop because of the elimination of out-of-synch inventory (work made early waits for work made late).

These are a lot of balls to juggle, and without advance planning some of them will be dropped. With advance planning, however, the inventory-raising influences can be offset by accurate time phasing of the inventory-reducing influences. For instance, bringing a late work center up to the level determined to be acceptable should, if at all possible, be done by transferring people from work centers running much less overdue. These latter work centers, therefore, cannot be contributing to WIP in the process of helping the former ones get more current, a process which does contribute to WIP. This emphasizes yet again the importance of having a flexible work force capable, man-for-man, of doing at least two jobs safely and efficiently.

As a further example, the ledger-keepers should be brought on-board the WIP improvement drive early. Some estimate, rough as it may be, should be made of the amount by which stock part delivery intervals will fall, and the presence and timing of reorders for stock adjusted in advance to recognize this and to head off the unwelcome influx of stock.

No further examples will be discussed, because the alert and responsible reader will study each factor and decide on his own plan, suitable for his own plant. However, this discussion does lead up to an important potential problem.

LESS INVENTORY MEANS LESS LABOR

Factories do not normally improve their turnover by abruptly increasing their throughput, because whatever level of business was available just before the change is probably still there after. So if WIP is to fall, total input has to fall as explained earlier (Fig. 5–13). The impact of this reduction is upon both labor and material; the simple fact is that, temporarily, inputs must be shut off (or throttled down) while output is maintained. Reducing staff temporarily is occasionally difficult and unpleasant. If it has to be done immediately after a drive to increase the output of laggard work centers, which probably required overtime, it can become a morale-destroying monster. And if it follows hard on the heels of a plea from shop management to the labor force to "assist and cooperate" in helping the company to install a better method, that company's credibility in the eyes of the work force may not recover for years.

These impacts, again, can be reduced or eliminated by advance planning. If the WIP control drive coincides with a business upturn and its impact can be spread over the expected duration of the upturn, this is ideal. We are not always that fortunate. If we are not, other methods can help:

● While bringing laggard work stations up to a current state, avoid hiring and overtime; instead run a temporary second shift with the experienced people; use people from the interchangeable-skills list on first shift where they can be supervised and helped.

● Time any necessary labor cutbacks for the less trying times of year, such as summer. Take advantage of retirements.

● Borrow against any contractual provision there may be for days of permissible layoffs without transfer. Part of the new plan is increased labor flexibility and reduced sudden surprises which deprive the work force of work; take advantage of this to reduce labor inputs on a planned basis. When the plan is in-place, there will be less need for days off without warning.

● Forewarn labor that a period of overtime may be followed by a period of short time—budget accordingly.

LESS INVENTORY MEANS LESS LABOR—PERMANENTLY

We are entitled to get, and will get, better labor efficiency when the WIP control plan is upgraded. This has to mean as much as 10% to 20% less labor required. This also is portrayed on Fig. 6–1. Again, planning is the key. Big firms can transfer people out, let the work force taper off through retirements, etc. But let there be no mistaking the message: Less work is needed to get product out of an orderly shop. This may be a place to take a thoughtful look at the work force. Appraise performance. Using whatever methods you feel are trustworthy, array your people on a normal distribution. Most will be adequate for the job. A few will be superior. A few are simply not cut out for your kind of work, for reasons of

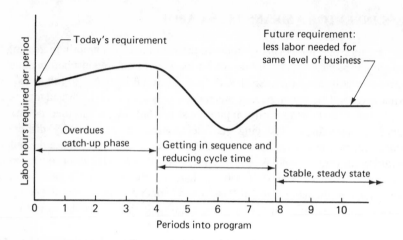

Fig. 6-1. How labor hours vary as WIP turnover improves.

efficiency, safe working, or whatever. Their eight hours a day may consist of three hours of useful work and five hours of creating problems for others. Now is the time to cut staff, and this is where to cut it.

LESS INVENTORY MEANS LESS PARTS AND RAW MATERIALS INVENTORY

Refer again to Fig. 5–13, where it was shown that a cycle-time reduction can result in *zero* inputs to manufacturing for a period of time. Your stores material controllers and your bigger suppliers deserve to be apprised of your intentions. They will appreciate knowing the inputs will be cut for some period. And, if there are open stock or blanket orders, it is essential that these be intercepted and stopped for a period to avoid unwanted inventory buildups.

FRONT-END OVERLOAD

As has been commented repeatedly in P&IC literature, one of the commonest errors in all manufacturing is to master-schedule more than the factory can make (Plossl 1973, p. 152; *Hot List* 1978).

The parts-inventory–inflating effects of this practice have been dealt with adequately elsewhere. Suffice it to say here that, the better the MRP system, the worse the inflation of parts and raw materials inventory will be. Now let's turn our attention back to WIP.

The effect of an overloaded master schedule is to put the factory into a very overdue position. This overdue position is partly fictitious, because no one really expects this month's production to be 200% of last month's. This has to mean that much of the overdues are not really overdue—or even due—at all. The consequence of this, in turn, is that someone has to tell the factory what is really wanted.

The next consequence is that scheduled dates are meaningless; and after that, that shop loads are meaningless. Since the factory must learn from its plan the right hours to work (schedule) and the right number of hours to work (load), and since the plan cannot be trusted, it has no option but to revert to the expedite mode, responding to the squeaky wheels, doing emergency overtime when someone guessed wrong, trying to hide surplus people somewhere when the load dries up, tripping over old WIP yet shipping late.

Nevertheless, some of the overdues are legitimate. They are the result of going late on genuinely needed product. But when the front-end of the system, the master schedule, is overloaded, who can tell which is which? We have an invisible division in the overdues: (1) overdue and needed, (2) overdue but not wanted.

This kind of plan cannot be effectively managed. The people on whom it is saddled (chiefly Shop Supervision and Production Control) are accustomed to being considered wrong most of their working lives. But the wrong was done long before the problem showed up in the factory, by the people who inflated the master schedule.

Traditionally, this problem is dealt with by the order–launch and expedite method. Orders for a great deal more product than can be made are entered into the system, and then as the requirements become more definite (because of customer orders, warehouse orders, stock finished goods shortages, or the pressures brought to bear by customers insisting that promises be adhered to), certain of the jobs are selected for expediting. This, of course, must be a mainly manual job and is very costly, because, first, people must replan vast amounts of detail work which has wrong dates. Even though expensive, this work is nearly impossible to do well. And secondly, it results in quite unforeseen loads being imposed upon the factory at unpredictable times. Work that may be in process in an orderly way has to be set aside while the expediting emergency is handled by breaking into setups, unplanned overtime, and similar expedients. Finally, shop supervision's only protection against being caught with surplus labor is to keep a big physical backlog on the floor ahead of the machines and to work as steadily as possible on it, allowing it to rise and fall as may be necessary to level the load on the men. During this process, the shop may work on jobs using such dates as it has. The typical priorities in such a shop are three: (1) do what the expediters are calling for, (2) do what's on top of the pile, and (3) do what the schedule calls for.

Since the expediters are usually very busy with hot lists, most time is spent on what the expediters are calling for, some on what's on top of the pile, and very little on what the schedule calls for. The item on the bottom of the pile may have been there for months; FILO has taken over.

These problems have led to the development of some very strongly held attitudes about overdues and rescheduling. Listen to some quotes and note the basic disagreements among them.:

"If you have 3,000 hours of overdues and can book 1,000 hours of work per week, then 2,000 hours needs rescheduling." (A consultant)

"I seem to be able to ship on time about 65% of what is on my shipping schedule. If I rescheduled my overdues, I'd ship about 65% of what was left. Don't talk to me about rescheduling." (A manager, manufacturing)

"When everything is late, the priority system has collapsed." (A textbook, paraphrased)

"Don't let 'em off the hook!" (almost anyone)

Opposite opinions like these hinder progress because they force confrontations and set up win-lose situations. But it is possible to develop cooperative, win-win situations, if the principles of synchronized production are understood, installed, and adhered to. This is the next subject.

MANAGING OVERDUES FOR PROFIT

These are the kinds of overdues:

1. Leftovers. We did this work long ago but didn't report it.
2. Not required immediately. We failed to un-expedite as true priorities changed, or we overloaded the master schedule with more work than we can do in the period.
3. Genuine overdues. We have fallen behind on work whose priority (its sequence with respect to the rest of the load) is still valid even though its dates may have passed.

The first and second types of overdues must be identified and purged from the system. They are the overdues which have given rise to the overzealous teaching that overdues are a mortal sin.

The third type should not be rescheduled because doing so commits us to rescheduling the rest of the load too, to maintain sequence (or priority). We can make the dates look better without improving performance. This is another way to say that a schedule is a sequencing tool and need not (probably should not) display a date for an operation. This is not to suggest that the operation date is unimportant and can be, say, dropped from the computer record. But, having been used to sequence the items on the schedule, the date should be suppressed from printing, since it is not helpful in answering the question the schedule should answer, "What do I do *next?*"

We all seem, unfortunately, to have lots of overdues of the first and second types. But we also have many of the third type, and these are useful management signals.

From these considerations a very simple and basic shop management modus operandi arises, one which is often overlooked; that is, to *work through the overdues in priority sequence without rescheduling.*

The Nub of the Problem

Our young science of production control is still beset by conceptual confusion. With apologies to those to whom this is old stuff, we will review some of the most dangerous of these areas of confusion as they apply to the disposition of overdues:

1. Load and capacity control is confused with sequence control. While related, these subjects are quite separate; while they must be dealt with together, they use different tools. When the practitioner recognizes instantly which problem he has and which corrective tools apply, he makes progress.

2. The presence of a lot of overdues implies we are expecting the shop suddenly to work off two or three times as much load as their recently demonstrated capacity. No such implication need be made; there is a better way to handle the situation.

3. If there are excessive overdues the "solution" must be to pour on the overtime. But this may make the situation worse, not better. For example, working out of sequence will generate overdues and shortage lists, even though the hours per day or piece count is sufficient to carry the load. Overtime will merely fill the shop with yet more unwanted parts. This is another case of confusing priority with capacity problems.

4. We draw fuzzy or no distinction between overdue at the plant or department level and overdue at the work center level. There are important and useful differences as explained earlier. There is probably no such thing as an entire plant which is overdue; what there is, chronically, is a plant whose *deliveries* are overdue because a few key work centers are overdue. And, curiously, these work centers are not likely to be the ones recognized by shop management as critical, nor are they the same work centers each week.

A Review of Principles

Let us restate briefly some principles developed at length earlier:

1. A plan for the protection of an article is sound if it displays two characteristics: (a) there is enough time to do everything required on every part, (b) there is synchronization between levels; each finish date of an item is the same as the start date of its parent, with some allowable exceptions.

2. That plan must be presented to the factory in two forms, (a) a load-and-capacity summary, (b) a schedule or sequence control. A set of each of these is required per work center.

3. Assembly can ship only at the pace of the most-late work center feeding it.

4. If all work centers are not abreast (i.e., a planned number of days early or late to schedule), up to 50% of the WIP is uselessly idle. Even if work centers are abreast, significant departures from schedule sequence will create similar amounts of useless, idle WIP.

5. The commonest reason for late shipment is late assembly start caused by late delivery of feeder parts. (This principle would qualify as trivial and its statement trite except that, through generations of management, it has been *one of manufacturing's most poorly solved problems.*)

We control best what we measure best. So let us review these principles with measurement in mind, to determine what might help us to ship more of our product on time. Principle No. 1 suggests we audit our plans (again, if necessary, even though it may have been done at the start of a WIP control drive—conditions change). Problems to look for will include items overlooked by Engineering, added after manufacturing began, with unsynchronized dates on them; interface trouble, where the identification structuring used by Engineering is not the same as that used by Manufacturing and a mechanized or manual translation is needed; and lack of control over date changes—the master scheduler must be the only authority for these. (The more powerful the computer programs, the more likely this trouble is.)

Principle No. 2 suggests that we check over our load summaries and schedules. Are all work centers running about the planned amount late or early to schedule? Are any exceptions planned exceptions, with reasons known and a time limit on the divergence? Are all work centers developing acceptable priority indices?

Principle No. 3 suggests that we identify the most-late work center feeding assembly and plan to boost its usable output. Questions to ask: Are we sure there is a capacity problem—or is the list of overdues merely masking the fact that we are working ahead on the schedule (showing a negative average days late), leaving behind too much work? To check this compare the work center's demonstrated capacity with the computer's calculation of an ideal booking rate. If demonstrated capacity is near the ideal booking rate, the capacity problem is probably under control. Then check the priority index. If the system typically gives a figure of 5.0 and this work center is showing 28.5, there is a priority (sequence) problem, not a capacity one. What is driving the work center out of sequence? Do we need a two-week task force from Purchasing to clear us up? Do the operators need some training? Is work arriving too randomly from upstream?

If there genuinely is a capacity problem at the work center, a skills listing can be brought into play. When transferring people temporarily from one job to another, try always to transfer *downstream* in the shop model (see Fig. 2–8). For example, it is better to transfer someone from the shear (a primary operation) to the brake or the drills (secondary operations), rather than from assembly to the brake or the drills. The reason is simply that, if one part of the plant is to be speeded up and another slowed down, it is logical to speed up that part of the shop closer to the shipping door and slow down that part farther from the door. The effect will be to increase outputs, decrease inputs, and give labor a chance at higher grade work. This makes the temporary transfers more acceptable and has a double-barrelled effect of lowering feeder inventory and increasing shipments.

Principle No. 4 suggests an audit of the amount of WIP on the floor and a thorough check of the input-output control system. Auditing WIP can be difficult in a job shop where piece count may mean little because the pieces change from hour to hour, and where dollars are not accumulated by Accounting or other functions, except in extremley sophisticated systems. However, piece count can be used if other measures cannot. And the cause will almost invariably be found in out-of-step working of the various work centers. It has often been commented that we get very good at expediting but usually ignore de-expediting; the same goes for work centers in the plant. If one work center needs to be speeded up by overtime, shifts, and so forth, then there is sure to be one work center that needs to be slowed down.

As commented previously, this is one of the most difficult of all points to impress upon the supervisory staff. We have trained them over the years to do what is available, as soon as possible; cutting back production on a work center which possibly is running behind schedule, in the interests of keeping balance with one which is even further behind, is foreign to their nature.

By now, of course, having dealt with Principles No. 1 through No. 4, we have already taken care of problems under Principle No. 5.

However, during this process, even if it is repeated several times during a year, we are bound to find more leftovers and changed priorities than we like. The importance of getting and keeping these out of the system cannot be overemphasized. Such records on our load summaries and schedules are destructive for the same reasons inventory record inaccuracies are destructive, and they are the same kind of problem. They obscure our real problems and create fictitious ones which, even though fictitious, prevent our getting at the heart of the difficulty. We must know where to speed up and slow down our working rates; we must know which work centers are being prevented from working in sequence. Our visibility of these two most fundamental problems in manufacturing is obscured and destroyed by fictitious overdues (leftovers and changed priorities).

Since this is such a serious problem, what can be done to minimize it without spending inordinate amounts of time as policemen; that is, how can the process of purifying the schedule be made self-policing?

Here is another opportunity to solve two problems at once. In the section on input control it was pointed out that the computer can readily be programmed to control the amount of work released by limiting it to no more than was reported last computer cycle, or some agreed multiple or fraction of that. Every shop "wants work"; one of the most difficult training jobs anyone has is to swing shop people over from wanting the work to be visible WIP, to being willing to accept that the work will come in time, even though it is not visible at this moment, that is, to have confidence in the system. When an organization has reached this point (i.e., its confidence in the system is good), the untidy clutter of overdues caused by leftovers and changed priorities will magically disappear or nearly so. The reason is simple:

As soon as the shop finds that the work released to it is half-full of things it cannot do (because they were done long ago or because no material is there to do them), purifying the schedule will become a positively religious rite. No foreman will be held responsible for doing the impossible, and since cleaning the "impossibles" out of his schedule is something he can do, he will do it with a will—and he'll keep it done. An old principle of systems work is that no one will continue indefinitely with a procedure which is not in his interest. Here is a case where the right procedure can be made to be very much in the interest of the key person who must do it and keep it done, who is the foreman in most plants, since he is responsible for booking-off labor.

Teamwork is needed, of course. If overdues which should have been rescheduled but weren't are present, others (generally Production Planning) have to take responsibility for talking to Management and to the computer and must do so promptly and conscientiously when they hear of such problems from Supervision.

To summarize this section on managing our way through overdues, we can say:

1. Much of the overdues on a shop schedule are jobs that are either not needed at all or not needed now. Get rid of them.

2. In absence of any major calamity (such as a strike in a supplier plant) which necessitates major deferral of entire parts of the schedule, the balance of the load, *even if past due,* should not be rescheduled because its *priorities (sequences) are still correct.*

3. The plant can work down its overdues by recognizing that the entire plant is not overdue, identifying the work centers which are, improving their outputs by transferring skills from earlier feeders temporarily into the backlogged work centers, and in that way bringing all work centers abreast (i.e., all planned amount late, or early).

4. The discipline needed to keep fictitious overdues (leftovers and changed priorities) out of the schedules can be maintained automatically by pacing the release of work to the same rate at which work is being reported.

There is a bibliography on this important topic on page 196.

EXPEDITING BY ORDER NUMBER*

To produce any assembled product, we must get matched sets of parts to the assembly department. The way we think about this problem will govern how we approach it in practice.

Typically, particularly in job shops, we think of assembly departments or subassembly work centers as needing matched sets of parts, but feeder work centers as working upon, and needing, only single items. This is dangerous thinking, and is an integral part of the order–launch and expedite mode of manufacture.

---

*Most of this material originally appeared in *Production and Inventory Management,* 4th Quarter, 1979.

Fine techniques like MRP have greatest success where the number of stock parts involved is highest, the number of manufacturing levels lowest, and the permissible customer variations least. Unfortunately, if we reverse these specifications (*few* stocked parts, *many* levels of assembly, *lots* of customer options), we have described the environment in which many of our firms must operate. Under these conditions, MRP must overcome generations of error in our thinking about what constitutes matched sets of parts.

Historically, most job shops have operated by identifying a point in time when assembly shortage lists should be made up and the process begun of chasing down each shortage. In big and complex products, this is done in several stages devoted to the important subassemblies. The importance of time has been recognized by spreading these start-expedite dates through the life of the order.

Of course the inevitable happens: buried in the mass of parts and information is a critical path. The assembly expediters encounter this (the experienced ones check these first) and, in many cases, find that the work remaining cannot be done in the time remaining; there are too many levels, too much work, to pass through.

Efforts to overcome this problem almost always end up in an attempt to "get all the machined parts" for customer order XYZ done "right away" (using any overtime needed, of course), despite the fact that four out of five of the parts probably cannot be used at once.

What has happened here? We have allowed the assembly department's very necessary order-number orientation to penetrate into the feeders, where it is disastrously wrong. "All the machined parts" for an order do not constitute a matched set of anything at all. They're an expensive security blanket that doesn't secure anyone against anything.

A job shop deals with a steady flow of different kinds of orders. The production paths of the various parts flow through various work centers at various times, supporting shipment of variously dated customer orders. This is a network of great complexity that changes like a kaleidoscope from hour to hour. Even in a week when nothing goes wrong, giving successive expediting attention to first this order, then that, can only result in chronic chaos. This is because the emphasis upon order number, which many job shops use extensively, is the wrong emphasis in the feeders, even though it is right in assembly.

In feeders like a machine shop, we often deceive ourselves by subconsciously feeling that we're dealing only with single items. After all, to machine that casting, all we need is that casting, right? Wrong! The output of that boring mill over a short period of time, like a day or a week, should consist of *sets of parts matched by date needed,* not by order number. Fig. 6–2 illustrates these two ways of thinking about matched sets: by order number (the wrong way, seen in the oval linkages which are not vertical) and by date (the correct way, seen in the oval linkages which are horizontal).

Thus, while we have assembly and feeder work centers, one of which we think of as dealing in matched sets of parts, the other only in single items, the fact of the matter is that we have a principle: *Every* work center in a factory deals with

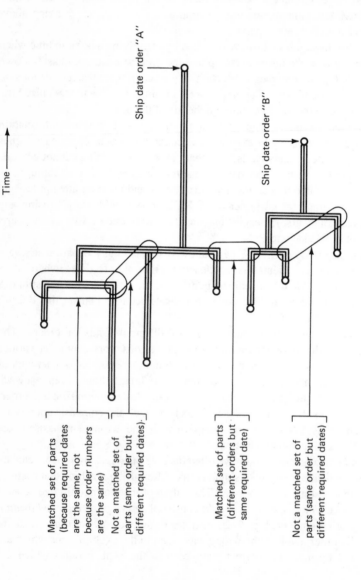

Time ——▶

Ship date order "A"

Ship date order "B"

Matched set of parts
(because required dates
are the same, not
because order numbers
are the same)

Not a matched set of
parts (same order but
different required dates)

Matched set of parts
(different orders but
same required date)

Not a matched set of
parts (same order but
different required dates)

Fig. 6–2. Model illustrating two different orders showing which are, and
which are not, matched sets for two different products with two different ship
dates and intervals.

matched sets of parts. The match is either on order number or on date. Determination of priorities (operation sequencing) *must always be on the basis of date*. (There are endless sophisticated priority-setting schemes; try to avoid them. Successfully working to simple date sequence will solve so many of the priority problems that further elaboration will become unnecessary. Working to date sequence is one of the "AA" items in any shop floor control system.)

A reminder: Only if the plan is good can this principle be applied. Refer to Chapter 2 for specifications of a good plan.

In a particular factory, one can easily find out if there is a genuine problem in this regard. Sit in on production meetings for a day or so. There are two warnings of trouble:

1. Most discussion is about order numbers and parts shortages at the assembly level, and what is being done about them. Feeder department discussions are still order-number oriented. The chairman insists on "promises" for parts, order number by order number, item by item.

2. Little or nothing is heard about the upcoming work center load and how it is to be handled (load and capacity control) or about specific difficulties that are preventing the work centers' running jobs in sequence (priority control). The only time these subjects emerge is when the foreman notices with alarm that the promises he is making add up to more man-hours than he has this week, leading of course to discussions of overtime.

This type of production meeting is characterized by far more reaction (to trouble we just fell over yesterday) than to action (to meet the upcoming load in an orderly way). Of course, in an actual situation, there's lots of both required; but the mark of good management is that there is much more action than reaction.

To summarize, then, every work center in the factory must work on matched sets of parts. But there is a vital difference between the matching criteria in assembly and in feeders. In assembly, the matching is by order or assembly number; in the feeders, by date. Many job shops permit matching on order number to penetrate into the feeders, thereby guaranteeing high WIP, high overtime, and missed shipments. Matching by order number in the feeders is the main tool of plants that are still in the order–launch and expedite mode. Jobs shops that are getting disappointing results from MRP can afford to check here for some of the trouble.

THE DESIRE FOR A VISIBLE BACKLOG

Many shop floor control problems, while very real, are psychological. For example, the instinctive objection of every line supervisor to the reduction in the security blanket of WIP often is, "I can't get my labor efficiency up if I don't have the work to do."

There is a changeover in thinking needed. Instead of planning manpower over an extremely short horizon (i.e., the man-hours needed to get through the visible pile of work at a work center), our supervision must be persuaded to plan manpower over a longer horizon (some days or weeks) based upon some numbers on a piece of paper.

The numbers had better be good. The shop supervisor's next performance appraisal depends quite a bit on whether the numbers are good. It is appropriate here to refer the reader once again to Chapter 2, on what constitutes a good plan, and to Chapter 5, "Preconditions." The numbers are, of course, a type of forecast, with all the shortcomings for which forecasts are notorious.

Therefore, credibility—not perfection—is the main requirement in the load summaries which we ask our shop supervision to use in planning their manning.

Lack of credibility in shop loads, caused by front-end overload, by managerial decisions to wrench the schedule around at the last minute, by failures of upstream work centers to do their jobs as planned, or by any of the other numerous reasons dealt with earlier, is the one single main reason that many shop supervisors chronically underman.

If the reader will think back over the P&IC literature he may have read in the course of a few years, he will realize that most of the shop floor control or capacity control articles end up emphasizing that the plant must get enough (or get more) product. The unconscious (and quite correct) assumption of most experienced writers is that, if there is a capacity problem, it is one of undermanning, not overmanning.

This is reasonable, given the options faced by the foreman. He can believe the load figures (if he has any—and many do not), man up to them, find that the work does not materialize, then be severely criticized for having surplus labor. Or he can go by his experience, ensure that there is a physical pile of work which is visible to him, and ensure that his men, in the memorable words of one often burned foreman, "Can go like _____ for a while without any idle time." (Recall that labor efficiency, which is only one of the criteria for successful operation of a multilevel factory, is the only measurement made on paper of the day-to-day shop management competence of many foremen.)

Thus, the desire for a visible, physical backlog is not unreasonable until the plan is made credible; and then a change is needed. A change must be made from a situation in which work center manning is governed by the physical, visible queue (and the noncredible load summary is ignored), to a situation in which work center manning and physical queue are both planned from a credible load summary.

Here we can draw a parallel with independent demand end-items. Such stocks require a safety component. Most of the time, the safety stock is not used. Occasionally, however, even the safety stock runs out. It is a principle of the management of such stocks that we cannot afford 100%, never-run-out service. At a factory work center managed by planning both labor and queue from the load summaries, it should be recognized that we will occasionally run out of work; but the advantages of high turnover, good deliveries, and overall high labor efficiency are worth it. Anyone wanting to know what the present safety stocks ahead of a work center are can use the same technique as we use for independent demand items. Any input-queue materials still there when the trucker delivers the next load, is safety stock. It's an easy and revealing check to make. It's not unusual to find safety stock to amount to many days of supply and to be larger than cycle stock (which is the amount the trucker brought) by many hundreds of percent. As has been commented before, we need to ponder the possibilities for FILO (first in, last out—remember?) in such a situation. It virtually guarantees that the work we want next will be the hardest to get at. And in actual situations, it often isn't gotten at; which is one reason we need expediters.

WHAT TO DO WHEN THE HOTLIST COMES FROM MANAGEMENT

Hotlist has become a bad word since MRP and other high-quality planning and execution techniques have been developed. But what can be done when the hotlist comes directly from management? Let us recognize, right at the start, that there will always be such lists. Wishing to be rid of them is like wishing for better forecasts, and is just that—a wish. And to hide behind them, blaming our falldowns upon them, is simply avoiding the problem. What we must do is learn how to minimize them and to cope with them when they come.

Management hotlists, management preference lists, or ship-for-sure this month lists, or whatever they may be called in a particular firm, have both honorable and dishonorable origins. They exist because:

- a job was taken on shorter than normal intervals,
- a late delivery penalty is involved,
- accumulated minor production lates are now threatening the delivery date of an important order, or
- expedite mode is the only method the firm knows to get production out. (The list contains those orders on which last month's expediting was most successful, and which the firm, therefore, has the best chance of shipping this month.)

The first three reasons apply at times to all firms. The last one should not apply to any firm at any time. If it applies to your firm you are urged to refer to the earlier parts of this text and return to this part later.

Management preference lists bring problems. For example, operating people (foremen, production control, operators) must work to two schedules: the formal one and the management preference one. This causes timing errors at all stages, since it is not practical manually to set operation priorities throughout the order. Preference orders get high priority whether they need it or not. This raises WIP because of unsynchronization and raises cost because of confusion, extra material movement, rework of damaged or lost components. It also sets up a vicious cycle, because the extra attention given to the preference orders drives other items out of synchronism, increasing the probability that they, in turn, will require preferential treatment.

In addition, operating people must depart from the formal system and feel justified, therefore, in not adhering to a synchronized schedule. This raises costs (because two systems are in use) and lowers work force discipline and morale.

A General Statement

For any product on the management hot lists, we are setting out to do the remaining work in a time shorter than we usually take. The "remaining work" may be the entire job in cases where we have agreed to it, or only part of it in cases where we have had serious production delays.

Particular Cases

Case No. 1. Order taken on short interval. There are two possible courses: (1) release the order into the system on its normal interval, (2) compress the interval to fit within the remaining time.

Method (1) will generate past-due dates immediately on some of the long paths of the order. This is anathema to many shop people, who feel they're being held responsible for lates they did not create. While this feeling is understandable, publishing less offensive (not overdue) dates is a little like giving chloroform to a motorist stalled on the track. It reduces the anxiety level but not the ultimate impact. Method (2) is usually the chloroform. The factory has been given less than its normal time to do its job, but the fact has been concealed from it: the information it needs to cope with the situation successfully is being withheld.

Method (1) has the advantage that it will bring the critical dates on the critical order right up to where the expediters are going to put them anyway; namely, ahead of other work which is on normal intervals.

Still another advantage of Method (1) is that it will call for preferred attention upon only the critical paths—not upon everything on the order, which expediting methods often do.

These characteristics make it possible to insist that the shop work to the formal system, thus preventing the penetration of the preference list into the factory as a separate conflicting priority. This higher priority will revert to normal by the natural operation of the system as the shop catches up.

Case No. 2. An order has gone late during manufacture for any of a number of reasons familiar to all. There are two possible courses of action: (1) reschedule the order for later delivery, (2) adhere to the original plan. Option (1), reschedule, should be taken only after management has reviewed the status of the order thoroughly and has exhausted every available method to overcome the problems that have developed. Even when this has been done, the decision is often rightly made to continue manufacture until some manageable stage of completion is reached, then hold the order. A manageable stage of completion, for instance, might be the finishing of a major subassembly which can be painted, covered, or moved into the yard. An unmanageable stage of completion might be partway through this subassembly, where scores of detail parts have to be either left where they are, cluttering work centers throughout the plant, or else gathered up and placed individually in storage.

Option (2), adhere to the original schedule, is a variation of the technique explained earlier for handling orders taken on short delivery. It keeps the late paths at the tops of the STS's of the work centers which must deliver them. This option, it must be recognized, will raise WIP because branches of the order not yet started will be started and finished on time, then will wait for the late branches to catch up. This may be an acceptable alternative. If it is taken, the order becomes a management preference order,and we want its labor operations to be right where this option will put them; that is, at the tops of the schedules of the work centers which are on its critical overdue path.

Case No. 3. An order has been rescheduled earlier to compensate for errors in forecasting, for slow flow of information from warehouses, or perhaps as a result of the flexibility granted to Marketing to set up planned orders, allow them to move inside the accumulated lead time, then alter their dates.

Case No. 3 is often the origin of most rescheduling troubles. The "flexibility granted to Marketing" is often a very unofficial one—it is the way the system has evolved over many years, and no one has ever taken a cold, long look at the effects and implications of this flexibility.

This goes back to one of the features of an ORP system misapplied in a dependent demand environment—which is the way many firms' inventory and production systems evolved over many years until about the 1960s. Under these conditions the firm can make some of almost any product because safety stocks are so inflated. Many firms became somewhat pampered (without realizing what was happening to them or what it was costing) by this ability and became very casual about last-minute schedule changes. After all, the factory seemed to be able to react well in most cases (although they did a lot of complaining), so why not use all the flexibility that's available?

When these firms moved to an MRP environment, sometimes insufficient recognition was given to a basic characteristic of MRP systems. It is this: Where the objective of an ORP system is to be *in stock* most of the time, on the assumption that there will be a need somewhat similar to last month's, the objective of an MRP system is to be *out of stock* except when a specific end-item demand has been exploded. Thus, a properly run MRP system is characteristically unable to produce anything at all which was not ordered outside the time fence. If a demand arrives inside the time fence, every component is an emergency—an unmanageable situation.* This may give rise to high safety stocks again, and leads us into the

---

*It might be argued that if such an order uses many parts common to other products, the statement is not true. But this implies other orders will be cannibalized, which dilutes and spreads out the emergency a bit but doesn't eliminate it at all.

situation where we have all the trouble and expense of switching over to MRP, but haven't reaped the benefits. If this sounds like a familiar situation to some reader, he should look to his forecasting, master production scheduling, and similar front-end fittings of the production system. There are many good reference sources which can be used to check out whether mismanagement of the master schedule is part of the problem—it usually is (American Production and Inventory Control; APIC 1977; Bourke 1975; Everdell 1972; Garwood et al (a); Greene 1970; Plossl 1973; Wight 1974).

THE "THEORETICIAN" LABEL

To many battle-scarred shop people, nothing is more useless than a "theoretical" person or a "theoretical" approach to their problems. But until we have a sound theoretical basis for what we are trying to do, we are merely lashing out in the dark.

> Using good theory saves administrative time, reduces anxiety, increases efficiency. . . . All administrative choices and judgments are based on assumptions, postulates and generalizations, whether or not the administrator realizes it. . . . Many [of them] do not realize they are busy on practical work based on hidden theory. . . .
>
> The "good practical man/woman" tends to belittle theory, stating that, "it might be good in theory but it won't work in practice." What he [or she] may fail to recognize is that his [or her] success is based upon a form of theory development known as trial and error. . . . This process is an uneconomical and painful way in which to develop skill. . . .
>
> Related to the "good practical man/woman" approach is a heavy reliance upon common sense. Someone has quipped that common sense is what tells us the earth is flat. . . .
>
> In summary, then, it is held here that hidden assumptions, trial and error, experts, tradition, law, and commonsense are not adequate guides for administrative practice, but that good theory is (Gue 1977, pp. 18–19).

Production and Inventory Control in the past few years has increasingly been the search for "good theory." And we can all be duly grateful for that fact. Lot sizing and safety stock formulae, linear programming, PERT, MRP, Gantt charts, ABC analysis, and the other tools in our kits have evolved because intelligent people gave thought to the theoretical principles behind the observation of everyday experience.

The proper object of scorn is the one who misapplies good theory or uses bad theory. Such a person is not to be dismissed as "just a theoretician" but pitied as merely a poor workman.

Thus, the successful P&IC practitioner is the one who has identified the correct theoretical base for what he is trying to do and has skillfully transformed this science into applied science in his own firm. But in doing so, his main defense against the scornful epithet of "theoretician" is his approach to those who have to get the job done on the firing line; and this means his language and the ways he chooses to express himself. If he persists in talking about normal distributions, cost tradeoffs, total cost minimization, and algorithms, he will be avoided and the dreaded theoretician label will be applied. If, instead, he can demonstrate his points with marbles in a matchbox (Belt 1978, p. 13) or from his own real-life experience on the shop floor (which his listeners don't have to know he has explained for his own purposes by use of "theory"!) he will at least get up to bat.

It pays to have had in one's background a stint at running a lathe, pushing a broom, or operating a 200-ton overhead crane. Like choosing one's parents, this is not always possible. If it isn't for you, rub shoulders with these people and with their foremen until you can talk their language. Until you can, your WIP control programs will go much more slowly than you and your boss might hope. And make no mistake; these people have plenty to teach the teachers, too! Such time is seldom wasted.

THE "ONE AT A TIME" SYNDROME

Problems are seldom what they seem, either in number or in kind. A single symptom may have numerous causes, some of them separated very far indeed from their results. An important order for a large piece of apparatus has, many times, and in many firms, been shipped late because, four months before the due date, the steel shop sheared a lot of the same thickness of plate to save handling and got the production sequence so twisted it couldn't recover. "Shipped late" was separated from its cause by a long time period and by many other events which obscured the original cause.

A different situation arises when several apparently unrelated problems exist which have, in reality, a single cause. For instance, complaints are heard from the field sales force that delivery intervals are uncompetitive, that the firm often ships late and seldom warns the customer of the probability. The manufacturing manager has more parts inventories than he likes or thinks he needs. The installation department reports an unsettling frequency of product dimensions not matching customer dimensions when the product is delivered. In this real-life case, all of these seemingly unrelated problems were traced to poor product structuring. This led to sluggish engineering cycles, slow manufacturing cycles because the product was unnecessarily different from job to job, unexpected production difficulties resulting from these steady small design changes, habitual padding of the intervals by salesmen or planners because of these uncertainties, considerable uncertainty until the last moment concerning exactly when the product might be shipped, and in the end engineering errors which leaked out into the field.

If we had considered each of these an independent problem, we would have spent fruitless months and years trying to solve them. As with product structuring itself, we need to find the parent-component relationship. Means-ends trees are a powerful tool in analyzing such situations. Their use in solving two seemingly separate problems ("we cannot ship on time" and "we have too much inventory") was illustrated earlier. We must look for commonality at the bottom levels of such a tree; places where fixing one will fix them all.

Quality assurance and quality control people for years have used the simple technique of sifting through problems looking for commonalities, secure in the knowledge that the firm doesn't have 50 quality problems today. It has one, two, or three at most, because they all group under one of the three. And Pareto tells us that one of the three is vital, one of the three would be nice to solve, and the third can be ignored.

Returning to the day-to-day problem solving which Production Control must do, we must never be satisfied to solve an individual difficulty without looking at least one or two levels up and down the cause-effect tree. We must identify what is the root cause of this and several related difficulties, so that we can spend less of our time firefighting and more of it problem solving. For example, in another specific case, the assembly department was plagued with stock shortages of a most mysterious kind. Physical parts inventories were often sufficiently short to stop a run. While it most often happened with a specific critical part, it happened frequently enough with all parts. The matter came to a head when the annual inventory revealed a serious dollar shortage which demanded a full-scale investigation.

In an orderly manner, all the causes which might account for such a persistent problem were identified. Everyone from Accounting to the ledger clerks and foremen were asked for contributions. The emotion was taken out of the situation by looking for only *possible* causes—not looking for a scapegoat. Having assembled a rather daunting array of possible causes, the analyst checked out each one in sequence of most probable to least probable, giving most time to the high probability ones on the list. This approach quickly paid off, because a significant number of the high-ranking candidate causes were found, in fact, to exist. Among them: duplicate identifications (in both directions—same part with two numbers, two parts with same number); inadequate or no identification of parts in storage; items missing from bills of material; and no formal parts withdrawal procedure that distinguished clearly between parts used in production and parts sold directly as spares. Experienced systems men and MRP practitioners will recognize at once the basic, underlying cause as *no formal disciplined system.*

But the organization did not stop there. Excited by its discoveries, it went back up the cause-effect chain asking what other, noninventory-related problems could such loose systems be causing? They found plenty. An expensive, high-powered sales-analysis system was working very badly. Clerks were overloaded with floods of corrections to various mismatch problems in the computer-operated parts of the system. Customers were receiving mislabelled goods. Scrap was being pilfered and sold. The sales manager complained that he was never sure whether he was losing or making money on a given piece of business because he could not be sure of his costs. Fig. 6–3 synopsizes this process.

There is a time to consolidate numerous seemingly different problems into one (such as the product structuring example) and a time to explode one problem solution into solutions for several (as in the "informal system" example). The ability to do this and the willingness to spend the necessary time today to avoid problems tomorrow is one mark of a good manager—of inventory or of anything else. Any person willing to tackle one problem at a time, solve it, and go on to the next is a born expediter and will remain one.

PROBLEMS NEEDING MANAGEMENT'S HELP

For each level in the organization, there are problems which can be handled at that level and others which have to be delegated down or taken up higher.

A principle of military, church, or industrial organization is that every matter should be settled at the lowest possible level. Conscientious inventory managers recognize this but they are in a bind. Typically, the information system in a factory is too weak to support confident decision making about what should be referred up higher, with the result that the inventory manager by default takes on more and more responsibility over matters over which he has less and less control, because he harbors the feeling that he should have these things under control, or at very least predict what is going to happen if they are not.

An example of this arises when management superimposes its priorities upon those already established for the shop. Now, these may be extremely good priorities and it may be best that they be followed. But as inventory and production management we owe it to our superiors to point out to them the consequences of the imposed priorities, and the results which spring from the way they may have been imposed. And it is here that our information system typically lets us down very badly. We cannot rapidly and confidently identify the overlapping effects upon other production of the imposed priorities.

Guidelines

Recognizing when a problem needs help from higher up is a mark of good management; much more so than struggling with it at a level where the necessary authority is lacking. Some guidelines may help:

1. Understand your own situation well enough to ensure that you know what you may and may not, can and cannot, do within its bounds. If you are the master scheduler, know enough about the job that you can stand up to an outside influence and either decline to change it or insist it can be changed, whichever is appropriate. And acknowledge when you're licked. If the foundry didn't deliver on Friday, know by 8:30 Monday which orders won't be shipped and get the word to your own boss and to whoever else should know, along with recommended schedule changes.

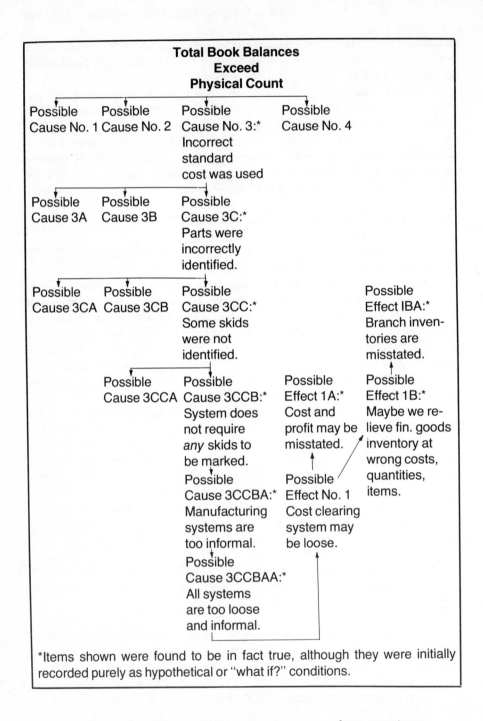

Fig. 6–3. Cause-effect tree tracing causes from symptoms.

2. Know and depend upon your information sources, so that consequences of certain courses of action can be identified quickly. Insist upon good information (current, accurate, accessible—remember?) and use it to keep your management aware of progress.

3. Recognize that flexibility and ability to respond on short notice to emergency requirements is the mark of a shop that will "make it" against competition. But know what you are getting yourself into when you have to change, and keep your boss and the troops posted on the consequences. Your management, too, needs training. If they find it easy, and the bad consequences well concealed and confused, they will impose changes that are unnecessary, impossible, or both. Only when you can confidently, calmly, and correctly offer them alternatives will you be considered a professional.

THE EFFECTS OF LOT SIZING

The models in this book are written as if the only problem the plant ever has is scheduling one customer order, complete from start to finish, with all quantitiies lot-for-lot. And, of course, many readers will be in environments which are very close to that condition. But most are not. Lot-for-lot is only one of numerous possible lot-sizing rules used by MRP.

Where intermediate level assemblies are truly stocked, it might seem that the rules for a good plan (synchronization, enough time) are immediately inapplicable. But such is not the case. "Enough time" remains as written: a fundamental rule which must not be violated. Synchronization, however, must be modified. Where lot sizing has called for more than the quantity per next assembly, for reasons of setup saving or service, the completion of the first item of the batch of components must coincide in time with the start of the first item of its first-schedule parent assembly.

Other items in the batch of components will await the start dates of the next order planned for the parent assembly; that is, a gap in time has been opened up and the item is awaiting a requirement. Depending upon the system in use, the item may wait in component stores as a stocked part or in WIP as a phantom; but financially the effect is the same—inventory is increased.

In this quite typical case, everything discussed earlier still applies, although the method of applying it may change. For instance, the establishment of lot-sizing rules is outside our scope. Lot sizes chosen depend upon the economics of the situation in a given factory. But within these constraints, use of the WIP control principles outlined here will assist in reducing WIP dramatically.

CASE STUDY: THE MANAGER'S INFORMAL SYSTEM

A young manufacturing engineer was assigned to shepherd an urgent, emergency repair order through a busy shop. Full of naive confidence that everyone he met would be reasonable and would see the necessity of making room for this work, which could enable an important customer to get back into operation, he went the rounds as he knew them: the planners, the information writers, the superintendents, the foremen. His frustration mounted as obstacle after obstacle was pointed out: the shortage of material, of cutters for soft copper, of skills for that particular bending job, of time in the shell blast and bake ovens. Chagrined, he returned to the manager of manufacturing to say it would be weeks before the repair could be completed.

"Come with me," said the manager.

The two of them made almost the same rounds. In only a few minutes, all obstacles seemed to melt away as if by magic. Yes, we could find that much material one way or another. The cutters were there after all—they just needed sharpening. Yes, we could swing the apprentice around to do the regular work while Joe bent this one. Well, we likely could squeeze a few more units a day through the shell blast and baking. Not sure what it might do to other production, but . . .

In the end, the repair job was done in just about the time the manager wanted. No one ever knew for sure what it cost in overtime, lost time, missed shipments, or other rippling effects and no one ever inquired. The organization really didn't care to know.

Question

What was "right" and what was "wrong" about what was done? Do you agree with the method of planning the manager used? Why or why not? If you feel this was not a good way to load the factory, and since the repair job was urgent, profitable, and needed by a good customer, what would you suggest be done differently?

Wight, O. W. 1974. Production and inventory management in the computer age. Boston, Mass.: Cahners International.

Gue, F. S. 1975. Input-output control in a job shop. *Proceedings of the eighteenth Annual International Conference,* APICS. Washington, D.C.

Running a job shop real time. *Infosystems,* Feb. 1978.

Sampani, P. 1977. Executing the company game plan. *Master Production Scheduling Reprints,* Washington, D.C.: APICS.

Mather, Hal F. 1978. Reschedule the reschedules you just rescheduled—way of life for MRP? *P&IC Management,* vol. 14, no. 1.

Chapter 7

Support from the Rest of the System

RESOURCE PLANNING

The *R* in MRP needs to be broadened, in most factories, to include drawings, tooling, specifications, services of outside suppliers, and other things we may not be accustomed to finding on bills of material. Most systems can plan them with little (sometimes no) modification, date them, and call for them in very routine ways. The more resources that can be planned within the framework of the formal system, the better WIP turnover job can be done and the fewer people are needed to do it.

Drawings

Drawings should be identified by the computer program and issued to the shop when needed. But care must be taken. The computer is a sorcerer's apprentice that will issue calls for thousands of unwanted prints if not given good selection logic to detect the difference, for instance, between standard drawing which the shop has on file and new drawings for a specific customer order or engineering supersedure. But a drawing call system is worth the trouble if it is a good one, and will usually free up the time of a good clerk who otherwise spends many hours a week requisitioning drawings. Such a subsystem can richly pay for itself in labor savings and also by preventing the release of drawings until they are needed, improving the shop's ability to issue a complete, current work packet with reduced filing-and-pulling and increased chance of using the most current print.

Tooling

Tooling should be on the bill of material. The tool is every bit as essential as any other piece of material and responds to all of the logic which calls up material. Tooling is stocked. It can be recorded in the system as a fake item master and, after being used in 500 pieces, can trigger a "stock replenishment order" which calls for it to be sharpened, rebushed, or whatever. It can and should enter into the system's eligibility test if there is one. A tool must be in a storeroom with its own bin number and should be withdrawn on a withdrawal tag. Most systems can digest tooling on bills of material without knowing the difference or requiring revision.

Specifications

Specifications fall into either the tooling or the drawing category, whichever the system and the people can accept most comfortably.

Services

Services, like tooling, respond to most or all of the material logic of many systems. If the system does not find the item on its ledger or item files, it will requisition Purchasing, giving the want date, which is a very useful way to handle a very failure-prone informal requirement in many shops.

LABOR RESOURCE PLANNING OUTSIDE THE LOAD SUMMARY

Our discussion has focused on shop loads that are visible within a fairly short horizon: ten weeks being typical. However, there is a definite need for a plan for capacity demands upon the factory which are expected in the medium term—say out to 12 or 18 months.

Such a plan tends to be driven by MRP's production plan rather than the master schedule. Specific end-items, let alone piece-parts, are not known; most probably, only forecast dollar volumes of sales by family are known.

It is best to keep this kind of planning separate from the kind of planning described in this book. It is, necessarily, quite coarse in two main directions: (1) It usually deals with the loads on entire departments, with no attention paid to individual work centers; (2) It usually deals with a very broad profile of load in which one load model represents an entire family which may have a good deal of variation. As a result, it inevitably departs from the detailed information needed for day-to-day operations. The user is fortunate if he finds the ultimate loads to materialize within plus or minus 10%, sometimes 15% or 20%. Nevertheless, dim visibility is better than none, and such a resource planning tool can be refined over a period of time until it is surprisingly accurate and extremely helpful.

Typically, a firm will develop a small, separate program in a convenient language (Fortran is better than COBOL if you have a Fortran programmer but no COBOL programmer!). The input to this program will be a deck of cards for each month to be forecast. Each card will call for the number of units of some particular product to be delivered in that month. Some of the cards may represent far-off firm customer orders; most of them will represent forecasts only.

The program will be arranged to recognize the product called for and to recall from its memory a model of this product. The model is simply a listing of the number of hours of labor expected to be needed per unit in each of the factory departments, and how far ahead of shipping month those hours must be worked. The program then adds each unit's contribution to each month from shipping month backwards in time (multiplied, of course, by the number of units) into each department's load, and assembles and prints the result.

The output of the program is a table having months across the top and departments down the left side. The contents of each cell so formed are, of course, the number of hours of load estimated for that month for that department.

Some firms become a little more elaborate and separate the lines into "on the book" (orders received but not yet engineered) and "yet to book," totalling and subtotalling, both down and across, as appropriate.

Such a portrayal of future load is shown in Fig. 7–1 and is extremely powerful if used with good judgment in identifying when and where loads are likely to go outside expected limits of capacity, skills, and so on. It can be an important component of the "gross capacity" test in Appendix IV, Block No. 20.

It is generally useless to try to reconcile the results of such work with the results of the formal scheduling-and-loading procedure. Where the detailed schedule-and-load process shows results different from the resource plan, it must be followed because it is, by now, superior information. But where the resource plan shows loads beyond the view of the scheduling-and-loading process, it must be

Standard Hour Loads Forecast For Next 6 Months Report Date 242.
Hours And Dollars In 1,000's. Mail to __________
Julian Date 10 May 198_

Sales And Hours	**Forecast For Month Of**						**FCST**
	June	**July**	**Aug**	**Sept**	**Oct**	**Nov**	**Total**
Objective Sales $	1577	1516	1577	913	929	1848	8360
Firm Orders $	1577	1516	1078	612	450	113	5346
Yet to book orders $	—	—	499	301	479	1735	3014
Sold standard hours	17	11	8	3	2	1	42
Yet to book std hrs	1	8	9	13	15	17	63
Total standard hours	18	19	17	16	17	18	105
Hours by department							
100—Details	5	4	5	5	4	5	28
200—Fabrication	7	8	9	8	7	9	48
300—Assembly	5	5	2	2	4	3	21
400—Test	1	2	1	1	2	1	8
ALL—Total std hours	18	19	17	16	17	18	105

Fig. 7–1. A labor resource plan.

respected as the only information we have. What the formal manufacturing plan and execution can do, however, is collect costs by product family and summarize them on a continuing basis to be fed back to those responsible for maintaining the resource-planning models. Continuous feedback of this kind will track cost increases and reductions, inflation, factory improvements, and so forth and will tend to make the resource plan more believable and dependable. (See Fig. 7–2.)

This kind of system, off-line from the main production-and-inventory planning and control system, is ideal for playing "what if?" games which are so

---

Standard Hours Analysis By Product Group For Orders Shipped Between Production Days 020 And 240.   Report Date 242.

Product Group	Standard Hours Required Per Unit In Months Before Shipping Month							
	6	5	4	3	2	1	0	Total
#92—Small. Average of 65 units built								
DEPARTMENT								
100—Details	—	—	—	16	10	—	—	26
200—Fabrication	—	—	—	5	15	30	2	52
300—Assembly	—	—	—	—	—	—	35	35
ALL—Total	—	—	—	21	25	30	37	113
#45—Large. Average of 23 units built								
DEPARTMENT								
100—Details	5	56	52	12	2	—	—	127
200—Fabrication	—	20	276	107	—	—	2	405
300—Assembly	—	—	—	—	18	142	24	184
400—Test	—	—	—	—	—	5	32	37
ALL—Total	5	76	328	119	20	147	58	753

Fig. 7–2. Computer-produced analysis of standard hours reported by type of product, by manufacturing department, and by time bucket, for recently completed shipments. "Standard" may include or exclude extra allowances, as governed by the accounting and shop practices of the firm.

essential to intelligent planning. This is one of the rare instances in which a plant manager will be found with a personal deck of machine cards in his desk. It is so simple to color code their edges for product family or for month of delivery, rearrange them, and try again. Once more, it pays to have a small, efficient, responsive, locally controlled program to do a small, very repetitive job. The manager forms the judgments and makes decisions based upon computer work done in a few seconds which would otherwise take him hours.

TIME FENCES

Fast reaction to change has been pointed out as an essential ability of modern manufacturing systems (Orlicky 1973, p. 10). Nevertheless, there comes a point beyond which change is impossible; the bullet has left the muzzle of the gun. Earlier than this moment, there are varying degrees of ability to change aim, timing, size of load, target, and so on.

Clinging too long to an original plan is self-defeating because the necessary change is then forced upon the organization after the damage has been done and over so short a time that further severe damage is probable. An example is manufacturing a volume and mix of stock products after the signals from the marketplace have indicated a change is needed. The result is large unsaleable inventories and low sales of goods in short supply: the damage has been done. Further damage is likely to be done when it becomes necessary to reduce the labor force drastically, followed shortly by a frantic search for additional labor of a different skill with which to build up production of the goods which are in short supply.

Refer to Fig. 7–3 for a picture of a typical set of time relationships involved in the master scheduling process.

These are the definitions of the various terms:

Production planning forecasts families of products over a rather long time period—typically a year. Individual end-items are not forecast.

Master schedule identifies specific end-items to be produced in the near future (i.e., in a few weeks or months).

Forecast horizon is the time from now to the end of the period being master scheduled.

Review cycle time is the frequency of revision of a master schedule. A master schedule that has a horizon of two months, say, could have a review cycle time of two weeks.

Accumulated lead time is the total time required from now to the time finished goods are delivered to stores or to customer if we start with nothing (no stocks of any kind). It will include time for system turnaround, procurement for raw materials, incoming handling, production, any intermediate waits (such as in stores), and handling into the storerooms. A key point needs emphasis in connection

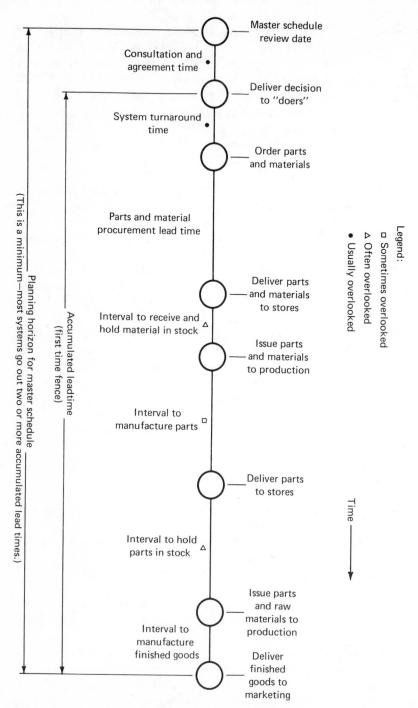

Fig. 7–3.   Time relationships and master scheduling.

with accumulated lead time. If we are manufacturing a standard product at a steady rate, we might consider our lead time to be, say, 4 weeks because we have a backup of stocks for some of the items; viz., those with procurement times in excess of this 4 weeks manufacturing time. But if we must increase our production rates, our lead time for the increase becomes the accumulated lead time, which might be 10 or 16 weeks, rather than 4. Thinking this through to its logical conclusion, we can see that a change in mix within the accumulated lead time (raising the demand for one product, reducing it for the other) simply cannot be accomplished without emergency measures being taken. This is because the parts needed for the increased member of the family cannot be obtained in time. Many factories attempt to manage by maintaining a reasonably level total load, but in the light of the accumulated lead time concept, this is far from a sufficient condition for effective response to the market.

System turnaround time is the time for the manual or computer system, or mixture, to deal with a decision such as to buy material. Note that a computer system which cycles once per week adds one week to procurement intervals.

A time fence is the period from today to some agreed day in the future between which production decisions (such as quantity and mix to manufacture) are protected. That is, Marketing and Manufacturing have agreed that, within this period, only limited (perhaps no) changes to quantity or mix will be made. There must, of course, be flexibility in such agreements; but it must be clearly understood by all concerned that the flexibility decreases markedly as the time remaining falls. Fig. 7–4 illustrates this.

As the day being considered comes closer to "today," less flexibility is possible. Little or nothing can be done to change quantity or mix of articles now on the production line (zero flexibility); whereas any reasonable change to quantity or mix can be imposed one year from now. A time fence specifies the degree of flexibility that can be accommodated between these extremes. Typically there are

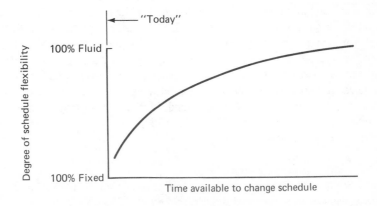

Fig. 7–4.   How flexibility decreases as time horizon shortens.

two or more time fences. The basic one is the accumulated lead time, within which it becomes rapidly more and more difficult to change quantity and mix.

Review timing

The production plan and the master schedule (along with the assembly schedule or shipping schedule for industries which also make-to-order) can be reviewed as often as is desirable and economical. These plans look at the market and its needs. If the market changes rapidly and is difficult to forecast, the interval between reviews will be short.

Typically the production plan is reviewed much less often then the master schedule. A change to the production plan usually indicates a major, basic change in the market—a large movement up or down in demand or a significant change in customer preference from product to product.

The master schedule is reviewed more frequently. This is because the cumulative effect of minor changes in demand can have major impact upon inventories, customer service, and productivity if not tracked and reacted to promptly.

Specific policies covering review timing and the degree to which the firm will respond to the market should be set by the management of the firm. On the one hand, it is desirable to react instantly to any change in sales levels or mix which the market might be signalling. On the other hand, it is desirable to freeze production rates and mixes for long periods of time in order to get maximum productivity of labor, material, and plant. Successful factories operate between these extremes.

It is good to work toward fast reaction to change without big penalties. Many plants try too hard for long runs, turning a blind eye to market shifts or to errors in the forecasts until it is so late in the game that an inventory disaster looms. It is then that the setups which were saved are swallowed up in the costs (in morale as well as money) of lost sales, temporary labor layoffs, and "white sales" to get rid of unsold goods at whatever the market may bring. Fig. 7–5 shows, in conceptual form, a curve which every firm has: its total cost of reacting 100% to the market, not reacting at all, and all points in between. While this figure cannot be fitted out with actual numbers because of differences among firms, nevertheless each firm does have its own numbers which it would pay to identify and record for policy guidance. The numbers are usually quite difficult to get, yet whether hard or easy to develop, they do exist and are ignored at our peril. Clinging to long runs and insisting upon firm long-range forecasts can actually bring on the problems such ostrich management is trying to avoid. It is better—and in the present highly competitive environment, essential—to strive toward developing an ability to react fast to market shifts. Fast reaction comes from:

1.   Short review cycle times.

2.   Short accumulated lead times. (Purchasing should fight off a lead-time increase just as vigorously as a price increase!)

3.   High quality information (information which is current, accurate, and accessible). Information from the field and from suppliers on business obtained and

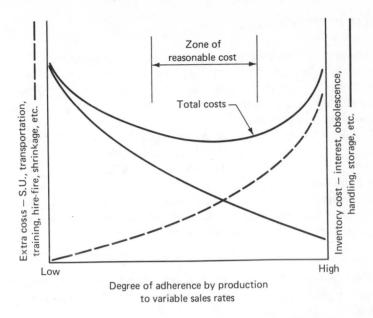

Fig. 7-5. How total costs change with various sales-production inventory strategies.

lost is received when fresh, analyzed at once, and made available to decision makers promptly in action-oriented form.

4. Use of a coordinated, multidepartmental method of using the available tools; agreement in advance of what constitutes an "out of control" signal; adherence to the agreed procedures until review of results indicates change is needed.

Again, the rules of a firm's game must be set by the firm; but a fairly common two-fence rule is this: From today to the end of the manufacturing lead time is time fence No. 1: *the schedule is frozen.* From today to the end of the procurement lead time is time fence No. 2: *between time fences No. 1 and No. 2 the schedule is firm.* If a change is desired, it can be requested and it can possibly be accommodated depending upon such things as safety stocking policies, labor skills available, and so forth. Normally, however, no significant change is expected in this zone and any request for one has to be approved by one higher level of management. Beyond time fence No. 2 *the schedule is as fluid as the various constraints inherent in the firm and its business will allow.* Such constraints include:

- the production plan,
- plant capacity, particularly on critical work centers, and
- management policies on market share, labor load leveling, supplier relations, and so on.

SYSTEM RESPONSE TIME

Any planning and control system, to be useful, must respond well to change. Further, even if the usual shortages, breakdowns, epidemics, and storms are spared us, the simple passage of time makes the plan obsolete, because planned work is finished and new work is fed in. The systematic answer to these problems is in rapid cycling of a net-change system.

Rapid cycling of a computer system has the potential to keep up with the happenings in the factory of which the computer is supposed to have a good model. It can assure that the formal system works and is usable. *Note:* the system has the *potential;* but it doesn't run the factory; people do.

How rapid is "rapid"? The only answer has to be, "rapid enough for the environment." For launching a rocket, one millisecond might be too slow. For raising cattle, one month might be fast enough.

Most factories get by on one computer cycle per week, some one per month. But this is rapidly changing in the direction of the on-line, real-time end of the spectrum.

A common error is to think that system cycling can be geared to the length of the product cycle—long for long-cycle products, short for short-cycle products. In fact, however, the frequency of cycling should be geared to entirely different factors which often suggest that long-cycle products need short cycling systems.

System cycling should be geared to how rapidly the manufacturing situation changes. Try ranking the factory from one to three on each of these criteria. A high score suggests a pressing need for quick responding systems.

1.   There are many different products or many variations of similar products, with widely differing cycle times.

2.   The product has many levels of assembly.

3.   There are many sources of input to the typical work center—purchased, stocked, and made-for-order items.

4.   There is high labor content.

5.   There is a large number of very different transactions per day, such as labor reports, material receipts and withdrawals, inspection approvals, purchase requisitions.

The maximum score a factory might collect is 15, and any factory with a high score should certainly be cycling its computer system no less often than once every few days.

Many shops divide their processing into two parts, on-line and batch. The on-line part, supported by a mini, cares for transactions that really must be on-line, real-time, such as material receipts and labor operation completions. Once a day or once a week, the mini talks to a host (or in some cases goes into batch-processing mode unattended at night, where response time is not a problem and inefficiency doesn't matter as much). The batch processing is devoted to functions that can or should wait. Things that can wait include, for instance, MRP processing, creation of accounting reports, and printing of the day's purchase orders. Things that should wait are ORP recalculations and other functions involving collection of data for some period and then smoothing it or combining it with historical information in some way. File searches, too, can often be done at night when the degrading of response time which they often bring with them is of no importance.

On-line, real-time systems offer such inticing possibilities to departments like Engineering (for file searches) that there is a risk of their being preempted for that although originally set up for Manufacturing's use. It is a paradox of industry that the functions often found to have on-line, real-time facilities (or something near it) are the functions needing it far less than does Manufacturing, where more things happen in an hour than happen in a week in some of the other departments. Manufacturing has mainly itself to blame for this. Over a period of a quarter century, Manufacturing has been so unsure of what it should demand from the computer that it has let first the programmers, then the systems analysts, sometimes the hardware peddlers—in short, almost anyone—tell it what it needs.

Historically, computer systems have had most success and least payoff in functions which are relatively rigid and almost inflexible, and were codified before the programmers had to code them (e.g., accounting). Computer systems have had the least success in areas where there is highest payoff (e.g., in manufacturing, where informal systems have been the norm and flexibility is so necessary). Computer systems do not cope well with the need for flexibility, although we are rapidly learning. And of course they cannot cope at all with an informal system. But then, neither can human beings cope with an informal system. But the difference between the computer and the human is that the human, after the mess has been created, can figure out some way to clean it up (at high cost).

Thus, with computer systems for manufacturing, it is necessary to know what is needed before shopping for hardware and software. Nothing new in this. But so far as response time, and such features as on-line, real-time are concerned, it is doubly necessary to understand the principles of manufacturing and to be able to specify those sytem features that will support those principles. On-line, real-time systems will continue to fall in cost, while the cost of learning how to use them will continue to rise. Some plants have put them in and taken them out in disillusionment. The problem was not always with the system; the problem was that the plant was trying to solve the wrong problem. Before high performing systems can truly assist a manufacturer, that manufacturer must have a soundly based, formal, well-functioning planning and control system in place; one which does not make the demands upon the people that are made by frantic attempts to reconcile useless CRT displays with what is actually going on in the informal system. Interestingly, if the plant does have that prerequisite, the felt-need for an OLRT system diminishes quite a bit. In the short run, the people in the plant are their own on-line, real-time system.

INVENTORY RECORDS

Every time a system is tightened up and formalized, record accuracy becomes a problem. It was a problem before the program started, too, but it could be overcome with excessive inventory, by expediting manpower, and with a high tolerance for shipping late and working inefficiently because of shop disorder (Plossl 1973).

As our tolerance for these things falls, inventory record accuracy comes out of the woodwork as one of the reasons (excuses?) for late starts and excess stocks.

Any WIP turnover improvement program will be no exception. Except that, to the usual interpretation of inventory record accuracy, we must add another: WIP record accuracy. This is usually governed by (1) the refinement we feel we need within the system (for instance, some firms rightly feel that product moves, as well as labor completions, must be formally reported), (2) the faithfulness with which production mileposts are reported as they occur, and (3) the frequency of cycling of the system.

Effective working of the formal system requires that the computer's model of the factory be accurate. And, since labor is inventory too, its status must be up to date. If it is, eligibility systems will work reliably; the system's signals will be useful and intelligible to the shop management who must react knowledgeably to them.

HELPING THE QUARTERBACK: INFORMATION THE MANAGER NEEDS

It was commented earlier that the shop manager's or superintendent's job is to ensure that the different parts of the factory are working in synch. His tools are the summarized summaries—load summaries by cost center and, if the shop is big enough, by department.

A common failing of many systems is to give far too much detail. At any moment, literally thousands of things are happening in the shop; its management can and must be interested in only the summarized status of all of them, with detail suppressed. When a WIP turnover improvement program goes in, the management-level summarized load summaries must be a primary output, not an afterthought or byproduct. The detail is the business of foremen, subforemen, and production controllers; the job of the manager is to identify major shifts of staffing and priorities that will demand his attention and direction.

Another management-level output of the system is the master schedule. This document, too, in many shops contains too much detail for the manager to manage. In 100% make-to-order shops, it should contain only the assembly schedule for customer orders, together with sufficient lower level status information that the manager can, at a glance, estimate such important matters as probable ship date. This will require that all lower level information (except perhaps that pertaining to items which are in some way threatening the ship date) be omitted. Again, the supporting detail is available to the actual shop operating people, displayed as may be logical in the particular factory.

In make-for-stock shops, the same principle should apply. In such factories, however, the master schedule for the management level tends to have extra information such as number of units built vs. number planned against an order for stock. Where certain products are manufactured continuously, batch control is essential. There may be no such physical entity as the "start" and "finish" of a run, *but there must be periodic batch counts against separate batch order numbers,* with scrap and shrink properly accounted for. Failure to do this invariably results in year-end surprises which seem always to go one way—toward writeoff.

INDUSTRIAL RELATIONS

Repeatedly we have mentioned the impacts upon labor which a WIP control program will have. Depending upon factory size, there may or may not be an industrial relations department; but there is invariably an industrial relations *function.* That function and its people must be brought on-board early and kept posted on progress. Contractual, legal, moral obligations to the labor force, and good business citizenship obligations to the community must be discharged.

MEASURING CRITICAL ACTIVITIES

A production planning system can be thought of as a model of what we would like to have happening during manufacturing. A production control system is one which keeps the model updated and accurate, so that manufacturing management can be an orderly process rather than a crisis-driven one.

Control is infinitely easier when the critical parts of the activities being controlled can be identified and their status and movements measured. One difficulty with WIP through the years has been that we have not been sure of what the critical activities are, let alone how to measure them and interpret the results.

One result is that we have measured the wrong things, or the easy things, or the visible things such as piece count and labor efficiency. While many of these things are good to measure for certain purposes, they do not point us in the right directions when we seek to ship on time out of a small asset base. For instance, both piece count and labor efficiency ignore the critical element: did we work efficiently on the *right pieces?* Close adherence to schedule is at least as important as the labor efficiency of the department, but usually is not measured.

Measurement, unfortunately, is filled with emotional overtones. If a foreman is judged on his adherence to schedule, he will bitterly oppose the release of overdue work into his schedules as recommended elsewhere.

Regardless of the difficulty of measuring, or of the emotional impact of the measurement, there is no alternative to measurement, if we intend to improve delivery performance and turnovers.

In a well-functioning organization whose people have confidence in each other, in the system, and in the objectives of the day's work, a great deal of the emotion can be removed from the measurement process by ensuring that all personnel understand that measurements of the kind we have recommended are intended to (1) prevent things from going wrong in the first place; (2) if things are going wrong, learn about it soon enough to do something useful to head off the trouble; and (3) if things have gone wrong, find out *what,* not *who,* is wrong, so that it can be fixed.

Perhaps one of the most helpful principles for the designer and user of a manufacturing (or any) system to follow is to make it difficult or impossible for the operating person (the subforeman, for instance) to be faced with a game of NIGYSOB. ("Now I've got you, you SOB!" See Berne 1964, p. 85.) To avoid "gotcha" games, performance indicators should be published within these guidelines:

1. The subordinate's boss should not receive information sooner, of higher quality for operating decision making, than the subordinate. A subordinate deeply, and rightly, resents a call asking him what he is doing about his average days late on some work center when he himself has not yet seen the report.

2. A subordinate should receive information about his own operation which is at least as good as, preferably better than, any information about it received by any other arm of the organization. For instance, the responsible supervisor should know his idle time, labor efficiency, overdues, or average days late before Accounting, Marketing, or any other interested department.

3. Especially in computerized systems, get permission of the "owner" of the information before searching files, or developing one-time reports or retrievals. Part of the mistrust of computerized systems springs from the fact that "my" information is invisible to me—hidden away on a tape somewhere—and accessible to some curious person who may want to demonstrate what a poor manager I am.

THE PERFORMANCE AND PERSONALITY OF THE SYSTEM

Plants committed to using formal systems are entitled to expect high performance from them.

Informal systems that have a formal façade provided by impressive printouts of schedules, load reports, or applications listings, do not require high performance. Errors in the reports go undetected or unnoticed because the real system—the informal one—does its own thing independently. Its own thing usually starts with a shortage list. Sometimes the shortage list is computerized too, with columns for "promises" and all the other trappings of an order-launch and expedite system.

Firms in this situation have a serious problem. It is very easy to make people—including themselves—believe they are computerized and they "have MRP," in short that they are doing all they can reasonably be expected to do to manage their deliveries, their inventories, and their costs.

But this is another case of measuring the wrong thing; in this case, input instead of output. Some firms spend hundreds of thousands of dollars per year on computer programs whose workings they do not understand and whose outputs could be produced by four intelligent typists using ditto masters, at half the cost.

Other equally expensive systems are so poorly documented, yet so built into the user's way of doing things, that the firm is, in effect, being run by the system. It was designed by someone probably now long gone from the firm. No present employee has a good understanding of what it does, and he is reluctant to change it for fear of bringing down a house of cards. If this is your state, you must get out of it, because your system will run you into the ground as other firms, with better and more flexible systems, become able to do easily and cheaply things you can hardly do at all. To measure output, it is necessary to audit any production planning and control system using the principles outlined earlier in "Fundamentals of Manufacturing an Assembled Product." If the system doesn't measure up, one of two situations will be found:

1. The system is incapable of producing the required outputs.

2. The system could produce useful outputs and could be modified to produce information such as average days late, but is full of poor data which makes, and will continue to make, all outputs of little use.

A system's outputs need not be 100% wrong to be useless. About 10% will do.

System credibility is the sine qua non of using a formal system. Using his hands, one manager memorably illustrated this truth:

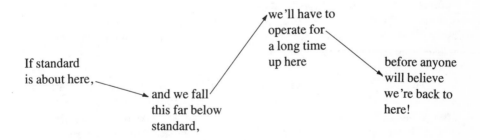

Within reason, any amount of time and effort spent getting the production system to obey the principles discussed in Chapter 2 and in getting rid of garbage data and known bugs is time well spent. We are asking other people to stake their reputations, careers, and paychecks on the quality of our system.

It would be tempting to write a long list of things that can happen and have happened to defeat computer and manual systems; but it would be dreary reading and would probably miss the main difficulty bothering the reader. These general guides may be helpful:

1. The users of the detailed information know intimately many of the unlovable characteristics of the present system; ask them. The cumbersome sort sequence, the date change that works forward but not backward, the labor report that sometimes "takes" and sometimes doesn't, must be smoked out and fixed.

2. Consider the people when designing outputs. Paper that is 132-column wide is a clerical monster; avoid it. Cards were meant to be ready by machines, not people; don't ask them to. A program provision that requires two lines of programming can result in printout books four inches thick; think before you print. The first thing many clerks must do when they receive outputs from the computer, is start computing; try to find the one extra step the program can take to prevent this asinine situation. Like a good radio communications receiver, whose quality is measured not by what it will bring in but by what it will leave out, a computer system must summarize, summarize, and summarize until it has left out most of what came in. The unattainable ideal is the entire status of the factory summarized on one 8½" by 11" sheet; unattainable, but how close can you come? On-line systems are great and have a lot of gee-whizz value; but don't force their users to sit and copy information off the screen by hand. There is a place for paper.

3. Every system has a personality. If it talks to the user in code, forcing him to remember (or look up) what some obscure acronym means, that personality is cold, mechanical, demanding, and unfriendly. Computer memory is no problem these days; force the computer to do the remembering and looking up and make it display helpful, spelled out, common language words and phrases even if they do require a fraction of a minute of extra print time. If the user has erred, make the computer tell him what he must do to get back on track. Particularly in on-line systems, make it easy for the user to recover and start again. One system we know has a "HELP!" command which overrides all others and prompts the user in a relaxed way back to the place he lost.

The designers of outputs need to remember, when they come to the user interface, how long their own struggles were with concepts such as synchronized production. The people who are to use system output will have their own difficulties with such concepts. These difficulties must not be worsened by our forcing them to learn unnecessary computerese.

SUPPORT FROM THE REST OF THE SYSTEM: SUMMARY

Resource Planning

Resource planning or rough-cut capacity planning beyond the load summary horizon will be found essential to the ongoing job of matching load to capacity. This system can and probably should be separate from the detailed master scheduling process because it necessarily uses very approximate inputs and cannot, for instance, explode by part number.

Resources

Resources include prints of the drawings, tools, specifications, bought-outside services, and subcontracts—everything, in short, which must be brought together before the product can be made. As much of this information as possible should be captured in the system and scheduled along with labor and parts.

Time Fences

Time fences must be established and drawn into the framework of manufacturing policy. The factory must be tuned to react as fast as it is possible for it to do; but it must be recognized that there are limits to this ability set by inescapable factors such as accumulated lead time. The closer to "today" the demand for change is imposed, the more costly and disruptive the change will be. A common two-fence system freezes the schedule out as far as the manufacturing lead time; keeps it as firm as possible from there to the end of the procurement lead time; and permits any reasonable change within the limits of the production plan outside that fence.

System Response Time

System response time should be quick enough that the factory does not wait for the system, but not so fast that excessive computer costs are incurred by re-reviewing a situation that has not changed. Response time can be determined only in a given plant. Many job shops can work well with a response time (time between computer cycles) of one-half to one week. Long product cycles do not automatically excuse long response times; the reverse may be true. However on-line, real-time systems are unlikely to be the first thing needed by the typical factory.

Measuring

Measuring the right things is a key concern of any firm with high WIP levels. Plan quality and plan execution are seldom measured but must be measured if WIP turn improvement is to be achieved. The criteria of goodness or quality of planning and execution are known and are not difficult to apply.

Inventory Record Accuracy

Inventory record accuracy (including timely labor reporting and move reporting) are, as always, central to success.

Summarizing Information

Manager-level information must be summarized. Much of the cost of system development can and should go to this objective.

Industrial Relations

The industrial relations function in the plant must be enlisted in support of the labor redeployment aspects of the program.

The System's "Personality"

Every system has a personality and a level of performance which is under the control of the user. The user must exercise this control to ensure that the system is "friendly," that it *works,* and that its outputs are in forms understandable to humans, even when this means a little inconvenience for the computer or the computer programmer.

CASE STUDY: PROTECTING THE TIME FENCE

A manufacturer of an industrial component felt he had excessive parts stocks. His product was highly engineered and complex in its way, but had only one or two levels of assembly and was subject to no customer specification whatever. Volumes were quite high and an MRP system was exploding requirements. Yet he had over 5 months of supply of parts. He assigned a small task force to find out why, and to take corrective action.

The task force dissected the 5 months of supply and found that over 60% of the dollar cost of inventory exceeded 5 months of supply, and that 25% of it had not moved at all for a year.

The task force then sampled the computer-produced listing of pegged material applications, one printed line in 50 systematically. They found 40% of the lines to be overdue and unreported. They wanted to know what contribution this was making to the 5 months of supply. They did this by multiplying each line dollar value by its months overdue, summing dollars overdue and dollar-months overdue, and dividing the latter by the former to get a figure they called "equivalent months overdue." By this method they estimated that 1.4 months of supply of parts was caused by this one factor—overdue applications.

Consulting with the production planners about this, with the pegged application list in their hands, the task force learned that many orders supposedly "overdue" were not really overdue at all—they had been held upon last-minute instructions from Marketing, who gave the final go-ahead on what to build during a given week, usually only one to two weeks ahead of time. Most part lead times were two to four months.

Consulting with Engineering about the parts which seemd to be dead (because MRP is not supposed to do this to a firm) they found that the commonest reason for their presence was that they had once been called for on active orders that had been held for long periods, then cancelled. A few represented badly managed supersedures.

Consulting with supervision, they found that production start for any given order was typically a week behind the nominal date ("gives us a chance to level out our loading a bit and for matching parts to come in"). They also found that the computer system didn't unload the pegged applications for one to five days after the actual withdrawal.

Consulting the computer's record of transaction histories by sampling one in fifty lines, the task force looked for excessive safety stocks and found them. (Safety stock is defined as what is left in the bin when the reorder comes in—whether that's how it was planned or not.) They discovered that, of their total active inventory (items registering receipts in the past twelve months), over 60% was safety stock as defined above.

Questions

1. Using the above information and making as few assumptions as possible, divide the problem into
    - master schedule management (changes within the time fence)
    - WIP management (shop floor control, etc.)
    - system problems (time phasing, etc.)
    - engineering problems (supersedures, phaseouts)
    - other

2. What do you think of using a 2% sample (one in fifty) to estimate such things as safety stock percentage? Do you approve? Why or why not?

3. If you are convinced that the product manager has more parts stocks than he needs, what first and most important one, two, or three things would you recommend he do?

Chapter 8

Summary and Conclusions

WORK IN PROCESS AND THE REAL WORLD

We have noted that, in the end, management's interest in WIP stems from financial considerations. The firm's objective is to make a profit from its investment. If the investment becomes too high, the profit necessary to justify it also becomes very high—often higher than can be obtained in the face of competition from leaner suppliers of the same goods. Thus, in firms with large WIP investments, the spotlight of management turns upon the control of this investment.

There is, as well, a growing recognition that there is something wrong with many long standing assumptions, such as the mistaken notion that we must have lots of WIP to be confident of shipping on time. Sadly, the more of it we have, the less of it seems to go out the door when it was promised.

Perhaps we should not be surprised to find that WIP control, in the end, depends upon our control over the *timing* of events—both as we have planned them and as we do them. Nor should it be a surprise that work which is planned well can be done well. Thus let us summarize and review the relationships between work in process and time.

Control of Timing: the Main Lever for Production Control

The standard cost of the product cannot be much influenced by production and inventory control once the factory is committed to building certain items over the short term—weeks or months. (It is worth repeating that P&IC has a great deal of control over the wasted, nonstandard labor time in any plant, because upon the success of P&IC depends the amount of hunting, moving, rework, and other lost motion involved in trying to run a plant glutted with too much WIP.)

What production and inventory control people can influence powerfully, however, is *time in inventory*–cycle time. It was explained that work in process inventory equals throughput rate multiplied by cycle time for the product. As a means of summarizing several of our earlier discussions, therefore, it will be instructive to consider an assembled product and ask: Why do we need *any* cycle time? Dissecting the question and examining the numerous answers will give us insight into better WIP control.

Consider the product illustrated in Fig. 8–1. If we required virtually no cycle time at all, Fig. 8–1 would look like Fig. 8–2.

216

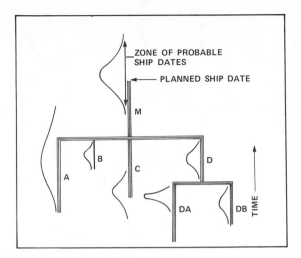

Fig. 8–1. How lateness and out-of-sequence working combine to determine how often the product is shipped on time.

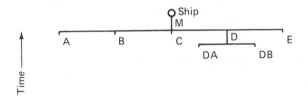

Fig. 8–2

One reason we need time, however, is to perform the labor operations on the parts. And so Fig. 8–2 becomes Fig. 8–3.

But we know that almost nothing occurs exactly as planned. Certainly the labor operations needed to build this product will not be ready to begin the minute they were planned to do so, thus, some tolerance must be provided in the plan (see Fig. 8–4).

Furthermore, the labor operations may take longer than planned, for any number of reasons. This gives rise to Fig. 8–5.

In addition, the factory must have some leeway within which to level their manpower load. It is not practical to work 18 hours one day, 2 hours or none the next. We have no simple way of knowing in advance how this demand will be imposed, so we must provide an additional allowance—some kind of judgmental average—to permit the shop to perform the operation, within reason, at a time which is efficient for them. So we have Fig. 8–6.

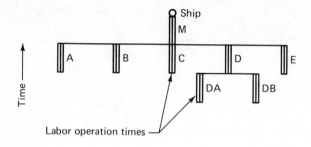

Fig. 8–3

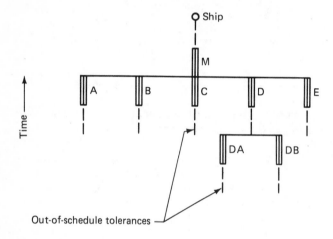

Fig. 8–4

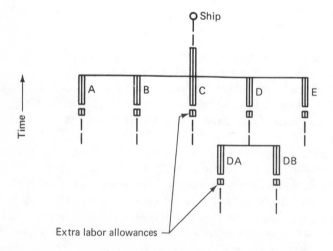

Fig. 8–5

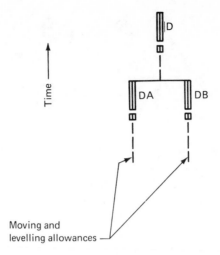

Fig. 8–6

We may have chronic difficulties in getting matching parts finished at the same time. These difficulties may show up as either planned-in or unplanned additional interval, giving rise to Fig. 8–7.

If for any reason parts are scheduled and made too soon, or if they must enter a storeroom and be withdrawn for the next stage of production (even if the movement is on paper only), additional interval (either for the physical movement or the system cycling time, or both) is required (see Fig. 8–8).

The cumulative effect of these phenomena through several levels of manufacturing will result in planned-in or unplanned slack all along the manufacturing path. Planned-in slack is visible as a deliberate gap in the plan between feeder finish and

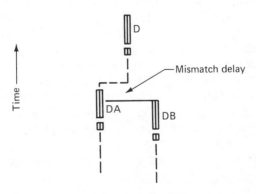

Fig. 8–7

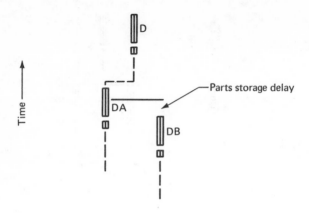

Fig. 8–8

assembly start. Unplanned slack develops during plan execution and frequently results in late shipment.

The result of all these processes, acting together, is that we "have WIP." Note that no value judgments were made in the above; the bad is mixed with the good. It is up to factory management—Supervision and Production-Inventory Control, chiefly—to eliminate the bad and minimize the necessary.

The Meaning of "WIP Control"

WIP control seeks to meet two main objectives: (1) minimize time in inventory, (2) maximize the number of on-time shipments.

Since product designers, factory engineers, and others control the product cost, which contains only the standard and nonstandard time allowances, P&IC's WIP control must take aim at the various kinds of slack in the plan that we have just outlined. This slack can be as much as 80% and more of the production cycle for the product and can be planned out, worked out, or, preferably, both. The methods for planning out the slack are dealt with in Chapter 2, in our discussion of the planning phase. The amount of planning required for products of any complexity at all is such a daunting task that many managements use false economy by shortcutting or ignoring the principles and living in hope that "the shop can sort it out." And, indeed, the shop always can, spending in the process more time and money than would have been needed in the first place, to plan the job right.

Money spent on improving the planning phase is seldom misspent. Money spent on shop floor control, productivity improvement, and so forth without checking out the planning phase is almost always largely wasted; and so are the human resources that must extend themselves so far and so hard to improve their performance of a faulty plan.

Once the plan is credible, working to it becomes easier. This is because shop floor decision making can become a more efficient process. Instead of selecting items to be expedited, the shop management can fall back on "bulk decision making"; that is, by working the right number of hours they know they can carry the load, and by working the right hours they know they can make the parts "we really need" and so keep the expediters off their backs. To take a purist point of view, shop management should be in the position where they neither know nor care what the individual items are, because they are working on a *flow* of product. The individual components of this flow, and the sequencing of these components, having been done correctly upstream, need not concern them. What must concern shop management, however, is that the pipe (the factory's capacity) is sized correctly for the flow (the load), and that the sequence, which was correctly planned, is adhered to.

Factory Structure

Each factory has a multilevel structure analogous to the structure of a product. Final assembly work centers are fed by subassembly work centers which are fed by single-item work centers, back upstream sometimes through six to ten or more levels. This structure evolves more often than it is planned, particularly in job shops. It is several orders of magnitude more difficult to change than product structure, and so product structure changes should be done with great care and with this in mind. Paths within this factory structure which are long and multilevel are subject to accumulations of cycle time caused by the additive effect of errors in planning and execution. The cycle times of product through these paths, therefore, depend critically upon how the paths are structured and how the paths are managed day-to-day and hour-to-hour. Product cycle time, therefore, is the result of strong interaction among product structure, factory structure, and factory management.

The Fundamentals of WIP Turnover and Delivery Improvement

Any WIP turnover and delivery improvement project falls logically into two parts:

1. Ensure synchronized production in which gaps and laps in the schedules are minimized.
2. Reduce the cycle times allowed for manufacture, with the confidence that plan execution will be supported by synchronized production through the life of every order.

Reducing cycle times before tending to synchronized production generally invites disaster.

Planning

A firm must work with estimates of requirements for labor and other resources which extend out to different horizons, for different purposes.

1. Long range. We must know what skills and facilities are likely to be needed to support the volume and mix of product expected to be needed many months or years hence. While this was covered briefly in Chapter 7 under "Resource Planning," it is not the main subject of this book.

2. Medium range. We must know what skills will be needed, in what quantity, by when within the next one to three months. We must, from this knowledge, determine how to staff. This cannot mean arbitrary hiring-firing, but must mean maintaining and deliberately, consciously using an inventory of secondary and tertiary skills so that our work force can follow the peaks through the shop. It is completely noncompetitive to level-load by letting backlogs rise and fall while the same number of men and women work on the same job for months at a time. Labor flexibility must be available and must be used.

3. Short range. For the forthcoming week or similar period, we must be prepared to work an agreed number of hours (of which we had ample warning through No. 2 above) upon jobs which are accurately sequenced. Easily said, this is hard to do, but it is the heart of successful shop management. We must be quite prepared to do unfamiliar things like slowing down the output of a work center which is already behind schedule, in order to apply the skills where the work is even farther behind. The plan to do these things must be the result of agreement among the key people who must see to it that they are done: shop supervision and production control. Thumbnail job descriptions of these people are as follows: Production control ensures the load can be done (assures eligibility), while supervision sees that it is done, efficiently and in sequence.

The System

The system deals with information, not data. The information must be summarized and must be good. Good information is current, accurate, and accessible. Good information is a paper model of the shop, with problems highlighted for action and several levels of summarization for several levels of management. Good systems, when they fail, often do so because of bad information. Good information depends upon good records (e.g., prompt labor reporting, item locations).

At the managerial level, the information system must present summarized reports which, in a quick perusal, lead management to where their talents are needed to break logjams.

Conclusion

Finally, to close as we started, better WIP control is in the end a financial consideration. The benefits are very concrete and not at all abstract. They include high on-time shipment percentages, lower product cost*, higher ROI, and a better share of the market. These benefits are real, tangible, and can be estimated with some confidence starting where you are. They should, indeed must, be estimated if the organization is to develop a unified drive toward agreed objectives.

---

*This is not a contradiction of what was said earlier, viz., that P&IC has little control of product cost. Generations of management have observed that, the longer a job remains in a factory, the more it costs, standard costs notwithstanding. Study of this phenomenon deserves the time of a Peter or a Parkinson.

Appendix I

Critical Ratio Priority Setting for Labor Operations

Critical ratio for establishing the priority of a stock item is a familiar concept (Plossl and Wight 1967, p. 296). An analogous technique is helpful in sequencing labor operations in a job shop under certain circumstances.

When a factory produces goods which have very different cycle times, and when these goods compete for capacity across the various work centers, shop personnel will either consciously or subconsciously treat them differently. Two jobs dated for the same day will be sequenced to favor the job which has to be shipped earlier.

This is not a bad rule. Its underlying logic is simple: there is less time to recoup errors on the short-cycle job than on the long-cycle job.

I have warned against elaborate priority-setting rules and recommended straight date sequence for the STS. About the farthest I would wish to depart from this recommendation is the use of a WIP-critical ratio test of this kind:

$$\frac{\text{Operation}}{\text{Priority}} = \frac{\text{Time still to go to order ship date}}{\text{Interval originally planned}} \times 10$$

The resulting number can be computer sorted to a priority sequence which may, at times, see operations sequenced ahead of others which have earlier dates.

Some words of warning and of definition:

1. Any number greater than 9 generated by the rule just stated must be left at 9 by the program, which then reverts to simple date sort of the STS.

2. If a plant decides to use this rule, it really must adopt the recommendation made in the text; that is, drop date from the STS. The sight of operation dates sequenced in what seems a random fashion tends to unhinge production control workers.

3. The numerator of the fraction is the ship date of the order (final assembled apparatus) minus today. The denominator of the fraction is the interval from final apparatus ship date back to the originally scheduled start date of this operation. The rule must not be applied over only one level at a time (unless that one level constitutes the complete order—a rare case) because its movements are so drastic that they cannot be followed by the factory.

4. This kind of priority setting is practical only in a computerized system where it can be recalculated every computer cycle.

Appendix II

An Algorithm for Generating a Priority Index

The purpose of such an index (called PRI in the text) is to indicate, in a single number, how faithfully the work center, department, or entire plant, adhered to the schedule during a given week. *Note:* This has almost nothing to do with how overdue the work center is. PRI is a priority control device.

Method:

1. Decide on what time a given operation shall be assumed to have been done. For example, if labor is reported weekly, Friday, assume every operation was performed the prior Wednesday.

2. Subtract the scheduled day number from the assumed work-done-day number. Carry the algebraic sign and store the result, along with the number of the work center which generated it.

3. Using the above data and a standard library routine available on most computers, compute the mean absolute deviation (MAD) or the standard deviation of the days-late readings. An example of a subroutine which gives standard deviation without making large computer resource demands is found in IBM's Scientific Subroutine Package, Manual Number GH20-0205-4, p. 29, Program 360A-CM-03X.

4. Print the result, up to 99.9, as a PRI for the work center. It is very desirable to consolidate the departmental PRI figures and the single PRI for the entire firm or plant, as well.

The Means-Ends Chain and Cause-Effect Tree: Useful Tools for Your Kit

We need all the help we can get in solving problems and taking advantage of opportunities. Sometimes this help is in the form of a disciplined, patient, step by step application of a proven technique. Any manager will soon come to grief if he depends entirely on inspired improvisation and extemporaneous brilliance to solve each problem as it arises.

Value engineering is such a technique. So is Kepner-Tregoe analysis (Kepner and Tregoe 1965). The means-ends chain is helpful in improving a complex situation (Newman and Summer 1961, pp. 270–73). The cause-effect tree or fault tree analysis is a related technique which can be used to attack difficult, multilevel problems in an organized way.

Figures A3–1, A3–2, and A3–3 are examples of means-ends chains devised to identify the possible means of improving ROI through inventory asset management improvement. They are for the entire company, for ledger controlled stocks, and for work in process, respectively. Such a chain is an orderly method, first of identifying objectives and subobjectives, and then of keeping the organization's energies channeled toward them, minimizing lost motion, tangential or conflicting activity, and drift. The steps in making a means-ends chain are:

1. State an objective briefly using the verb-noun method of value engineering. Be sure you use this verb-noun approach. Example: "Improve shipping stock months of supply by 20% before year-end." It often helps, when making the first pass, to omit the specific numeric objective and say merely, "Improve shipping stock months of supply." Participants are more likely to agree on the principle than the number, which can come later.

2. Identify all significant means to this end. The question is, *"How* can inventory turn rate be improved?" First results tend to sound trivial and naive, like, "Increase output" and "Reduce inventory." Do not be discouraged or feel foolish.

3. Carry the questioning down to the lower levels. Perhaps one "means" is "redistribute safety stocks away from slow-movers to fast-movers." But to do this, we must (a) know how much we have, (b) know where it is by item number, (c) determine how "safe" it is keeping us, (d) review our customer service policy (if we have one!). Now we've hit pay dirt. The cynic will comment, "Why sure. Of

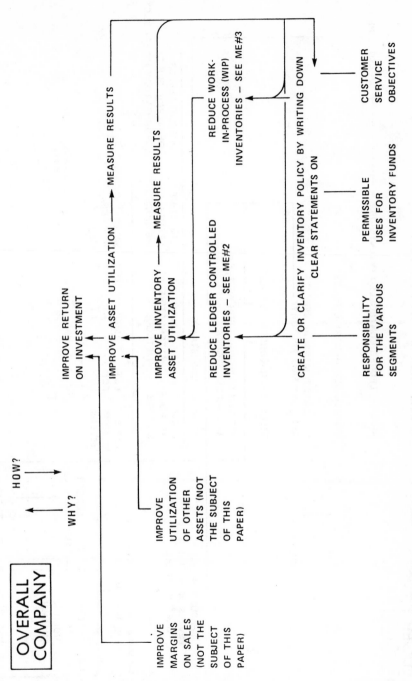

Fig. A3-1. Opportunity analysis matrix example.

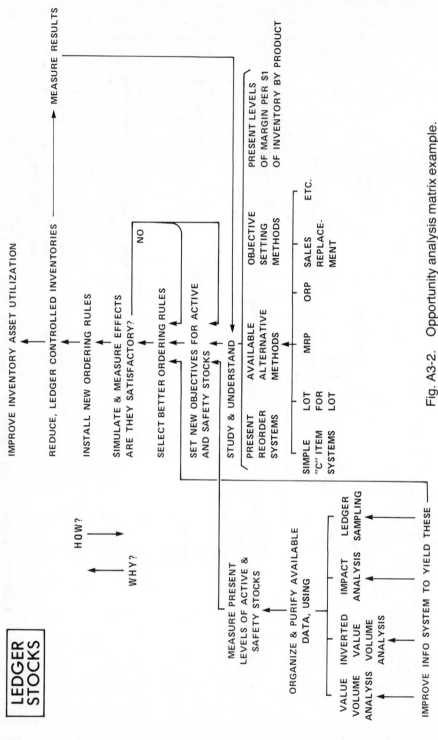

Fig. A3-2. Opportunity analysis matrix example.

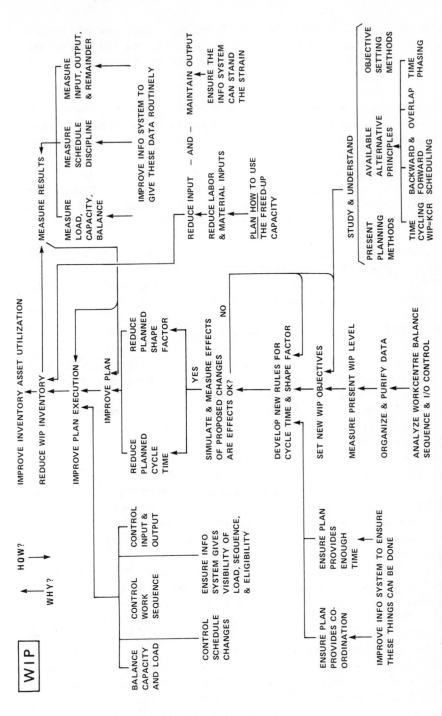

Fig. A3-3.   Opportunity analysis matrix example.

course. Obvious. We do that all the time.'' In response to such comments we need to ask a couple of questions: (1) If these suggestions are obvious, what have we been doing about them lately? (2) If one or more has us thinking, what do we propose to do about it?

Most of life's troubles arise from overlooking the obvious. That man wouldn't have had his auto accident if he had stopped at the sign, or obeyed the speed limit, drinking law, or whatever. Don't let pursuit of the obvious deter you; the obvious gets ignored every day.

The resulting tree is 100% objective oriented. Each element contributes to an objective (or, except for the bottom elements, is itself an objective). It answers the questions, ''How?'' (looking down the tree) and ''Why?'' (looking up the tree). It will quickly pinpoint objectives for which we do not have the means, as well as activities which do not support useful objectives.

Caution: The means-ends chain does not guarantee that the best means to each end have been identified. Nor does it suggest that everything identified absolutely must be done. These are typical management decision-making activities from which the orderly convenience of the means-ends chain does not spare us.

THE CAUSE-EFFECT TREE, OR FAULT TREE ANALYSIS

A similar line of thinking can be applied to specific problems which are serious enough, complex enough, and possessed of enough contributing causes, to warrant such an analysis.

Briefly, the top level is a short statement of the problem, stated a clearly as we can manage to do so. Below this are arrayed the possible causes. *Note well:* This is a speculative phase, not an analytical or fault-finding one. Typically a small group of people (such as a manager, manufacturing and one or two of his foremen and controllers) are working on the problem. It is necessary only to agree that if this condition exists, then it could cause the problem. It is not necessary, and often not possible, at this stage to say whether it exists or not. Taking the problem apart in this objective manner tends to take the emotion out of the work, reducing defensiveness and promoting creative discontent. It is best done by a ''9,9 manager'' (Blake and Mouton 1964, p. 10) whose people trust him not to turn upon them if they discuss candidly (later in the exercise) their own shortcomings or those of others— including, perhaps, the manager. The two opportunity analysis matrices, Figs. A3–4 and A3–5 illustrate this process applied in a work in process environment.

When we arrive at the first level of possible causes, the results tend to seem very trivial. After all, if you have a variance you either spent too much or budgeted too little, which doesn't sound very helpful or instructive. At this point, though, we should take to heart the words supposed to have been used by Lynn Townsend when he took over the Chrysler Corporation in the depths of their financial and market difficulties in the mid-fifties: ''Why, I know what your trouble is. You're spending more than you are earning.'' Starting from there, he turned the corporation around

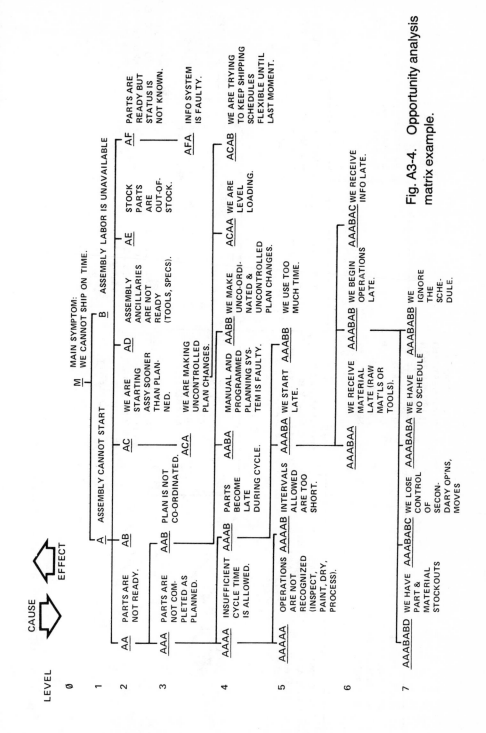

Fig. A3-4. Opportunity analysis matrix example.

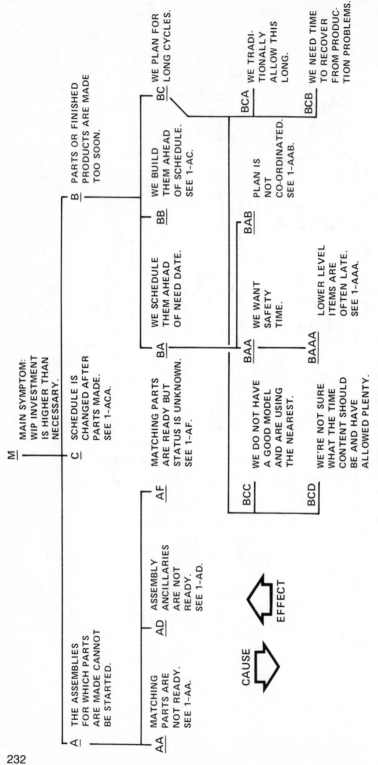

Fig. A3-5. Opportunity analysis matrix example.

in a few years, altering the whole industry's concept of a product guarantee in the process.

So before we dismiss these first-level possible causes as obvious or trivial, let's go one or two levels further. We'll soon find paydirt and opportunity aplenty. Some of the lower level causes you see on these charts seem far fetched (e.g., "We ignore the schedule"). However, each of these causes is there for two very good reasons:

1. It is, hypothetically at least, one possible way to account for the symptom immediately above it.
2. Experience has shown that it really happens.

Most of our overall inventory excesses are the results of simple fear. The ever-present unofficial inventory policy is, "Don't run out." This seems reasonable. It's superficially logical that having lots of stock on the shelves will result in fewer stockouts. It seems reasonable that starting a job early into the shop will improve its chances of being finished on time.

And it seems superficially logical that reductions in inventory will reduce our chances of doing all these good things—shipping on time, serving over-the-counter customers well, and so forth.*

So if we go along with these seemingly "logical" conclusions, we would expect to be able to set up two opportunity analysis matrices with completely different causative factors. These symptoms might read like this:

1. We cannot ship on time. The above "logic" would suggest that several of the reasons would be connected with attempts to cut down inventories.
2. We have too much inventory. This, we might suspect, is partly because of our efforts to ensure that we ship on time.

But a curious thing happens when we begin building in the lower levels of the matrix. We find that:

> MOST OF THE CAUSES OF EXCESS INVENTORY ARE THE VERY SAME AS THE UNDERLYING CAUSES OF OUR INABILITY TO SHIP ON TIME, AND ONLY ONE OR TWO MINOR ONES HAVE TO DO WITH INSUFFICIENT STOCKS.

So a somewhat better grade of logic suggests that:

> ACTIONS WE TAKE TO IMPROVE OUR INVENTORIES WILL ALSO IMPROVE OUR ABILITY TO SUPPLY OUR CUSTOMERS AND TO SHIP ON TIME.

---

*This is, after all, only commonsense. Commonsense, remember, is what tells us the earth is flat.

Appendix IV

Model of a Net-Change System for a Maufacturing Firm

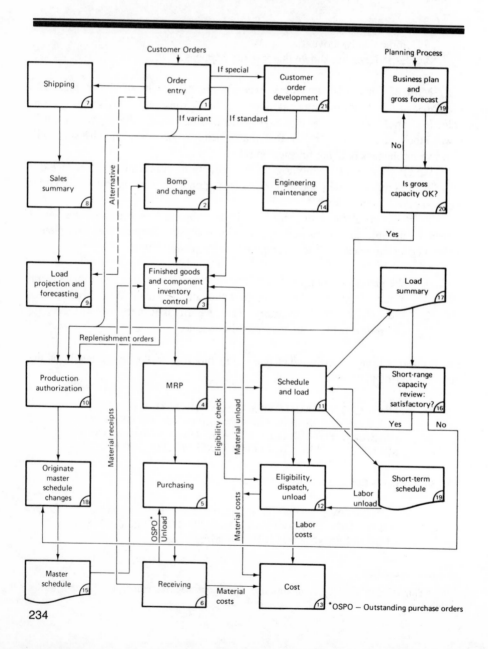

Appendix V

Solutions to Cases

CHAPTER 2

Answers to Case Study Questions

Question 1: The ship date does not necessarily govern the start date because of labor content, process times, order quantities, etc. In this case, Order #2 should start first since it has the earliest start dates in it.

Question 2: Order #1 is for some component for which we do not know the parent: however on the assumption that the scheduling system is working OK, the parent must be due to start early in April. The informal system will work OK: the parts will be ready just about when needed. Similarly, the parent for Order #2 is due to start in mid-April: however the informal system will have Order #2 parts ready at the end of March, throwing up two weeks of useless stock (whether officially called "WIP" or not matters very little).

Question 3: A very possible scenario for Work Center "B" is as follows: (a) Since Order #2 is for a parent order due in April, its parts are not expedited by the informal system on Day 540, which is in February. The work center could be short of work at the time. (b) March is the "month before shipment" for the parent of Order #2, and so it is expedited. But there is too much labor content in Order #2 for it to be done routinely: overtime will be needed because the shop started late. (c) March is also the "month before shipment" for Order #1, and so it is expedited in March. But it finds itself competing with Order #2 for machine capacity, which is short because the machine is already on overtime. (d) The parents of both orders #1 and #2 may be shipped late: #1 because there was a shortage of capacity, #2 because such a big job was started too late.

Discussion of Case Study

The reader should understand that this model, laid-out simply as it is, illustrates a problem that can never be so simple and visible as this in the factory but which, nevertheless, happens constantly. The main lesson is that poor priority control can lead directly to what superficially looks like a capacity problem, but is not. The secondary lesson is that priority control and load-capacity control cannot be dealt with separately but must always be considered together.

CHAPTER 4

Answers to the Questions for Case Study: The Cost of Capital

The cost of capital tends to be used as a policy variable, and has for long been recognized as such when used in the EOQ formula.

For example, the division using the 3%–12% rule probably has cash flow problems and wants to apply a powerful disincentive for exceeding a preset level. Whether this is an effective way of accomplishing this end is another question which will probably result in hot discussion. There is no "answer."

Firms can at times recognize at least two, sometimes three, different costs of capital.

1. Tangible, hard-money dollars which will not be spent if the inventory is not owned. This excludes even bank interest, and typically is from 3% to 6%.

2. Tangible plus managed costs, which include bank interest, direct costs of handling and storing, etc., and which may run from 12% to 18%.

3. Strategic costs, which include all the above plus fixed costs of warehousing, insurance, etc., on the principle that sooner or later another increment of investment will be needed to house inventory if it continues to grow. This may run as high as 35% even for ordinary firms.

Which of the costs is used in a given situation depends upon the situation of the firm. No. 2 is often a reasonable fit in an ongoing business.

The firm that ignores the time element in WIP is sure to have several hundred percent of the WIP it really needs. Saying "We have to have it—it's good, sold inventory" is born of ignorance or is a copout.

Submitting an appropriation request for increases in inventory is a useful reminder that inventory, as any other investment, must pay. However such a practice must be accompanied by (a) a means of identifying a "good" level of inventory, (b) mechanisms for controlling to that level.[1] [2]

---

(1) Plossl, G.W., *Manufacturing Control, the Last Frontier for Profits,* Reston Publishing Co. Inc., Reston, Va., 1973, p. 75.

(2) Sirianni, N.C., *How Much Inventory is Enough?* Reston Publishing Co., Inc., Reston, Va., forthcoming.

Answers to the Questions for Case Study: "All Our Factory Inventory is in WIP"

1. There is no "right" turnover figure. However, the case information indicates that all sales are made from finished goods which came from WIP. Hence the WIP turnover is

$$\frac{20/\text{day} \times 240 \text{ days/year}}{\$1,766} = 2.7 \text{ times/year.}$$

For a light industrial good, this has to be considered "low." Industry figures for this kind of good range from 2 to 8 and more.

2. No, it cannot be true. This is an Accounting convenience. Parts and raw materials are ordered through MRP and come into stock, hopefully for a brief time (this is an objective of MRP) but nevertheless into stock.

3. Since the cost during assembly (manufacturing) cycle varies from 90% to 100% of final cost, we can estimate the shape factor "S" to be the average, or .95. From this, therefore, the WIP needed to support output of $20/day on a shape factor of .95 is:

$$\text{WIP} = .95 \times 120 \text{ days} \times \$20/\text{day} = \$380.$$

4. The difference between $380 and $1,766 is, of course, very significant. Among the things which could account for it are:

    (a) Most of the inventory is not WIP at all, but is parts stock.

    (b) The cycle times are actually much longer than the factory people assume. (This often happens—we tend to think of what we would like our cycles to be, not what they actually are).

    (c) Lateness or errors in reporting material issues.

5. Some further calculations are in order. For instance, if we accept that $380 is needed to support WIP, then we have $1,766 − $380 = $1,386 in raw material and parts. If 90% of product cost flows through these segments ($18/day), and we guesstimate* that the MRP system has driven the shape factor down from its ORP level of 0.5 to something less, say conservatively 0.4, then

---

*ORP controlled ledger stocks are assumed to decrement on a shape factor of .5. That is, as shown in all text books, the usage is assumed to be a straight or nearly straight line dropping from the maximum (just after resupply) to the minimum (the safety level). One objective of MRP is to *time* the inputs so that the material is consumed almost at once. Shape factor is therefore no longer .5 but is something else, smaller—in a tightly run MRP shop, it could be as low as .1 or .2. In the above we use .4 so as not to overstate any case which may develop, and because we really don't know what "S" is.

the parts-raw material inventory needed to support this level of production is:

$$(\text{Parts \& RM Inv.}) = 0.40 \times C \times \$18/\text{day}$$

Operating people, when questioned, estimated that parts and raw material are in the shop about 1 month before being consumed in production, so "C" = 1 month and the above formula solves for Parts & RM Inventory = $144, contrasted sharply with the actual parts and raw material estimate of $1,386. The turnover of parts and raw materials which is implied is $18/day × 240 days/year//$1,386 = 3.1 times per year, while inventory standard* turnover of $18/day × 240 days/year//$144 = 30 times per year.

At this point, the specialist should hypothesize about the reasons for the obvious excesses. Among the possible reasons which should be brought out are:

- (a) Parts are on hand but unapplied.
- (b) Parts are on hand too soon.
- (c) Parts are on hand awaiting matching parts.

Using fault-tree analysis thinking, and with the aid of operating people, the specialist could identify potential reasons for each of the above, for instance (a) could be caused by uncontrolled supersedures, last minute cancellations of orders for low-activity end items, etc.

Discussion of Case Study

The alert and careful reader will become aware that the figures developed to date are still very hypothetical (for instance, we do not really yet know whether the excess is in parts, raw materials, or WIP). Any ongoing investigation should begin by gathering figures sufficient to estimate where the problem really lies. Then the list of potential reasons for each problem can be expanded, giving main attention to the segment which has been identified as the main contributor. However, what we *do* know for sure from the above analysis is that, as the Operations Manager suspected, our so-called "WIP" inventory is far too high by almost any measure and richly deserves further analysis and corrective action, which will probably extend upstream to Marketing and Division Management, downstream to suppliers and the shop.

---

*A "standard" is not the same as an objective. It merely shows a hypothetical minimum inventory toward which the unit should be working, and reveals the difference between where the unit now is and where it might be if there were no machine breakdowns, no strikes, no weather troubles, no retirements or epidemics, etc. In the case above, the difference between actual of 3.1 and standard of 30 indicates there is *plenty* of room for setting an objective between the two, such as an improvement from 3.1 to 6 within 12 months.

CHAPTER 5

Discussion of Case Study: The Superintendent's View

Readers can be expected to complain that there is insufficient case information to answer the questions. For instance, some may feel a knowledge of specific hour loads into the future is essential. This was available but was omitted from the case material to force attention upon two or three major problems which are all too plain from the condensed, management-level information presented.

A thoughtful reading of the case should make the reader aware of the following points: Work Center BA should be slowed down or stopped, since its product cannot be used for some days and will merely create clutter. There must be standby capability, but routine production can be stopped.

If possible, BA's skills should be applied at AA, which is the latest work center in the plant. Even if the operator(s) from BA are not highly skilled or fully efficient in AA's work, their efforts will be better used at AA than at BA, which is probably in the process of running out of work in any case.

The fact that the plant as a whole is less overdue than the most-overdue work center indicates among other things that a lot of expediting has been necessary, or that some of the load is not really needed in some of the feeders and is being left behind without harm to production. Note, for instance, that work center AB is reporting work 5 days ahead of schedule, its priority index shows it is working quite well in sequence, yet it has 3.3 weeks of overdue. What is in this overdue? Is it junk—unreported completed work? Is it, perhaps, work on orders for stock that has been set aside in the rush to complete customer orders (which by now are probably stopped farther downstream because of shortages of stock parts!)?

Some thought should be given to the entire factory's ability to carry its load, since it is 3.2 weeks overdue. This is a complex problem involving oncoming loads, both visible and not yet visible, short-term and long-term. Further, before automatically assuming that overtime or more staff is needed, the wise supervisor will recognize that the reduction in confusion which will result from shutting off the flow of useless WIP from BA may so improve his labor efficiency (by eliminating searching and clearing out floor space) that he will begin overhauling his overdues without additional labor in-plant hours.

A good load summary will, of course, lead shop management to a choice of other things they could well consider doing. For instance, BA's condition of being almost current, far ahead of the rest of the plant, may have been the result of a decision one month ago to put it into that position because of an oncoming, highly visible peak in the load which was at that time five weeks off.

Perhaps one of the most important points to be brought out in any good discussion is the fact that averages are a deadly sedative that will put us to sleep where we need to be most alert. For example, the entire factory is, apparently, much less late than its most-late work center. This is a measurement made in many factories, and it goes like this: we can generate 3000 productive hours per week and we have 2000 hours of overdues, therefore we are less than a week past due. In such a factory, however, the very people who make such calculations seem puzzled by the fact that most jobs are shipped up to four or five weeks late. The reason, of course, is as pictured in Fig. 2-20 and Fig. 2-21 where the combined effects of unsequential working and unbalanced working are shown. Typically, only one or two work centers are pacing the plant, contributing relatively little to the comfortingly small hours of overdue, but contributing mightily to lateness of shipment.

This points, yet again, to the necessity of applying the Pareto principle (ABC analysis) to problems as well as to other things. In any such array of information as this case contains, there will be a ranking of problems. The most-overdue work center can be readily identified (it is AA) as can the work center with the poorest adherence to schedule (BB)*. If shop management has time and energy for only two problems this week, these are the ones: improve the manning at AA and the material supply to BB.

Answers to Questions for Case Study: Input-Output Control in a Fabricating Shop

1. Readers should note that there is a difference between *planned* cycle times and *actual* cycle times. The project *did* reduce the *actual* cycle times by ensuring that (a) Parts were not made too far ahead, (b) Parts were not made late, thereby holding up already-made parts still further. The reader should be aware that such a project should narrow the distribution of actual operations dates around the average days-late, which reduces time the average job spends in the shop; and that stock parts in the WIP stream will get their proper priority attention and therefore stock-part shortages, which hold up production and lengthen the cycles of the waiting parts, should be reduced.

2. Fig. 5-10 is the key reference here. Readers should note that the shop performance has been improved by bringing work centers abreast and reducing their degree of departure from schedule. The result will be that parts will be ready in matched sets to go into their parent items on the planned dates. There should also be comment that Fig. 5-10 shows that many parent parts such as "D" now seem to have open space (slack) at the starts of their manufacturing intervals, indicating that, under the improved conditions that have been established, parts are being made sooner than they are needed. The clearly identifiable stage in which this factory

---

*Work center MA, which is slightly worse, is bypassed this week because it's an assembly work center: experience and good judgment tell us that it is not likely to do much better than the worst performing feeder, and BB is clearly that.

finds itself, therefore, is that it has mastered synchronized production and is ready for cycle time reduction. This is the "further potential" about which the question inquires. The wise student will cautiously estimate that there may be "a little" or "a lot" of potential, depending upon many factors not brought out in the case material.

3. Labor efficiency could be expected to rise for one or all of the following reasons: (a) Reduced confusion and clutter leads to steadier work with less waiting and rehandling. (b) Constant followup by supervision in the interests of the schedule has a byproduct effect upon productivity: every conscientious workman wants to see his part of the work go well, and if the boss is following up daily he has a chance to find out exactly what has to be done, how well he did last week, etc. (c) Provision of matched sets to each subassembly stage leads to smooth production, particularly when little or nothing has to be moved out of the way to get at the matched set. Students role-playing the factory manager's job should be expected to comment that a careful study of factory facilities (such as parts storage at secondary workstations in- and out-queues) would be warranted. Readers should note that the careful separation of priority (sequence, schedule) problems from load-capacity problems will lead to less emergency overtime. This is because, even though a plant may work "the right number of hours" (load-capacity balancing), if it works the "wrong hours" (loss of priority control), the capacity has been consumed making the wrong things and emergency capacity (overtime) will have to be provided to make the right things.

4. As the factory manager, the reader should consider a planned reduction of the cycle times built into the computer-housed models. He should do this by identifying those departments where most front-end slack seems to have been opened up by I/O control (refer to Fig. 5-10 again), and reducing them first. He might also consider doing a Manufacturing Cycle Efficiency study along the longest, high-cost product path to identify areas which have not yet yielded their maximum potential: he would find the reasons for the low m.c.e., correct them, then go through the I/O control, cycle time reduction sequence again. The reader should also conclude that at least equal weight should be given to the structure and characteristics of the factory as of the product in doing this kind of work.

CHAPTER 6

Discussion of Case Study

Several things happened. The manager tested the young engineer and had not gotten the desired results: he set about to show how it was done. It is a moot point whether all he taught the younger man was good. However one lesson having, at the same time, little to do with production and nearly everything to do with production, is that simple, sweet reason is not sufficient to get the job done. The power of office, either held directly or clearly and unequivocally delegated, is a powerful motivator. There are others, too, which outrank sweet reason.

The manager imposed his own priority on a shop already busy, without inquiring what would happen to the rest of the load. Only one foreman ventured an opinion that there might be a capacity problem, and he hastily withdrew in the face of his boss's boss's obvious determination.

Since the factory made a complex product of which the repair job was only a part, inserting this extra load with no notice could well delay regular production—but the effect would not show up for some weeks. After studying the case, the reader should be able to conclude that jamming extra work into a factory without appraising its impact on costs and upon another work creates chaos, which is doubly troublesome because cause and effect are so far removed in space and time. This is a place for Master Schedule management. A capable Requirements Planning system should be able to answer the obvious "What if?" questions and make possible a solution which would minimize cost and confusion and, perhaps most important of all, not undermine the production system upon which the factory depends for guidance. The manager had imposed a second set of priorities outside his normal system. If the shop ignored them and went on with their regular work, supervision would quickly be on the carpet. If they ignored the formal system, other shipments would suffer and supervision would be on the carpet. Heads I win, tails you lose.

One way to handle such jobs would entail some sequence of steps similar to the following:

1. Identify critical material, labor, and machine requirements and their timing, and play these against the existing load. In the case, it is apparent that the supply of soft copper, the bending skills, and shell blast-bake oven capacity were critical. A good computer with good "What if?" capability in the software is very helpful: but if the critical items can be accurately identified and time-phased, it may not be absolutely essential.

2. Where there are capacity or material shortfalls, determine an earliest possible date by which the critical work could be done or material obtained. This is no time for parochialism: another division or another firm (even a competitor) may be able to bail you out. Remember: your customer is in trouble and will gladly pay you for *saved* time as well as for the product.

3. Feed these decisions into the system, scheduling both backward and forward from the critical activity or event, so that the necessary shop work will be included in the outputs of the formal system with an appropriate priority, and so that the job will be properly synchronized within itself. *It is usually impossible to synchronize a product built outside the formal plan, and avoiding the formal system to "save time" is nearly always a snare and a delusion: it takes longer in the end.*

Chapter 7

Answers to the Questions for Case Study

1. There are three categories of parts: 60% over five months supply (including 25% not moving), and all else (40% by subtraction). A three-item model of such a ledger might look like this:

Item	Balance on-hand dollars	Activity Dollars/month	Months of Supply
1.	25	0	Infinite
2.	35	5	7.0
3.	40	15	2.7
Totals and re-sulting months of supply	100	20	5.0

Further, the active stock is 60% safety. Many practitioners will suggest that an MRP system should need no more than 10% safety, so this means that 60% of 75% of total stocks, or 45%, is safety, while 10% of 75% or 8% would be a more suitable level, a difference of 37%. This 37% might be called "questionable safety stock." Overdue starts account for 5% (1 week of supply in 21), and system lags for 3% (average 3 days delay in 105). This leaves 29% of total stocks we would have to call, "mismanaged safety stocks."

To clarify these relationships, we can draw a barchart which starts (Line 1 at the top) with 100% of the inventory and then splits up this bar into segments. See below.

2. "Mismanaged safety stocks" are a big 29% of total parts inventory. Safety stocks protect against uncertainty. Clearly, the uncertainty has been imposed by the firm itself by its habit of changing the master schedule inside the parts leadtimes of four to eight weeks. One of the fundamental differences between ORP and MRP systems is that *ORP systems seek to be in stock, while MRP system seek to be out of stock* except for specific requirements exploded from specific end-items. It follows that, under MRP, if you don't forecast it, you can't build it . . . unless, of course, you hold large safety stocks, at which point *the performance of a firm with a badly managed MRP system becomes indistinguishable from its performance before it switched to MRP*.

3. WIP management seems to account for only 8% of the excessive stocks. But this text should alert the student that inactive parts in the stores have their counterparts on the floor, where parts have been withdrawn, started into work, then stopped as the schedule changed. Money spent on unneeded parts is paralleled by labor spent on unneeded assemblies. Worse, the resulting confusion reduces the factory's efficiency in producing the goods which really are needed, since several

Line 1		Total Parts Inventories —100%			
Line 2	25% Dead	Active Inventory 75%	{ 40% fast moving { 35% slow moving		
Line 3		60% of 75% = 45% Safety Stock			Working Stock = 30%
Line 4		Questionable Safety Stock = 37%		Allow-able Safety = 8%	Working Stock = 30%
Line 5		Mismanaged Safety Stock = 29%	Late Starts & Sys-tem Delay 8%	Allow-able Safety = 8%	Working Stock = 30%
Line 6				Realistic Target Parts Inventory = 30 + 8+ 4 = 42%	

things must be moved to get at the one which is needed. Further, factory capacity is being wasted to produce parts which will enter the slow-moving or dead category. Engineering problems with phase-outs will be severe because it is very difficult to get a clean cutoff when so many of the stocks move so slowly. The case gives insufficient information to estimate a percentage with much accuracy: but it is certain that much of the 25% dead and some of the 35% slow parts are the result of hard-to-manage supersedure.

4.   Sampling invariably is criticized by some who feel it is not representative. Experience indicates otherwise. In any mass of information of more than a few hundred items, sampling will give amazingly accurate estimates of the true situation. Statistical procedures and tests are out of the scope of this text: but one warning must be sounded. It is to select a sampling method that avoids conscious or unconscious bias. In the factory environment, systematic sampling (e.g. one labor card in every 100) seems to work best. Try to arrange things so that the adequacy of the sample can be checked by multiplying the result of the sample by the sampling ratio and comparing the result with a known figure, such as an Accounting statement. Reasonable agreement between the two figures should be obtained.

5.   The product manager could profitably write a firm policy on time fences and master schedule management. The structuring of his product may be the

source of part of his trouble: bills of material could well be tested, along with their relationship to the master schedule, particularly concerning treatment of options. There is little doubt that much of his WIP, not even mentioned in the case information, is held—"not really needed." He could profitably sample materials on his floor to estimate the dollar value of this segment. These are among the many "next steps" an alert reader might suggest.

References

REFERENCES

American Production and Inventory Control Society. *Master production scheduling training aid*. Washington, DC: APICS.

American Production and Inventory Control Society. 1977. *Master scheduling reprints*. Washington, DC: APICS.

Anthony, R. N. 1960. *Management accounting*. Revised ed. Homewood, IL: R. D. Irwin.

Belt, Bill. 1978. Input-output planning illustrated. *Production and inventory management,* vol. 19, no. 2.

Berne, Eric. 1964. *Games people play*. New York: Grove Press.

Blake, R. R. and Mouton, J. S. 1968. *Corporate excellence through grid organization development*. Houston: Gulf Publishing Co.

Blake, R. R. and Mouton, J. S. 1964. *The managerial grid*. Houston: Gulf Publishing Co.

Boston Consulting Group. 1968. *Perspectives on experience*. Boston. Now available from University Microfilm International, Ann Arbor, Mich., Ref. # AU39.

Bourke, Richard. 1975. *The bill of material: key building block*. Pasadena, CA: Bourke & Associates.

Buffa, E. S. 1961. *Modern production management*. 2nd ed. New York: Wiley.

Carruthers, John M. 1976. Product structure charts: key to designing and controlling modular bills of material. *Proceedings of the Nineteenth Annual Conference, APICS*. Washington, DC.

Cool, W. R. and Reece, James S. 1978. Measuring investment center performance. *Harvard Business Review*, May-June.

Everdell, R. 1972. Master scheduling—its new importance in the management of materials. *Modern Materials Handling*, October.

Gall, John. 1975. *Systemantics—why systems work, and especially why they fail*. New York: Pocket Books.

Garwood, D., Orlicky, J., Plossl, G., and Wight, O., et al. *Materials requirement planning*. IBM publication G320-1170-0.

Garwood, D., Orlicky, J., Plossl, G., and Wight, O. Structuring the bill of material. IBM publication G320-1245-0.

Greene, J. H., ed. 1970. *Production and inventory control handbook.* New York: McGraw-Hill.

Gue, F. S. 1976. Dollar-days: another handle on inventory opportunities. *Production and Inventory Management,* vol. 16, no. 2.

Gue, F. S. 1975. Input-output control in a job shop. *Proceedings of the Eighteenth Annual International Conference, APICS.* Washington, DC.

Gue, F. S. 1976. Notes on the length and content of the short-term schedule as used in a heavy-job shop. *Production and Inventory Management,* vol. 17, no. 1.

Gue, L. R. 1977. *An introduction to educational administration in Canada.* Ryerson, Toronto: McGraw-Hill.

Hayakawa, S. I. 1964. 2nd ed. *Language in thought and action.* New York: Harcourt, Brace, and World.

Hessler, H. and Cline, C. 1960. The DuPont chart system. In *Readings in Cost Accounting, Budgeting, and Control.* 2nd ed. W. E. Thomas, Ed. Cleveland: Southwestern Publishing Co.

Hoffman, Robert F. 1977. Structuring a product data base. *Proceedings of the Twentieth Annual Conference, APICS.* Washington, DC.

Hot list. Jan.-Feb. 1978. Atlanta: R. D. Garwood, Inc.

IBM. 1975. *Communications oriented production information system,* vol. 2. IBM Publication G-320-1975-0.

IBM. 1978. *Communications oriented production and inventory control system.* IBM Publication G-320-1978-0.

Kepner, C. H. and Tregoe, B. B. 1965. *The rational manager.* New York: McGraw-Hill.

Mather, Hal F. 1978. Reschedule the reschedules you just rescheduled—way of life for MRP? *P & IC Management,* vol. 14, no. 1. Washington, DC: APICS.

Newman, William H. and Summer, Charles E., Jr. 1961. *The process of management.* Englewood Cliffs, NJ: Prentice-Hall, Inc.

Orlicky, J. A. 1973. *Net change MRP.* IBM System Journal, vol. 12, no. 1.

Plossl, George W. 1973. *Manufacturing control—the last frontier for profit.* Reston, VA: Reston Publishing Co., Inc.

Plossl, George W. and Wight, O. W. 1967. *Production and inventory control principles and techniques.* Englewood Cliffs, NJ: Prentice-Hall, Inc.

Ruch, William A. 1978. The relationship between inventory and return on investment. *Proceedings of the Twenty-first Annual International Conference of the American Production and Inventory Control Society.* Washington, DC: APICS.

Running a job shop real time. *Infosystems.* Feb. 1978, p. 102.

Sampani, P. 1977. Executing the company game plan. *Master Production Scheduling Reprints*. Washington, DC: APICS. p. 5.

Shone, Kenneth J. The queueing theory. *Time and Motion Study,* 1960 and 1961. London, England.

Sirianni, N. C. 1980. *Inventory: how much do you need?* Reston, VA: Reston Publishing Co., Inc.

Sirianni, N. C. 1975. WIP—things we can do. *Proceedings of the Eighteenth Annual International Conference of the American Production and Inventory Control Society*. Washington, DC.

Skrotzki, B. G. A. and Vopat, W. 1945. *Applied energy conversion*. New York: McGraw-Hill.

Waddell, H. L. 1952. Work sampling. *Factory Management and Maintenance*. New York: McGraw-Hill.

Wight, O. W. 1974. *Production and inventory management in the computer age*. Boston: Cahners International.

Zimmerman, Gary W. 1976. The ABC's of Vilfredo Pareto. *Production and Inventory Management,* vol. 17, no. 1.

Index